Symposia

Salvator Dali, *Paris and Helen of Troy*
© 1998 Fundación Gala-Salvator Dali/Artists Rights Society (ARS), New York

Symposia

Plato, the Erotic, and Moral Value

Louis A. Ruprecht, Jr.

STATE UNIVERSITY OF NEW YORK PRESS

Published by
State University of New York Press, Albany

© 1999 State University of New York

For information, address State University of New York Press,
State University Plaza, Albany, NY 12246

Production and book design, Laurie Searl
Marketing, Dana E. Yanulavich

Library of Congress Cataloging-in-Publication Data

Ruprecht, Louis A.
    Symposia : Plato, the erotic, and moral value / Louis A.
Ruprecht, Jr.
    p. cm.
    Includes bibliographical references and index.
    ISBN 0-7914-4263-2 (hardcover : alk. paper)
    ISBN 0-7914-4264-0 (pbk. : alk paper)
    1. Plato. 2. Love—History. 3. Ethics, Ancient. I. Title.
    B398.L9 1999
    184—dc21   98-31973
                                                                        CIP

10 9 8 7 6 5 4 3 2 1

for my grandmother

ἀλλὰ παράγαγ᾽ αὔταν . . .

Some say an army of horses
others say an army of men
still others say a sea of ships
is the loveliest sight on the dark earth.

But I say it is whatever you love.

It is painfully easy
to make this plain to anyone.
For the loveliest of women,
Helen herself, laid waste the heart

of a noble husband—all this for love.

Trailing beauty, she sailed to Troy
forgetting her child, utterly
forgetting the parents she loved.
She was led away, led there by love . . .

[And this calls Anactoria to mind to me]

I would rather see her beloved step,
the glittering light in her shining face,
here with me now, than all the glitter
of all the arms of all the footsoldiers

in all of vast Lydia.

—Sappho of Mytilene

Contents

Preface

Books raise questions. At their best, that is the great gift of books. The paradox of books has something to do with their inability to answer questions with anything even roughly approximating the clarity they boast in posing them. And the danger of books lies in the likelihood that they will ask too many questions at once, thus losing focus and clarity. The best books are often those that raise one question repeatedly, perhaps even systematically. I have tried to write such books, more often than not by focusing upon a single word. In my first book, *Tragic Posture and Tragic Vision: Against the Modern Failure of Nerve*, I was from beginning to end concerned with the complex meaning of "tragedy"— what the word meant to the classical Greeks, what it meant to the Hellenistic Jews and early Christians who became intrigued with the genre, and with this noble Greek idea, and what that same word has come to mean still later in this, the modern period. In my second book, *Afterwords: Hellenism, Modernism, and the Myth of Decadence*, I became interested in the word 'modern'—especially the ways in which that word has become a sort of (vaguely) proper noun, intended to define a particular time-period whose borders prove to be beyond drawing, once you begin seriously to examine them. There is no cartography for an epoch, nor for a human soul. The rhetoric of "modernity" seemed to me inseparable from an equally vague and ungrounded sense of nostalgia for a better, and now bygone, era. That era is, more often than not, supposed to be "classical," and Greek. I reject such polarities as "ancient versus modern," just as I reject the nostalgic whimsy for an illusory and fantastic golden age. So, I think, did Plato.

This book may appear to be less single-minded. It has something to do with erotic thought in Greek antiquity—primarily in Plato's work— as well as with the ways in which that thought has been appropriated by contemporary thinkers who are interested, so they claim, in the same ideas. It is a book that is devoted primarily to the constellation of ideas surrounding the perplexing Greek word, *erōs*. Three words, resulting in three books: on Tragedy, on Modernity, and now on the Erotic. The three concepts are linked, as I hope to demonstrate in this third volume.

The book, such as it is, has grown out of a seminar that I have been invited to teach in several religion departments at various institutions. In the course of so doing, I have noticed something surprisingly constant in these varying academic venues. Just as I note the presence of the word 'body' in an astonishing number of book titles these days, so I note the presence of the word 'sexuality' in college courses across all sectors of the contemporary curriculum. Students may study "sex" in any number of departments: from anthropology, to biology, to psychology, to women's studies. There will come a day, I strongly suspect, when "Sexuality Studies," or something very like it, comes to name a concentration at many secular universities.

In each of these areas, what one is allegedly studying is *the body*, the body in the grip of *extreme physical desire*. Students do not need yet another venue in which to study the strictly bodily side of such matters. Nor do they need another forum for discussing orgasms. The mass media, I suspect, provides a sufficient venue for that. As I began to ask myself what the discipline of religious studies might have to contribute to such an apparently overworked topic, it seemed to me that there was indeed something missing, something that religious studies might be in a unique position to provide.

The study of sexuality is, naturally enough, about bodies and bodily pleasure. I freely admit that. But by shifting attention to "the erotic," we are also, equally and inescapably, attending to souls in pain. Soulful pain as well as bodily pleasure: to the degree that souls cannot be neatly separated from bodies (as I suspect that the Platonic, *and* the Jewish, *and* the Christian traditions all claim that they cannot be), then eroticism defines a complex continuum of pleasure and pain. Even a cursory review of the pop culture that clothes sexuality and eroticism in our own day and age tells us as much: perhaps most jarringly, in the Valentine image of a human heart, pierced by an arrow. Love is depicted as a mortal wound, a hole, a hole in our once-complete (and no longer so) embodied selves. Love is mortal. Love is a battlefield. Love is like a kind of dying. Sappho says all of this, and Dali depicts the idea in all of its stark serenity. Sappho also insists that *erōs* is the most beautiful thing on this darkly fertile, strange and perplexing, loamy orb of earth. The erotic paradoxes run deep.

Human sexuality, when viewed through such a subtly "religious" lens, is perhaps better described by the term *erōs*. That is what the

Greeks called it. One large task for this book will be the attempt to *translate* that word, to say in a modern English idiom something about what this term might have meant in ancient Greek. *Erōs*, and *erōtika*, do not denote "sexuality" in any crass or simple way, popular jargon notwithstanding. It is my own view, presented at the tentative end of this study, that the best English translation for the Greek term, *erōs*, might just be "true love"—this, and not simply "sex." The distinction between sensuality and sexuality is one our own culture is in some real danger of losing altogether. I hope to recover it for my own purposes here.

Plato, much to my surprise and eventual delight, became a sort of intellectual lodestar on this journey, both in the classroom and in my own more private work. As I have read and re-read his most popular dialogues—*Symposium, Phaedrus, Republic*, and *Phaedo*—I have been impressed by several things. First and foremost, these dialogues were all written around the same time, in the so-called Middle Period of the philosopher's development. It was in this period, so I learned during my freshman year in college, that Plato began to break from his master, Socrates, began to speak in his own voice, even if he still put the words in Socrates' mouth. Allegedly, it was here, in the Middle Period, that Plato developed his own most influential ideas: the doctrine of the forms, his more overt hostility to the body and to the very idea of embodiment, and with this, his condemnation of poetry as, at best, a sort of seducer's craft, attentive strictly to matters of bodily and emotional appetite.

What no one seems to have noticed is the sudden appearance of *erōs* at this same time, and in these same dialogues. I will go so far as to refer to this as Plato's "Erotic Period," not his "Middle Period," so as to make the point plain. As I puzzled over Plato's sudden and rather shocking interest in erotic matters, I found myself no longer certain of some things I thought I already knew about the man and his philosophy. The somewhat controversial claims I will be offering in this book are, first, that Plato's "theory of the forms" is the most exaggerated, and underdetermined, notion in the entire Platonic corpus.[1] Plato does not ask "the forms" to do nearly as much work for him as some Platonists have asked it to do. There is no "form" of justice. There is no "form" of *erōs*. There is no "form" of knowledge (*Parmenides* 135d). And so on. Secondly, I will try to rehabilitate Plato's philosophy from the accusation, made especially eloquently by Martha Nussbaum, that it is unreasonably hostile to the body, that physical embodiment is, somehow, simply a problem for Plato. I see no real evidence for this claim in the dialogues of the Erotic Period. Rather, I see a rich and multilayered analysis, a really very sophisticated and quite modern one, that denies the body— and poetry, for that matter—none of the complex attention it deserves. We do not find a full-blown theory of forms, nor a dismissive hostility to the body, nor an outright dismissal of poetry, in Plato's Erotic Period. Rather, what we find is a first-rate thinker at work on difficult questions, admitting all of their complexity, and highlighting them as worth thinking about. I will devote the better portion of this book to a *defense* of the emphatic connection Plato makes between truth and love, thus pointing to the still more profound connection he makes between loving and a more philosophical kind of knowing.

And now comes the danger more clearly into focus—danger is never far off, when the topic is erotic. The danger lies in a sort of solipsism, a kind of never-ending-ness. Erotic discourse threatens to become an abyss, a black hole rather like the ones our latter-day cosmologists find so fascinating. No light escapes them. They remain perennially in the dark. Once you begin talking about it, you cannot stop talking about it. There is no end to *erōs*. There is an end to you, and there is an end to me. Our bodies, their edges, their mortality most of all, set clear limits to each one of us. There is a place where I end. It is the place where you begin. Yet the love we create together in erotic communion has no such clear limits. That is still another enduring paradox. Love blurs even the clearest lines. *Erōs*, Plato suggests, is neither precisely mortal nor immortal, but rather something "in between." *Erōs* blurs that precise line *between* "self" and "other," *between* "you" and "me." That is just what it does to the human soul.

There is no end to *erōs*. It simply begins, then, once begun, it slowly becomes impossible to speak, or think, of anything else. Monotheists have often worried about this. The beloved so completely occupies the lover's attention that the thought of God all but disappears. As Juliet knew well, Romeo no sooner erupted into her life than his "gracious self" became "the god of [her] idolatry." She speaks of her passion as "infinite," a quantity that is traditionally thought fit for divinity alone. Is there something about the outrageous phenomenon of human loving which brings divinity in its wake? Divinity is infinite; we are not. And yet . . . every lover knows the inverted truth of the matter, that the soul in love has, as Socrates suggests in the *Phaedrus*, gotten back its wings. There are no limits, in the soaring shadow of love. Small wonder, as I say, that the scriptural monotheisms have had a notoriously difficult time with *erōs*. Small wonder that nineteenth-century Romanticism—a complex of movements in the visual arts, in literature, and in philosophy with which I have some real sympathies—was always thought to be potentially and dangerously irreligious, flirting with idolatry at nearly every turn. They celebrated the wrong god. *Erōs*, a curiously middling sort of divinity, according to the *Symposium*'s portrait, always stands at the gates, threatening to make the more traditional pantheon disappear in post-Olympian shadows. Such implications are part and parcel of the erotic life. This, as I say, every lover already knows.

It would not be possible to thank every one from whom I have learned about the intimate constellation of issues which I will be describing here— about risk and vulnerability, about pleasure and pain, about the fineness and spirited eloquence of human loving. Since it is an organization that has been under considerable seige of late, it is a real pleasure for me to be able to thank the National Endowment for the Humanities, which graciously sponsored my own research in two successive summers. In the summer of 1993, I was selected for participation in a six-week institute entitled "Beyond the Text: Teaching Religion and Material Culture," under the gentle direction of Mark Juergensmeyer and Richard Carp. It was here that I began reading the Greek lyric tradition seriously, working especially closely with Sappho's poetic fragments. Then, in the summer of 1994, I was again selected for participation in a seven-week NEH Institute entitled "Plato and the Polis," directed this time by Diskin Clay and Michael Gillespie. This provided me with the extraordinary opportunity to read Plato's *Republic*, which I had read previously, and Plato's *Laws*, which I had not done, in the company of a remarkable communion of philosophers, classicists, and political scientists. I had not originally seen these as related ventures, but they came to be. *Erōs* must ultimately find a home in the *polis*, after all, must somehow be domesticated there. Yet it cannot *be* domesticated; that is the moral dilemma. This, I was delighted to discover, Plato already knew well. Out of that fundamental insight, the mere intuition of a subtle connection, this book began to take its (admittedly tentative) present shape. It was Robert Detweiler, then a professor in the Institute of Liberal Arts at Emory University, who convinced me of this over a lunchtime conversation I have not forgotten, and who first insisted, gently but persuasively, that I write this book.

I have countless friends who also deserve better thanks than I can provide. Let me thank some of them in three separate groups. First, there are my students, who, in the course of the past six years, have so deeply influenced my own reflection and, I hope, my sensitivity to these matters. In particular, I should like to thank Vicki Andreadis, Brooke Baxter, Laura Brown, Caroline Coleman, Kim Cotter (now Fowler), Hugh Cruse, Sarah Ferguson-Wagstaffe, Roger Fowler, Michael Gundlach, David Hart, Lisa Henry, Matt Huff, Amy Klapper, Lang Lowrey, Laura McIlwain (now Cruse), Danielle Muñoz, Ann Parker, Corinna Sampson, Ommeed Sathje, Doug Schontz, Heather Sheats, Ryan Short, Jason Silverman, Ryan Slater, Adora Spatz-Glenn, Justin Stacy, Ayesha Tanzeem, Aron Tremble, Carrie Wilson and Rebecca Zuspan. Each of them performed that most magical of services; they taught their teacher.

Secondly, there are a handful of scholars who have helped me to think about these matters by writing, to me and through me, about them. The late Marguerite Yourcenar has been my own most cherished literary companion since I completed my graduate training. Her *Memoirs of Hadrian* seems to me an unparallelled literary and spiritual accomplishment about which I have written elsewhere. Less well known, not nearly as well known as it deserves to be, is her lovely set of poetic reflections entitled *Fires*. This is not a book I read so much as I live with it. The same may be said for Anne Carson's lovely little volume, *Eros The Bittersweet*, which has been impossible for me to use in my classes because, whenever I read it, there is simply nothing left for me to say. Her book made me wonder seriously if I had anything left to add to this vast topic. Luckily for me, there is no end to erotic discourse. With each passing springtime, new love songs float across the nation's airwaves. So it has proven possible for me, even still, to write this book. In so doing, I have relied extensively on Martha Nussbaum, who is such an indelible presence in my footnotes. I have been savoring her philosophical reflections on the nature of human loving for so long that I can scarcely remember how these matters looked to me before she showed me how they appeared to her. *The Fragility of Goodness* is another charter text for anyone involved in this good work.

That marvelously interdisciplinary journal of theology, the arts, and humanities, *Soundings*, represents the first venue in which my own written work appeared. Since then, the *Soundings* editor, Ralph V. Norman, has become a significant champion of my work and a cherished friend. He and his staff—as well as the Department of Religion and the University Honors Program at the University of Tennessee at Knoxville—have continued to provide a venue for my thoughts and have been eager boosters of my own research interests. Without the challenge that my presence in their pages represents, I would find it literally impossible to conceive of the grand hybris of writing books at all. I am more grateful to them than I can properly say, but want at least to thank them here for their kind permission to reprint portions of two essays that have appeared previously in the pages of *Soundings*.

I have also been richly blessed with the kind of discerning and self-less editorial assistance of which most writers can only dream. Since the major ideas in this book first were birthed some four years ago, they have been helpfully nurtured, amplified, and nudged toward maturity by the editorial staff at the State University of New York Press. I am especially grateful to Jane Bunker for her help in acquiring four anonymous read-ings of an earlier manuscript draft, each of which called for helpful addi-tions and rewriting which have thoroughly improved my arguments. It was also Jane Bunker who secured permission to pursue this project to that tentative kind of completion we call "books." I am also grateful to Laurie Searl for the care she has devoted to a book not her own. This book is infinitely better for the loving attention paid to it. How much bet-ter the book could be still is known to no one quite so well as myself.

Finally, there are other well-loved friends to thank. To the degree that *erōs* is all about limiting the limitless, I will confine myself to men-tioning only two. Barney L. Jones was my chief mentor in the long col-lege years. He very graciously gave up that role, preferring the far more complex and demanding role of friend. And so he has been, ever since I graduated from Duke University in 1983. He has done what no friend ought to have to do: he has read every word I have ever written, not once, but many times over. I find myself unable to think anywhere quite so clearly as when I am with him, walking the beach near his home in Bridgehampton, New York, surveying the limitlessness of an ocean that nevertheless always manages to be confined within a horizon, and a shoreline. An essential part of his presence in my life has been his wife, Marjorie, who has been so singularly generous and unsparing of his time and energy. If love always brings with it the possibility (I would say the *inevitability*) of jealousy, then it is remarkable to me how fortunate I have been to work among friends who do not live in the grips of that most grasping of human emotions.

Still, *erōs* ultimately has something to do with taking risks. It involves accepting the fact that we are not finally in control of some pretty essential human matters. It is all about responding, in fitting ways, to things whose origin lies very much outside of us. It is about liv-ing in the passive, as well as in the active, voice. *Erōs*, the poets insist,

involves us in the acceptance of a wound. As a bowshot. From elsewhere. We do not choose the wound; it chooses us, paradoxically, if we
are deemed worthy of it. Because this is so, *erōs* is all bound up in moral
questions, questions about the appropriate place of risk, and of vulnerability, in the creation and enrichment of a human life.

On a brilliantly cold January afternoon in the winter of 1935, on a train
shuttling its fateful passengers from Cape Breton Island to New York City,
sat a young nurse who, from the evidence of photographs I have seen
taken at roughly this time, was a stunning beauty. Her skin virtually
shines, serene and transluscent; her face—most especially in the eyes—is
expansive, welcoming, and vigorously alive. She was returning to New
York against her better judgment, having been called down to assist a
patient with whom she had previously worked and who required round-
the-clock care just then. Her hesitancy derived from the fact that she was
preparing to move from her home in Sydney, Nova Scotia, to the Philippines. She had boarded the train in Sydney late in the evening, at some
time after 10 PM, and after passing the first night traveling southward and
westward, the train stopped to pick up transferring passengers in Monc-
ton, New Brunswick. The man who would be my grandfather—and thus,
genetically speaking, fully one quarter of the man *I* am—was among them,
just returning from the Christmas holidays on Prince Edward Island. Several hours into the trip, they met, and the rest of their trip lay in the playful hands of the very powers I will be trying to understand in this book.
  Wonderfully charismatic, an inventor by trade, an enormous grizzly
bear of a man, but also the gentlest person she had ever known, Louis
Ruprecht was a widower, and forty years her senior. By the end of that
long first day and the ensuing evening, all of it spent deep in that earnest
kind of conversation one may occasionally have with newfound friends
in precisely such settings, my grandmother knew that she was not going
to the Philippines, or anywhere else for that matter. Her destiny lay elsewhere. Six weeks later, the two were married. And, in a sense far more
literal than most of us can tolerate thinking about for long, it is only
because of this bold decision that I exist at all.
  So, with winsome memories of a grandfather I never knew, and with
the very grandest gratitude to a young woman for answering the call of
that playful, wingéd god, this book is dedicated to my grandmother,
Geraldine Murray Ruprecht.

Acknowledgments

The frontispiece, Salvator Dali's *Paris and Helen of Troy*, is reproduced here with the kind permission of the Fundación Gala–Salvator Dali/Artists Rights Society (ARS), New York.

"Endings," "The Fist," and "Love after Love" from *Collected Poems 1948–1984* by Derek Walcott. Copyright © 1986 by Derek Walcott. Reprinted by permission of Farrar, Straus and Giroux, Inc., and Faber and Faber Limited.

"Bypassing Rue Descartes" from *The Collected Poems 1931–1987* by Czeslaw Milosz. Translated by Renata Gorczyniski and Robert Hass. Copyright © 1988 by Czeslaw Milosz Royalties, Inc. Reprinted by permission of The Ecco Press.

Portions of Chapter 2 have appeared previously as "A Funny Thing Happens on the Way to Mantineia" in *Soundings* 75.1, and are reprinted here with permission.

The editorial staff at *Soundings* has also graciously granted permission to reprint a passage from Martha C. Nussbaum's "Reply" in *Soundings* 72.4, as well as the map on page 44.

ON BEGINNING CAUTIOUSLY

or, What Do We Mean By Ethics?

Sie sind den christlichen Gott los und glauben nun um so mehr die christliche Moral festhalten zu müssen: das ist eine *englische* Folgerichtigkeit.

They have gotten rid of the Christian God, and cling all the more tightly to Christian morality. That's *English* consistency for you.
—Nietzsche, *Twilight of the Idols*, "Skirmishes"

The title of this book, *Symposia*, is a candid description of an emphatic authorial intention. I envision these independent, but intimately related, chapters as literal "symposia," as repeated passes at the same material, repeated walks over some of the same rough terrain. One chapter builds on the insights, or rather, on the sense of wonder, ideally achieved in the last. Or, to shift the metaphor, which is a very large part of what modern philosophers attempt to do: these chapters represent philosophical attempts to peel away one layer of the onion after another, in order to see more clearly what lies in the heart. My title also deliberately recalls Plato's *Symposium*, of course; that winsome dialogue serves as a sort of lodestar throughout this book and lies literally at its heart, in the second chapter. The book is a meditation, in large part, on what I will call Plato's "erotic philosophy," so suprisingly prominent in the Middle Period dialogues.

But the real argument is in the subtitle, I suppose: *Plato, the Erotic, and Moral Value*. Erotics and Ethics: that is the important (Platonic) connection I am attempting to trace. Viewed one way, there is a certain obviousness about this connection. Sexual activity has historically been among the most highly regulated, legislated, and litigated of all human activities. Its value, its place in a properly ordered human life, is also one of the most vexing and hotly debated of all philosophical and theological questions. We tend to regulate what we fear the most. We tend to normalize those very realities and relations that we all worry may not be susceptible to norms in any simple way. It is where the lines get blurriest that we seem intent on drawing them most sharply. There is no cartography for the human soul.

That is why, viewed another way, this alleged connection between erotics and ethics seems most peculiar. *Erōs* is an outlaw deity, refusing to respect social conventions or sexual boundaries. He is customarily portrayed as a child, armed to the teeth with painfully disruptive darts. The tragic and comic stages in antiquity were impressively peopled with sexual transgressors. The power of the erotic is portrayed as overwhelming, whether humorously or disastrously so. The Greek lyric poets (not to mention the Romantics, with whom I also see myself in conversation) have, more often than not, knowingly celebrated the singular hypocrisy of lip-service fidelity, often while coyly advertising their adulterous "amores" for all to read. And they have been, some of them in any case, in times more puritanical, exiled for their candor. There is clearly a connection between the erotic and the ethical domains. But what in the world can it be?

As my subtitle indicates, I intend to use Plato's vast resources for assistance in thinking through this devilish question. But I come at the question, inevitably, with a host of modern concerns, many of them quite different from Plato's own. For starters, it is not entirely clear to me what we mean by "erotic," nor what we mean by "ethics," when we use these words today. The words are so heavy, so fraught with philosophical significance, that they run the very real risk of meaning everything to us . . . and therefore nothing at all. I find myself wrestling with a very modern notion of what we wish "ethics" to be, but I have found an ancient account of "the erotic" to be a singularly helpful standpoint from which to think these thoughts through. It is precisely that dialogue—from antiquity, to our modernity, and back again—that I have tried to display in this book.

One final paradox should at least be acknowledged here at the outset. I have found no modern moralist more engaging, none more illuminating, and none more innervating than Friedrich Nietzsche. I will devote most of this introduction to a rather personal reaction to his thought, although after that he will become a more subterranean, less visible presence. My understanding of what we wish "ethics" to be, the work we moderns wish it to do for us, is deeply indebted to Nietzsche's profound and restless question-posing. If I do not fully accept his answers, my debt to his work is no less for that. I call this fact paradoxical, because Nietzsche is himself so relentlessly critical of Plato, another philosopher in whom I find many of my own questions helpfully advanced. Plato, after all, not Nietzsche, appears in my title. In this introduction I will try to say why that is the case. The way I read Plato, the questions it occurs to me to ask of him, are powerfully influenced by Nietzsche's meditations on modern ethics and the moral life. What I notice in Plato at the end, however—something I do not think Nietzsche was particularly well suited to see—was a patient insistence on the importance of the erotic in the construction and completion of a moral life. In this book, then, I will try to illustrate something of what I think this all means. But in order to do so, fittingly enough, I find that I must tell a story first, and a personal story at that.

I

I received my doctoral degree in Religious Studies in the spring of 1990. What I would like to do, by way of cautious beginning, is to reflect a bit on the way in which that degree—what it means, and how it is perceived—has changed in the ensuing six or seven years. The degree changed for me personally because I became ever more deeply involved in the texture of archaic and classical Greek thought. The *public* change in the perception of my degree was made all the more dramatic because it began at a time when I just so happened to be living outside of the country. After I finished my coursework, I arranged to move to Greece, where I had previously worked on an excavation in northwestern Crete, where I managed somehow to rough out a dissertation, and where I ended up staying for two years in all. It seems to me that some of the essential changes I will be narrating here took place in that decisive transatlantic interim between 1988 and 1990, during what became, albeit in retrospect, *my* "Grecian journey."

I was faced with an interesting sort of moral dilemma—if that is the right term for it—whenever I traveled in those years. On planes and trains alike, I seemed always to be seated next to a somewhat older person, vaguely reminiscent of one of my own grandparents. These women and men invariably—very much like my own grandparents, now that I think about it—were deeply interested to learn that I was pursuing a doctoral degree. And, of course, upon learning this their inevitable next question was, "What exactly are you studying?"

This was the moment that presented an acute moral dilemma. My official course of study was housed in a program somewhat grandly entitled "Ethics and Society," but it was part of a much larger system called "the Graduate Division of Religion." Technically speaking, then, there were *two* appropriate answers to the question: "ethics" or "religion." My answer, by and large—and I am not too proud to be admitting this—depended entirely on whether I had other things I felt the need to get done on the plane.

If I had the time, and wanted to talk—as Socrates seemed always to want to do—then I would say that I studied religion. That answer pretty well guaranteed that I would be involved in a discussion that would surely last until the plane landed, and quite possibly longer. *Everyone* has an opinion about religion. The remarkable thing—I suspect that this is a little-recognized feature of life in North America, one more example of our cultural peculiarity—is that people in this country want so badly to discuss religion among themselves. On the face of it, it seems a rather personal matter, the kind of thing about which we might simply agree to disagree, and in any case *not* to discuss in polite society.

Not so in North America. Religion, which we pretty well all agree has no constitutional place in our federal or state civic institutions, and which we all pretty well agree has been *privatized* for the good of the body politic, is nevertheless one of the most *publicly* discussed matters in this society.[1] We try to keep it out of public debate—no wars are quite so intractable as religious wars, not even our much-touted "culture wars"—yet religious issues refuse to be so sidelined, creeping forever back into civil discourse and the political process, even and especially when we are most deliberately trying to keep them out.

So it went on the planes and trains of my own graduate trajectory—when I had the time to talk. If I did not have the time for conversation (let's say that I had a book to read or a paper to write, a not uncommon dilemma in those years)—then I would never think to mention "religion." I would simply inform my neighbors that I studied "ethics." For whatever reasons, this was a conversation-stopper. Hearing this, my adoptive grandparents invariably turned to their in-flight magazines, or else to their presumably more interesting neighbor to the right. I was located on the left, somehow, simply by naming myself "an ethicist."

II

What is going on, I began to wonder? Part of the answer, of course, has something to do with the ill-defined place which intellectuals have in North American society. We who work in universities can only pine away for the Parisian intellectual scene, in which philosophers are public figures, interviewed prominently in the newspapers. Along the Seine, thinking is sexy, as we suppose everything in Paris to be.

By contrast, here, on the North American leg of my intellectual journey, no one ever really asked me for information, much less for guidance, in any of these conversations, whichever way I answered. If I said that I studied "religion," then they proceeded to talk nonstop until we landed. They might ask me for a few informational points of clarification, and perhaps for a little story or two which they might share around the supper table. But I was under no illusions about what was obviously my completely dispensable part in this monologue-duologue. That is the bizarre paradox of religion in North America: everyone has an opinion about it, and yet the opinions seldom seem to divide us the way they might—the way they continue to do, in places like Bosnia or Northern Ireland. The important thing here seems to be to have a religion, *any* religion. So long as you are religious—no matter the way—things move along. Conviction of a curiously undefined sort seems to sell. Even Native American and yogic spiritual traditions can be turned into commodities here. Ours is a religiously saleable society.

Things were, if anything, even more confusing when I admitted that I studied something called "ethics." If we are confused in this society about religious matters, then we are doubly confused about matters moral. I will return to that point, to say a little more about why this might be so. But first I want to press the question: Why should the claim that I study something called "ethics" have provoked such consternation and *silence?* What is so off-putting about "ethics?"

As the careers of too many politicians and televangelists illustrate, we in this society do not like moralists. We especially bristle at the thought of being told what to do or what to think. Normative claims sit uneasily with us, especially to the degree that we accept a vaguely Protestant narrative that insists (somewhat disingenuously) that "we" left Europe to get away from all of that. The Pilgrims crossed the ocean, not so much in search of religious freedom, which they already had found in Holland, than in search of arable land. But let that lie. Nothing delights our tabloids and newspapers more than a vocal moralist who is subsequently caught with his or her hands in the cookie jar. *Why* are we so delighted? Why should *moral failure* delight us? To be sure, we are delighted to catch "them" in hypocrisy, it seems, women and men guilty of violating the very rules they themselves preach most publicly. Yet our own hypocrisy in being so thoroughly delighted is equally grave—we, after all, seem to be saying that "we" do not wish to judge moral matters in the way that "they" do. Save, it would seem, when it suits our purposes.

I offer this scenario as one possible explanation for why "ethics" was in such ill repute in the late 1980s in North America. Political and religious hypocrisy seemed to be in the air. I had the distinct feeling that those with whom I spoke sensed moral judgment coming from me, as a natural outgrowth of what I studied, long before I ever opened my mouth. Ethics, it seemed, was something that a lot of North Americans thought we'd be better served without. They were visibly tired of it.

What I want to suggest now is a little silly, because I will be making an observation about this society as if I stand *outside* of it, and of course I do not. Moreover, if I am even roughly correct in this, then we stand too close to these developments to know what they mean yet. Proximity can be a philosophical problem in such cultural affairs. Still, I did stand outside of this country for two years or more; the country looked and felt quite different to me when I came home again.

Something changed seismically about seven years ago, as nearly as I can tell. When I returned and began having these same conversations again, I noticed something really quite remarkable—remarkable, at least, to me. Quite simply, the moral situation was reversed. And I was left with a troubling personal question: Had the country changed, or had I?

My first clue that something had changed was that I never seemed to be getting my work done on airplanes or trains anymore. The answer to enquiries which had been met with a stony silence in the past was now generating great interest. And the things which had been the source of so much interest before were no longer so interesting. People seemed frankly bored with religious matters. It was *morality* that got their attention.

So it is that I began to have the kinds of conversations that I can narrate now. I can confidently assume that it will be intelligible, that the reader may even have had a version of it him or herself. Feeling pressed to get an article written (notice this change, too—"papers" had become "articles" in the interim, a testament, perhaps, to my dawning postdoctoral self-importance), I offered what had been a real conversation-stopper before: namely, the fact that I had taken my degree in "ethics." But this answer was no longer met with the stony silence and vague discomfiture that it had ensured me in years past. Instead, people's interest was piqued. "Good for you," was the most common reply in the nineties, "we need more of that in this world." We need *more* of something called "ethics," I was now being told, not less of it. What, besides the so-called Gulf War, had happened while I was away?

And now the still, nagging voice to which Socrates had taught me to be attentive kept asking me the famous Socratic question, famous above all for its aporetic indeterminacy: "What is it?" Ethics, I was being told now, was a matter of the gravest cultural importance. "We need more of it," I was told. But what in the world did they think "it" was?

III

Answering that complex question requires a change of venue. Quite fortuitously, I fell into a temporary position at Emory University, where I was blessed with the opportunity to teach for fully five years (in departments of Religion and Classics, tellingly enough). It seems to me that, if we want to understand the common North American preoccupation with ethics in the 1990s, then we need to attend to what has been happening at our major universities. Intellectuals in this country may not have the public status that they enjoy in Paris, but they do have an interesting way of working behind the scenes in this country, setting certain essential social agendas and helping to define some of the buzzwords which make the North American moral motor hum. Most young people go to college in this country now, and they learn, among other things, how to *argue* there, how to argue about moral matters.

Now, I will not endeavor to describe some narrative fiction called "*the* North American university." Rather, I will continue to reflect upon what my own experience was like, there and then, at Emory. This is, after all, a *story* every bit as much as it is a piece of moral reflection,[2] *and* an introduction to a book about the "erotic" dimension of Plato's thought.

At Emory, we shared the widespread public sentiment that "ethics" was something we needed more of. We oversaw the creation of a new office that was called "The Ethics Center," but whose official title was the somewhat more ponderous "Center for Ethics in Public Policy and the Professions." Such "ethics centers" are emerging at an astonishing number of institutions: from Emory and Georgia State and Georgia Tech—all three of them in Atlanta—to Harvard and Princeton and Duke, and other elite private institutions. Even the U.S. Naval Academy in Annapolis has gotten into this business, along with the other three national service academies, which were required to install a coherent "ethics component" into their mandatory curriculum (thereby eliminating the last elective course the midshipmen had in a long, four-year academic career). Coupled with these developments, "ethics conferences" have recently come of age as well. Much as "the body" came into academic fashion ten years ago, and much as "the erotic" became fashionable more recently, so now "ethics" has become an uncommonly attractive academic commodity. That is the larger development I am trying to comprehend: the newfound prominence of "the ethical."

Our Ethics Center was an office in search of self-definition (as were we all), but some initiatives were pretty clear, pretty early on. Above all, the Ethics Center was responsible for defining an academic concentration, of sorts, by tracking every course offered anywhere in the college which had an "ethical" component (whatever that meant). You cannot major, or minor, in ethics at Emory University, not yet, but I suspect that one day within the next five years you will be able to do so. This is a shocking development.

Now, the emerging list of ethics courses was, I think, a telling one, and I would like to pause here to reflect upon it, briefly. As nearly as I can tell, what count as ethics courses in the contemporary university break down into two distinct groups. On the one hand, we teach ethics classes that present a series of "hard cases," courses in which nothing is ever really resolved, but in which we do demonstrate a remarkable facility for seeing two or more sides to every issue. So we descend into the alleged morass of gay sexuality, abortion, the death penalty, and nuclear deterrence.

Having said that, I am well aware that any number of these issues are not intractable for a great many people, that many of us will have strong opinions on one side or the other of any given issue—but that is precisely the point, in an increasingly pluralistic intellectual environment. We teach both sides of these issues, admitting to the presence of strong convictions on both, and leave the matter formally unresolved in this way. The same strategy characterizes the early Platonic dialogues, of course. Students, after all, must be free to make up their own minds.

We gain a moral sensitivity to the moral complexity of every policy question, to the fact that people on all sides share an equal fervor and conviction. We customarily gain a vast skill at living with that type of moral perplexity. We all are encouraged to become moral pluralists of a sort. We are taught to feel more at home "amid fragments,"[3] perhaps even to forget what whole moral structures looked like, "once upon a time."[4]

Now, this dead end—what Plato called an *aporia*—brings me to a second way of teaching ethics, when we don't know precisely what the word means, an approach even more disconcerting in its way. That is to teach courses on what I would call the "self-evident." You don't need a college course—and you certainly don't need a Ph.D. or a pluralistic education—to recognize Nazism as morally problematic or the death camps as a moral scar carved into the very texture of this turbulent century. You do not presumably need a moral theory to teach you this. Moral intuitions are thought to be quite sufficient. Gone here is the moral perplexity, gone are the various shades of gray. Everything is suddenly clear and distinct—precisely as our other "ethics" courses teach us that moral matters can rarely, if ever, be. It has been suggested that the way North American students flock to such courses is indicative of the fact that they are thus nurtured in the belief that our "cultural values" actually are still intact, even when we know deep down that they are not. If we can draw one really sharp line, then our values must not really be incoherent, and we are not really living "amid fragments." If we can still talk about "ethics," then perhaps our beliefs are not in the same disarray that we fear they are. Perhaps our foundations are still stable and secure. We cling all the more tightly to a fallen morality *when* it falls, much as Nietzsche suggested.

This point invites emphasis and clarification. The history of the Holocaust is an essential piece of the story of the European twentieth century. And the story must not be forgotten. Yet such a course, devoted to such a topic, is not "ethical," precisely speaking, in the same way that our other courses were. Rather, such courses are perceived to be "ethical" in an apocalyptic intellectual environment where book titles like *Ethics* After *Babel*[5] or *Ethics* After *Auschwitz*[6] or *Ethics* After *Hiroshima*[7] make an immediate kind of sense. By invoking Auschwitz and Hiroshima, we seem to be suggesting that we do, indeed, live amid moral fragments at the end of the millennium—even and especially when we are telling ourselves, a little wistfully, that we do not.

With that caveat in place, let me return for one moment more to the airplane, where I have just been congratulated for what I do. What does this woman or man think that I teach his or her grandchildren in college? Am I one of the ones who problematizes everything, or makes everything clearer? Am I the person who will help Jack or Jill learn how to make clearer and better moral choices? Or am I the person who will help them become essentially, and eloquently, confused? If I am being congratulated, then what am I being congratulated for, exactly? If ethics is something we need more of, then what in the world is it—in the public perception, and in my own?

My tentative observation about my own students' four years of college, and the so-called ethical training that most of them receive there, runs as follows: Our students are being trained with coherent and even admirable intellectual goals, yet I would suggest that they are designed to be discrepant with each other. Students are taught to see two sides to every issue—except for the ones where they don't. Students are taught to "tolerate" things—except for what we tell them is "intolerable." Except for intolerance itself. And, with the rosy moral lenses they have been given through which to view the world, the brutal fact that some conflicts are less tractable than others, that some moral issues simply will not go away, is lost on them. It has been argued that this is the ultimate fate of political liberalism, by the way.[8] While I do not agree finally with that diagnosis, it *is* possible to read certain cultural landmarks in precisely this way.

This issue came into singular focus during the recent Chinese diplomatic visit. Our administration insisted on talking about universal "human rights." The Chinese kept talking about "cultural difference," and about "national sovereignty," using our own language to silence us quite effectively. The only argument left to the U.S. administration seemed to be the hopelessly vague idea of "being on the wrong side of history." And that is where the conversation stalled. It was somehow all quite unsatisfying *and* disturbing. For these are intractable moral arguments, and no amount of moral theory or classroom conditioning will make them more easily resolvable—unless we arbitrarily decide to silence one side or another.

Now, this is rather uncomfortable news for those of us who, according to Nietzsche, cling all the more tightly to a morality when we know that it can no longer be firmly grounded. And so I ask my original question, again, but with a new twist. Not "What is ethics?" this time, but rather, "Why am I being *congratulated* for teaching it?" It seems almost more trouble than it is worth.

IV

I would like to suggest a somewhat different approach to the purpose of an ethics classroom, one closer to the Platonic notion of what "ethics" entails. I take seriously the etymological idea that "ethics" (*ta ēthika*) is about what the Greeks called *ēthos*, that is to say, *character*.

Most of the decisions, the really "ethical" decisions, we make every day are neither so interminable as complex cross-cultural political debate, nor so self-evident as the rather abstract statement that "genocide is wrong." Rather, our ethical lives are lived at a remarkably rich, and bracing level of everydayness. Interest in the "everyday" is something that has preoccupied much moral theory of late. Consider:

- My friend is in need, having just broken off a long-term relationship, yet I made dinner plans for this evening weeks ago. Do I cancel them?
- Another friend is soon to marry, I think mistakenly. Should I say something? Dare I say something?
- I'm about to "borrow" a stamp from the office, because I did not have time to visit an ATM today . . . should I? Isn't this technically stealing?
- I am a vegetarian—neither for health nor for religious reasons—and I've been invited to come along to a dinner with friends of friends. They serve meat of one form or another—in the words of a friend of mine, "something with a face." Should I eat?

These are all lovely examples of rather urgent moral dilemmas, illustrative of the rich moral complexity of human social life, the sheer adventure of daily living together in groups.[9] They all involve *desire* in one form or another, as Plato saw so clearly in the Erotic Period.

I take Plato's claim to be that *erōs* is one of the human being's primary and most fundamental moral gestures. We decide when and where to commit ourselves to another person, erotically and romantically. We anguish over when, and where, and why, to sever such a bond. Each of these issues is agonizing, each in its own way. Each requires a very particular kind of courage and conviction and practical wisdom. Lives can be disrupted by this, hearts broken, and persons involved in the disarray they leave behind do not survive the experience with their characters unscarred. Yet each of these issues is very far from the medical clinic, or the missile silo, or the death camp (I am not suggesting that these places are morally equivalent, although I recognize that there are some who make precisely this connection, in ways which I find morally misleading). Most of us live most of our lives in this rather more *intermediate* moral domain, a place that Plato called *metaxu*, "in between." Most of the moral life takes place in this vast arena of "in-between-ness." Where ethics is thought to be nothing more than the confrontation with hard cases and with calamity, this rich and rather obvious fact is easily forgotten.

We may well gravitate to ethics courses to help us identify "the sort of persons"[10] we would like to be, and to anticipate our daily responses to some of life's everyday moral dilemmas. Some call this "values clarification"; some call it other things less kind. Martha Nussbaum has put this point well in response to a series of essays devoted to her own moral viewpoint and its recovery of "the Aristotelian way":

> We have friends to love and help and enjoy, children to raise and educate, a city and country and world to make better. We have death to face well, our appetites to educate and to manage. There is generosity to friends; there are parties to give, kind and amusing and gracious remarks to make. There is learning and understanding; there is justice. Being human in the Aristotelian way leaves no time for wallowing, clearly. It is the job of a complete life.[11]

Using this elegant insight as a sort of springboard, let me reiterate now the main point that I have been rather long in making. In the past several years, I have quite suddenly come to be congratulated for the same thing that elicited scorn or silence seven short years ago: the teaching of something called "ethics." And I have suggested one working hypothesis to help explain this dramatic change.

The diagnosis is Nietzsche's. We cling all the more tightly to the language of moral standards at precisely the moment when we suspect that they cannot be grounded. We can actually and cogently preside over the death of every classical theological idea we have ever had—about providence, about justice and its relation to the natural order, even about eternal life—and still cling to the same moral standards, all the while. We can claim most loudly that we are a "Christian nation" in the very moment when we are most clearly not so, culturally, anymore.[12] We do away with a God, Nietzsche says, then cling all the more tightly to that same God's morality. That may or may not be "English consistency," as Nietzsche would have it, but it *is* clearly a response to an apocalyptic perception[13]—the perception that things are falling apart, and that our center cannot hold. Beasts, blond or otherwise, are forever slinking toward Bethlehem to be born.

In the final analysis, I do not follow where Nietzsche leads, but I find much truth in his diagnosis of modern culture and its confusion about morality. Nietzsche has helped me to understand what I see going on around me in the university. And I consider him one of the most perceptive and provocative thinkers about moral developments in the past century and a half. He developed his unique philosophical vision out of a sustained, lifelong encounter with what he called "Greek" thought. He taught as a classics professor for fully a decade before poor health forced his early retirement. And before criticizing Nietzsche, I want to defend his intuition for just a moment more.

Remember his claim: "they have gotten rid of the Christian God, and cling all the more tightly to Christian morality. That's *English* consistency for you." Walk into any Unitarian Church in North America, and what you will in all likelihood find is precisely what Nietzsche was talking about. Earnest and morally serious persons, seriously engaged in doing some of the good and hard work that so desperately needs doing in the larger society, yet feeling vaguely uncomfortable, even embarrassed, every time the name of 'God' or 'Christ' is invoked. They may read the *Bhagavad Gita*, or even Plato in such a church, but not the New Testament. That, I think, was the trend Nietzsche anticipated so clearly. He adds:

> In England one must rehabilitate oneself after every little emancipation from theology by showing oneself to be an absolute fanatic for morality. That is the *penance* they pay there.[14]

"For others of us," he continues, "it is otherwise." Be sure to notice that the operative assumptions behind Nietzsche's analysis are twofold. The first is that things have come apart—*which is to say that they once held together*. I am very suspicious of that nostalgic claim. In any case, Nietzsche's second assumption follows from his first.

> When one gives up on the Christian faith, then one tramples the *right* to a Christian morality underfoot. It is absolutely *not* self-evident . . . Christianity is a system, an integrated and *total* perspective on things. If you remove the central notion, the belief in God, then you shatter the whole thing: you no longer hold anything necessary in your hands. Christianity sets before us the view that man does not know, *can* not know, what is good and what is evil for him: he believes in God, who alone knows this. Christian morality is a command; its origin is transcendent; it stands beyond criticism, beyond even any right to criticism. It possesses the truth only insofar as God is the truth—it all hangs or falls with the belief in God.[15]

That is the assumption I question most emphatically. This romanticized and idealized picture of the past—as a golden age, or as a coherent world of seamless beliefs—leads almost inevitably to a postured despair about the contemporary situation. The ancients—classical or Christian, it hardly seems to matter—become the measure of our modern fall from grace. Things never have held together so seamlessly; God's commands are seldom clear; there is no such "system," religious or moral or otherwise. Moral perplexity seems to me to be one of the permanent features of human social life. Not every case is a "hard case," but every society has its hard cases. And it is necessary, somehow, to find a way to live with the moral life's hardness. This Nietzsche himself tried to do (*sei hart!*, his Zarathustra tells us),[16] with only partial success.

There is another, a more *hidden* assumption—hidden, in part, because it is completely unstated—that makes Nietzsche's insights so grand and so compelling. It is, I think, the same vague intuition that has animated all of my conversations on planes and trains in the past decade. It is an assumption about what ethics is. And here we meet a shocking paradox: Nietzsche never tells us what he thinks ethics is anymore than my adoptive grandparents did.[17]

Wondering why that might be so has led me to some further observations. One of them I have already mentioned. That is the notion that the contemporary fascination with ethics has something deeply apocalyptic about it. Ethics is the place to which we turn in order to come to terms with matters of moral enormity like state-sponsored executions, federally funded abortions, the decision to wage war and how to wage it, the texture of institutional genocide, the decision to stockpile or to use nuclear weapons and other weapons of mass destruction . . . in a word, matters of life or death.

To be sure, each of these issues is fraught with matters of pressing and even outrageous moral concern. Yet there is an ethos of the bazaar,[18] an ethos of dinner parties (which Plato and other Greeks so popularized as institutionalized *symposia*), an ethos implicit in meeting persons whom we do not yet know, especially when the meeting takes place in a culture, or a language, not our own. These are all primarily cosmopolitan matters, the fundamental ethos of the great Mediterranean city.[19] There is an ethos, finally, of loving attentively and well, the character of which may have *everything* to do with the proper fashioning of human lives and moral selves. These things, too, bear attention in any ethical discussion about the sorts of persons we aspire to be. Loving, Plato seems to suggest in the Erotic Period, is an outrageously moral and spiritual human gesture. So it is that this book, which wanted initially to be about religion and morality, could not directly be about either one. For *erōs* kept getting in the way. This, as even Nietzsche was forced to admit,[20] we ought to have learned from Plato.

V

So, I begin again with the old Socratic question: *What is ethics?* My hypothesis goes something like this: Every society, like every language, has its buzzwords. Buzzwords do not *need* to be grounded. Simply by invoking them, the moral argument has for all intents and purposes been made. Speak of "rights," or of "the separation of church and state," at least in North America, and the argument has largely been made. 'Good' and 'evil', as Nietzsche saw with such astonishing clarity, are two particularly interesting examples of such buzzwords.[21] Especially, he went on to argue, in the post-Enlightenment *European* world. Many others would, I think, agree to that diagnosis—if not to Nietzsche's rather jarring proposals for a cure.

I began this meditation with a suspicion that one of the buzzwords in this culture is "religion." "Tolerance" and "multicultural" are two others (I will return to them in the conclusion), and I strongly suspect that "modern" has become one as well. Now I wish to add "ethics" to this august list. It is not that these words mean nothing, but rather that they are *supersaturated* with meaning. They do not mean too *little*; we almost ask them to mean too *much*. Now, clearly, these or *any* society's buzzwords need to be interrogated. That is one task that "ethics," of the Socratic and Platonic sort, ought to be about.

But there is more to this matter, and in order to get at this properly, I think that we need to go back *behind* Nietzsche, *behind* the Enlightenment, back to the same Greeks with whom he was attempting to think— especially to Socrates who, as even Nietzsche was forced to admit, set so much of this ethical agenda for all of us. "Socrates," so he confesses to himself in 1875, "if I am to be honest with myself, is so close to me that I feel myself constantly at war with him."[22]

Nietzsche began his career as what we would today call a classicist (and what the Germans of his own day called *Philologen*). It was an impressive title for a relatively new discipline[23] that had everything to do with the German Romantics' preoccupation with Greek literature. That is one reason, by the way, that Nietzsche eventually left the field. He simply couldn't bear what was being published in Germany in the name of "the Greeks." And when he tried to publish something different— namely, *The Birth of Tragedy*—he was essentially exiled for his trouble.

To listen to the German classicists tell it, Socrates and Plato (and through them, *all* of the Greeks) were wonderfully congenial conversation-partners, precisely because—lo and behold—they shared so many nineteenth-century, Protestant, Prussian moral tastes. They were, so said the academic establishment, "speaking our language." "Their" buzz-words—justice, moderation, courage—were like "ours," or so it was believed at the time.

Nietzsche's classical revolution, if that is not too strong a phrase (and I do not think that it is), consisted of the scandalous claim that Plato was *not* really the greatest Greek who ever lived, and neither was Socrates. Nietzsche suggested that there was an entirely different Greece, an entirely different ideal, that animated Greek literature in the generation or two *prior to* Socrates. Nietzsche called this "the tragic age." And he insisted that "the Greeks" were much older than classical scholars thought, an insight that the next hundred years of classical scholarship did much to confirm. As he put the matter in an unpublished essay in 1876:

> Men today marvel at the gospel of the tortoise and the hare— ah, those Greeks simply ran too fast. I do not look for happy times in history; I look for times which provide suitable soil for the *cultivation* of genius. I see such a time in the period prior to the Persian Wars. One cannot learn enough about it.[24]

There is a world here not dreamt of by our classicists, Nietzsche suggested. It is a world where moral matters are not primary, a world where *tragedy and erōs* are the primary concerns.

I would like to hang onto this Nietzschean insight, while at the same time blurring one of his sharpest lines. I do not want to have to choose *between* the tragedians and Socrates, *between erōs* and Platonic philosophy; I want them both. And indeed, I think that we may have them both. For the tragic and erotic traditions are the ones to which Socrates and Plato are responding. Their notion of what "ethics" entails is deeply indebted to these prior genres. "Ethics" has everything to do with tragedy, with facing up to failure, and with erotic passion. That is the singular insight of Plato's Erotic Period.

If you consider the matter—as I have been doing for quite some time now—my colleagues in moral philosophy on the nation's major mass-transit lines all look to ethics as a way to solve "the problem of perplexity." Whether by providing us with clearer answers, or else by assisting us in living without them, "ethics" somehow has been conceived as being in the business of perplexity. So it is that the question of morals and the question of truth are linked—precisely as Nietzsche links them. He tells us that the two are inseparable. And now, living after the collapse of the truth-standard (Nietzsche's much-touted "death of God"), morality will have to go as well. The distinctly modern retrieval of "the ethical" is part of a much larger modern fixation on the apparent groundlessness of moral appeals, and the enduring difficulty of securing universalizable moral judgments. We worry about this at the United Nations, and worry about it in our increasingly multicultural college classrooms.

To my mind "the Greeks" tell a rather different moral tale. They investigate the moral life only after they have turned our intellectual kaleidoscope a quarter-turn or so. Their buzzwords are not like ours—not even some of the ones, like *erōs*, that we think we understand. Their moral world does not look immediately like ours, in part because their understanding of what "ethics" entails is so vastly different. I want to suggest that the tradition of Greek moral thinking was far more concerned with the inescapable phenomenon of *moral failure* than it was with *moral certainty* or with "finding *the* right thing to do." The Greeks were far more comfortable than Anglo-American philosophers (at least after Nietzsche) are with the idea of *moral intuition* as a necessary first step in a moral argument,[25] with the idea that we know what we should do far more often than we do not. *The Greeks did not deny the existence of moral perplexity; they simply were not obsessed with it.* We seem to be obsessed with it just now.

This crucial distinction seems to be one of the major realizations of twentieth-century Continental thought, especially that which sees itself in dialogue with Martin Heidegger—and therefore, of necessity, with Plato as well. Heidegger's *opus, Being and Time* (to which I will return briefly in chapter 3) had everything to do with *using* the resources of Greek thought to rethink the idea of "truth" in ways that do not rely quite so heavily on Enlightenment. That crucial claim is, if anything, made even clearer in a lecture course Heidegger offered in 1925 on Plato's *Sophist.* Here, developing the etymological point with which he remained fascinated throughout his life—namely, that the Greek word, *alētheia*, seems to connote an "un-forgetting" or an "un-covering"—Heidegger notes:

> If we hold fast to the meaning of truth as unconcealedness or uncoveredness, then it becomes clearer that truth means the same thing as compliance. . . . This is objectivity correctly understood. The original sense of this concept of truth does not yet include objectivity as universal validity or universal binding force. That has nothing to do with truth.[26]

Taking this insight on as a major moral insight has been a growing pre-occupation of a great many contemporary thinkers. And it is far from accidental that Plato is the starting point for much of that thought. It is that Platonic starting point that I am interested in recovering in this book.

Let me use an example from my own classroom to illumine this point. I recently asked my students to tell me what they thought the notorious Socratic maxim—"virtue is knowledge"—might mean. Not surprisingly, they began to reflect on the ways in which this claim, if true, would mean that virtue is the same thing for all rational persons. That is to say, virtue is *universalizable*. That's just the way we are trained to think about ethics today.

It took a lot of digging (and a lot of pushing, to be honest) to get them to take seriously the idea that Plato's interest was in moral failure, rather than in moral certainty. The implication, for Socrates, seems to be that, if virtue is a kind of knowledge, then it may—just may, now—be teachable. Even that is the wrong metaphor. Virtue may be *learnable*, not teachable.[27] The focus on *teaching* implies that the decisive activity is the *teacher's*, whereas a focus on *learning* admits that the decisive moral activity is the *student's*. No ethics center, no book, and no teacher can *make* you virtuous. All we can hope to do is to nurture the process of moral development along. Moral development is not the matter of a semester, but rather of a lifetime. Any approach that denies this infantilizes its students, requiring them to aspire to a form of "goodness" with veiled threats, and without telling them why it is good to begin with.

The irony of Greek moral thinking is that, confident though they were in the preliminary value of intuition, they knew well that we violate our most certain moral intuitions, all the time. This is the fact that presented them with perplexity. St. Paul is speaking in a good Greek idiom when he notes, with some astonishment, that he continually does the very thing which he knows he should not do.[28] That experience—of standing outside oneself, virtually watching oneself fail—is an essential moral moment. And no human experience lends itself to these moral gestures quite so readily as *erōs*—a word that rather curiously fails to appear in the Greek New Testament.[29]

It was only a curious brand of eighteenth- and nineteenth-century German, then Anglo-American, scholarship (mostly classical studies, but also philosophy and theology) which first conceived of ethics as a discipline for finding moral certainty. We inhabit that world of expectations still, often enough, in our universities and in the "ethics centers" they are promoting. These expectations may have everything to do with what has changed in the nature of my airplane conversations in the past seven years.

By contrast to such modern ideas, the Greek concern with moral failure was an explicitly *psychological* one. Nietzsche is nowhere more wrong than when he claims to be the *first* philosopher who was also a psychologist.[30] He knows well that Plato was one, too. After all, it was Plato's realization—*not* Socrates', I do not think—that we will need to attend to the nature of the human soul if we are to understand how a person with perfectly clear moral intuitions can violate them so dramatically with his or her very next breath. How can we know the good and not do it? Socrates asked (*Meno* 70a, 87c, and passim). Plato's answer was a *psychological* answer, an attempt to say what it is about the human soul, and what it is in the nature of human loving, which creates this paradox and this precise problem (*Phaedrus* 246a–257a, *Republic* 435b–441d).

In the centuries after Plato, all three of the major Hellenistic schools took this moral insight for granted. Theirs, too, was a concern with moral failure (and emotional disruption) rather than with moral certainty.[31] Moral truth was not yet thought to be "universal binding force." And when we look back on these philosophical schools through the lens of nineteenth-century scholarly assumptions, it is very difficult for us to see them as they were. The way we slice the intellectual and cultural pie simply is not like theirs. What should we call Stoicism? Skepticism? Epicureanism? Are they therapy? Or philosophy? Or religion? The simple fact—which is, of course, like most things worth knowing, not simple at all—is that these movements are all three things at once. It is *we* who have separated these practices—philosophy, religion, psychology, reified now in a rigid and artificial departmental system at our major universities—in a manner that may well confuse more than it illumines.

In any case, that same Hellenistic environment contributed essentially to the creation of a new religious ethos that continues to influence decisively the North American moral landscape—that of Rabbinic Judaism on the one hand, and that of Christianity on the other. So it is that this obscure little chapter in the history of Greek philosophy becomes one of the most essential chapters in coming to terms with how we have become who we are now. This is one reason, I think, for the persistent Jewish and Christian interest in the so-called classics. These Greeks can tell us, I think, some important things about our own moral discussions, on airplanes and in marketplaces and elsewhere.

They can tell us a great deal about the ways in which we fail. They can tell us a great deal about the ways in which we love. The Greek erotic vocabulary is unusually fertile and flexible. By comparison with a Sappho or Socrates, it is a great shame upon us that we should have

made 'love', to borrow a phrase from T. E. Lawrence,[32] the shortest and
most irrelevant of our syrupy monosyllables. It would take a god, Plato
tells us in the *Phaedrus*, to say with any specificity what the soul, and
what knowledge, really *are*. But human beings are best equipped to say
what such things *are like* (*Phaedrus* 246a). We live in the realm of
metaphor and analogy whenever we are thinking morally. And the
metaphor to which Plato's Socrates most frequently returns, in the
Erotic Period, is to *wingéd erōs*. The way we love, he scandalously suggests, has everything to do with the way we come to know, and the
nature of that to which we aspire in the first place.

This, too, Nietzsche might have known. If it were possible to have
a Nietzsche without the apocalyptic posturing, without the radical split
between tragedy and erotics on the one hand and morality on the other,
and without the senseless badgering of Platonic thought, then I would
consider him *the* philosopher for this generation.[33] But as things stand, I
am drawn ever more passionately to Plato. Or at least so I have discovered myself to be, for the purposes of this book.

Chapter One

SYMPOSIUM, THE FIRST: PLATO

or, Cosmology, Ethics, and the Poets

ENDINGS

Things do not explode,
they fail, they fade,

as sunlight fades from the flesh,
as the foam drains quick in the sand,

even love's lightning flash
has no thunderous end,

it dies with the sound
of flowers fading like the flesh

from sweating pumice stone,
everything shapes this

till we are left
with the silence that surrounds Beethoven's head.

—Derek Walcott

In this chapter, I take up the vexing question of Plato's relationship to poetry—and thus, at least implicitly, his philosophical relationship to human emotion and human desire. I will suggest that there is a profound structural similarity between the *Symposium* and the *Republic*. This proves to have important ramifications in a number of areas, but the essential point—which has not been made before, to my knowledge—is that we are witnessing the "break-up" between Socrates and poetry in the *Republic*. His relationship to poetry is framed as an erotic one. Now, such erotic relationships never simply end; rather, they change, often dramatically so. So, too, does Socrates' relationship to poetry endure, even while it is changing, in the course of the *Republic*. This serves as a crucial metaphor for the erotic life, which I will then try to develop in subsequent chapters.

But what did Plato mean by "poetry?"[1] After all, *poiēsis* is a Greek word that merely denotes a kind of "making." Socrates and Adeimantus are envisioned "making" a new kind of ideal city. There are a great many things that can be "made" with words, and thus there are many kinds of "poetry." There is *epic* poetry, the kind of which Homer was the paradigm. There is *tragic* poetry, which Aeschylus and Sophocles and Euripides made famous. There is *comic* poetry, of which Aristophanes serves as our only complete classical example. There is *epinikian* poetry, the celebratory athletic poetry that Pindar popularized. And there is *lyric* poetry, poetry designed for the lyre, a set of musical traditions which most specifically address, as a genre, the concerns of the lover in love. Sappho composed such music with her words, and according to one later epigrammatical tradition, Plato himself is alleged to have termed her "the tenth Muse" for this reason.[2]

It seems to me that when Plato thinks of "poetry," he is thinking of literary genres which ask what it means to be vulnerable, which expose the limits that fragility and risk impose on the creation and sustenance of a fully human life. In that sense, the larger category of "poetry" that Plato has in mind is indeed "erotic"—whether it be Homeric, Sophoclean or Sapphic. But that simple fact, easy enough to say, will prove to have more implications than are customarily dreamt of in our philosophies.

I

Let me turn then, first, to poetry—to tragic and lyric poetry, which was probably the kind with which Socrates and Plato both began. I must confess that I have never precisely understood Plato's position on poetry. Some of this is due, no doubt, to the complexity—if not actually to say the inconsistency—of the philosopher's views. And certainly Plato's relationship to an extraordinarily rich contemporary poetic tradition—tragic and comic, lyric and erotic, and finally even epic itself—*is* exceedingly complex. The traditions themselves were exceedingly complex.

And so, too, is the philosopher who turned his attention so frequently to them. This is a complex relationship between two complex phenomena: Can erotic relationships be of any other kind?

Nowhere is Plato more complex than when he turns to poetry. Tradition has it that he had tragic and poetic aspirations himself. Actually, the traditions associating Plato with poetry in his youth are legion. In addition to briefer traditions which claim that Plato was involved in competitive wrestling, or in painting, there are no fewer than eighteen independent anecdotal traditions, spanning fourteen centuries and no fewer than three religious traditions, associating Plato with some form of poetry in his youth.[3] Indeed, "in varying combinations, nearly all genres of poetry are attributed to him."[4] Plato is portrayed as a dithyrambic choreographer, as a lyric poet, and as we have seen, as an epigrammatist. But, whatever else Plato was believed to be, the subsequent anecdotal tradition is *unanimous* in saying that Plato wrote tragedies. Perhaps Proclus' commentary on the *Republic* (fifth–sixth century CE) provides the most fitting narrative account for our purposes.

> Now, nothing else seemed to prepare Plato for his subsequent career more than this: Socrates happened upon him for the first time when he was hurrying on his way to the tragic festival. Socrates showed him that nothing of ultimate value for human beings comes from such kinds of imitative arts [*mimēsis*]. So it was that Plato took to writing up these Socratic sayings in which Socrates illustrated how tragedy had neither any pedagogical nor useful purpose, but stood instead at a three-fold remove from the truth of things. Such imitation of things partakes of neither knowledge [*epistēmē*] nor correct opinions [*orthē doxa*],[5] nor even of thought [*dianoia*] itself, but rather aims at the irrational [*alogia*] side of things.[6]

Plato certainly had the dramatic touch, and the requisite skill for poetry in a tragic register. Anyone who has read the *Phaedo* knows this well. The dialogues that Plato designed to spread the word of Socratic investigation (that word being *ti estin;* "what is it?") are, themselves, highly charged *dramatic* set-pieces.[7] Here is a man who, for all the criticism he launches against rhetoric as a profession, is possessed of high rhetorical skill himself, as well as the stunning poetic ability to wear many masks when he is writing. He makes Isocratean speeches which rival anything the rhetorician himself composed (*Phaedrus* 237b–241c). And he similarly mimics the style and the content of *all* his chief writerly rivals. Here is a man of consummate poetic and dramatic skill, for whom the writerly craft is precisely that: a *technē*, a craft. For Plato, writing is a craft every bit as much as philosophy itself is. The two crafts are in fact married, inseparable.

Yet Plato is as critical of *technē* at times as he is of *poiēsis*, or very nearly so. To be sure, in his most antidemocratic moments, he places artisans and technicians fairly low on the ladder of philosophical merit. So we are faced with a paradox—a whole series of paradoxes, in fact. Plato criticizes rhetoric, yet he uses rhetoric. He criticizes dramatic poetry, yet he uses dramatic and poetic techniques. His mentor, Socrates, is equally critical of craftsmen, yet he was himself allegedly a stonecutter, or else a sculptor, by trade (we never see Socrates at work, other than when he is philosophizing). His premier student, Plato, allegedly bans the poets entirely from his ideal political union, or *politeia*, yet he continues to use poetry, Homer and Sophocles especially, to make some of his most enduring philosophical points—even in the *Republic*, and even after the ban. Plato is, in fact, often in the habit of quoting Homer immediately after telling us that he no longer wishes us to read the poets at all. Surely Plato cannot be unaware of these inconsistencies. Has he gone mad? Is he somehow celebrating irrationality? What in the world is going on?

This is one of those questions that cannot be answered straight up. It seems a better intellectual strategy to get at it obliquely, to come at it from the side, if you will. In order to simplify this topic, which is not simple in the least (isn't that a part of Socrates' genius and seductiveness, his ability to do this, time and time again?), I would like to underscore two assumptions that are rather "traditional" and comparatively noncontroversial in most Platonic scholarship. I will use them both as working hypotheses in this short book. It is my hope that reminding ourselves of several obvious points—such as the ones I have enumerated above— may help us in understanding a fairly essential and enduring Platonic paradox. It will turn out that understanding Plato's relationship to poetry requires us to understand the Platonic notion of *erōs* first.

II

The first assumption I will make is that Socrates was indeed the founder of a revolution of sorts in the realm of philosophical enquiry. What had counted as "philosophy" before his time—namely, the probing cosmological speculations of the so-called Ionian philosophers— gave way, under pressure of the Socratic example, to a new order of enquiry, believed by Socrates to be a *higher* order of enquiry, or at least a more *fruitful* one. Cosmology gives way to moral philosophy.[8] The examination of nature gives way to the examination of the political and moral life, the lives which human beings make for themselves, in the *polis*. The search for beginnings and first causes gives way to the quest for appropriately human ends (*Apology* 20d).

I must confess that I have come to appreciate this Socratic insight better after having made my own tentative forays into the work, and the often bizarre world, of our own epoch's cosmologists and their candid description of their own speculative procedures. For we, too, have an abundance of such "natural philosophers" in our own day and age; we simply call them "theoretical physicists." The late Carl Sagan was one of the most popular and eloquent of them all. Sagan's book *Cosmos*[9] sold over five million copies internationally, an astonishing figure. The viewing audience for his television program of the same name was estimated to be far larger. Most significant for my purposes is his description of the pre-Socratic Ionian tradition of speculative (largely cosmological) enquiry.[10] This is the tradition of which he himself wished to be a part. It was in Asia Minor, he notes, that the vast work of intellectual liberation began.

> For *thousands of years humans were oppressed—as some of us still are*—by the notion that the universe is a marionette whose strings are pulled by a god or gods, unseen and inscrutible. Then, 2500 years ago, there was a glorious awakening in Ionia. . . .
>
> And so it was that the great idea arose, the realization that there might be a way to know the world *without the god hypothesis*, that there might be principles, forces, laws of nature, through which the world could be understood without attributing the fall of every sparrow to the divine intervention of Zeus.[11]

There then follows an appreciative, if brief, sketch of the careers of Thales, Anaximander, Hippocrates, Empedocles, Democritus, and Anaxagoras. Sagan does not want to call them "pre-Socratic" because "their main function was [not] to hold the philosophical fort until the advent of Socrates."[12] Sagan wants to rehabilitate these thinkers on their own, not on Socratic, terms. In fact, he prefers the Ionian period, because it was allegedly trying to free itself of "religion" altogether. Now, such a claim, of course, has a great deal of evidence to overlook. That view constitutes the main reason that Sagan does *not* like Pythagoras, or Socrates, or Plato, or even Aristotle: they all continued to think theologically in precisely the ways that Sagan decries.

And so Sagan is forced to make a host of stunning claims about this "alternative" Greek tradition of speculative enquiry. He claims that Plato and Aristotle were comfortable in a slave society (we never get a sense of what he means by "comfortable," but Plato's *Republic* would not have had it, and Aristotle freed his own slaves upon his death). They both offered philosophical justifications for political oppression (to claim this in this way is an unforgivable caricature of both philosophers, since the only "oppression" Sagan really has in mind is "religion" itself, of *any* kind). They taught the essential separation of the body from the mind (a fairly standard and predictable charge of which I will try to acquit Plato later in the third chapter). The *post*-Socratic philosophers also separated matter from thought, divorcing the earth from the heavens—divisions, all, says Sagan, "that were to dominate Western thinking for more than twenty centuries."[13] In actuality, Sagan does not like Socrates, Plato or Aristotle (or Empedocles, for that matter, although Sagan himself remained ambivalent about him) because they continued to speculate using "the god hypothesis," not merely using empirical evidence about "the cosmos." Socrates, for his part at least, insisted upon the priority of moral *over* cosmological speculation, which proves to be a matter of some considerable complexity, as we shall shortly see.

They are an odd bunch, by and large, these cosmologists,[14] couching some of the most rabidly antireligious sentiments in the specious rhetoric of objectivity.[15] Let me cite just one peculiar example of this far more general peculiarity. Stephen Hawking and a colleague, in reflecting upon the irregular orbit-structures of the stars around Cygnus-1, disagree as to whether there is in fact a black hole in the vicinity. The manner in which they have elected to negotiate this dispute is quite telling, from a moral point of view:

> There are other models to explain Cygnus-1 that do not include a black hole, but they are all rather farfetched. A black hole seems to be the only really natural explanation of the observations. I have a bet with Kip Thorne of the California Institute of Technology that in fact Cygnus-1 does not contain a black hole! This is a form of insurance policy for me. I have done a lot of work on black holes, and it would all be wasted if it turned out that black holes do not exist. But in that case, I would have the consolation of winning my bet, which would bring me four years of the magazine *Private Eye*. If black holes do exist, Kip will get one year of *Penthouse*.[16]

These cosmologists playfully think and write as if there are no moral implications to what they do, effectively severing a relation—between virtue and knowledge—that Socrates was very much interested in maintaining and nurturing.

Socrates tells us that he himself briefly flirted with the cosmological speculations of Anaxagoras, but that he rather quickly came to the conclusion that it was a dead end, philosophically speaking (*Phaedo* 97c–99d). It is all well and good to conclude that "mind" (*nous*) orders the universe, he tells us, but it is another thing to explain *how* that is done, and what the *moral* implications of this hypothesis might be. The crucial point, in Socrates' opinion, is how such cosmological speculations play out *in practice*. What is their *moral*, rather than their *epistemological*, payoff? It was Anaxagoras' studied refusal of all such moral or evaluative language—'good' and 'better' and 'best'—that finally led Socrates to reject his method. The explicit disavowal of such a moral standpoint among the natural philosophers inspired Socrates to set out on a different tack. This initiated what he refers to as his "second sailing" (*deuteros plous*, *Phaedo* 99c),[17] and the articulation of a mature method of philosophical enquiry that stayed with him to the end of his life, a noble enough end depicted in this selfsame dialogue.

Socrates seems unwilling to detach thinkers from their thoughts, given his own profound commitment to the relation between the thinking of thoughts and the propriety of human action. To the degree that virtue is indeed a kind of knowledge (*Protagoras* 361a–c, *Meno* 87c), then one must know well, not merely know a lot (*Apology* 17d–18c). Sometimes, it is important to know when to stop seeking new knowledge, and to rest content with the knowledge you already have. An investigation of nature has a human value, a moral value, or else it is not worth pursuing. There is no value-neutral moral enquiry, not even Socrates' own (*Apology* 26a). The accumulation of knowledge is not an end in itself, not for Socrates. To that degree, natural philosophy is subordinate to moral philosophy. That conclusion, I suspect, marks the essence of the Socratic revolution.

Now, Plato did not maintain this same hierarchy consistently in his own philosophical speculation. Indeed, later in his own career, long after Socrates' death, and especially in those dialogues where he abandons the pretense of speaking through Socrates' mouth, Plato admits a high level of significance to such cosmological speculation. By the time he writes the *Laws*, that which is "in accordance with nature" (*kata physin*) is defined quite precisely as good, and that which is "against nature" (*para physin*) is conceived as crime (*Laws* 636a–e).[18] Natural speculation, like the geometric speculation apart from which no one might enter the Academy,[19] achieves an independent value that it had not had in Socrates' homier and more homespun discourse. But this is a much later *Platonic* development, not a Socratic one, an insight that relates to my second philosophical assumption.

But first, a brief point of clarification is in order. Plato may *seem* to be substituting one cosmology for another in his so-called "theory of the forms," another essential speculative innovation of this same period in his intellectual development. I am insisting that he does not. First of all, the theory of the forms is surely the most overrated and overemphasized part of Plato's entire body of thought. It was far more important to later Platonists than it was to Plato himself. Plato is not above poking fun at the doctrine, in some of his later dialogues (*Parmenides* 129a, 130b–d, 132b). Secondly, it is important to note that Plato is attempting to fore-ground moral value, as opposed to cosmological sophistication, in his mature theories. Finally, and crucially, there is another essential specula-tive force that Plato introduces into his analysis, at precisely the same time as the idea of "forms," and that is the concept of *erōs*—which is "a sort of a god," as we shall see in the next chapter. I will be making much more of "the erotic" than I will of "the forms" in this book.

III

Ever since Friedrich Schleiermacher's pioneering work on these mat-ters in the early nineteenth century, there has been a great deal of energy devoted to the parsing of the Platonic corpus, to the relative dating of dialogues, and to the articulation of their chronological relation, one to another. Surely there are limits to all such historical and philological guesswork,[20] yet I think that the general contours of the picture that has emerged from this close philological work are probably and essentially accurate. The general view is that Plato's writings fall into four major periods.[21] The first group of so-called *Early Dialogues* are among the most "dramatic" portraits of Socrates that we possess. They are shorter works. Their dominant preoccupation is with moral enquiry, more often than not with the close interrogation of a single buzzword in the tradi-tional Athenian moral vocabulary. So we puzzle over "courage," or "friendship," or "piety," and the like. These dialogues represent, or rather they *display*, the Socratic revolution, which placed moral enquiry at the forefront of all philosophical speculation, and made ethics the

most fitting sort of "first philosophy." Among these critical early dialogues are the *Apology*, *Charmides*, *Crito*, *Euthydemus*, *Euthyphro*,
Ion, *Laches*, and *Lysis*. The *Protagoras* and the *Gorgias* probably represent the last of this series, and taken together, they manage the transition to the next phase of Plato's intellectual development.

The period of what I am calling the *Erotic Dialogues* was perhaps
anticipated by the *Meno*, with its remarkable conviction that knowledge
(*epistēmē*) is actually the recollection (*anamnēsis*) of preexistent forms
that the soul knew once but has since forgotten (*Meno* 85d). This second group of Platonic dialogues is among the finest in the corpus, from
both a literary and a speculative point of view. Here Plato discovers (or
perhaps *re*covers) the doctrine of the "forms" and gives it a kind of
rhetorical and poetic resonance it had not had before: in such extraordinary dialogues as *Phaedo*, *Phaedrus*, *Republic*, and *Symposium*. Recognized less often, but at least as important in these dialogues, is the
emerging portrait of the human soul that was developed as an attempt
on Plato's part to explain the desperate and enduring problem of *moral
failure*. In the earlier dialogues, and building upon the apparent Socratic
conviction that "virtue is knowledge," Socrates had been unable to give
an account of why the moral agent who actually knew the good might
yet fail to do it. Philosophy, at least when its "knowledge" is certain,
ought never to fail. Yet it does fail, of course; or rather, its proponents
do. The mature doctrine of the tripartite soul—made clearest in *Phaedrus* (253c–255a) and *Republic* (435b–441d)—is, in part, an attempt to
address this emphatic moral dilemma.

For the Early Dialogues leave us with an enduring *aporia*. Now,
an *aporia* is *not* simply the experience of argument, nor of agreeing to
disagree. That, in Plato's view, is a rather *un*interesting event, philosophically speaking. An *aporia*, by contrast, is the experience you
have when the thing you have always thought, and the language you
have always used, has proven to be inadequate, and you do not yet
see your way clear to a new way of thinking or speaking. That experience, the one Socrates seemed so expert at inducing with his questions, *is* philosophically interesting. The Early Period dialogues consistently lead to a confrontation with the inadequacy of one or several
of the premier Athenian buzzwords, and we do not yet clearly see
how to thicken and enrich the meaning of these terms—"ethics" least
of all. As it turns out, a proper understanding of *ta ēthika* requires a
proper understanding of *ta erōtika*, first. That is the bold hypothesis
of Plato's Erotic Period.

Here there is a problem of squaring the Socratic belief that virtue is knowledge with Socrates' playful claim not to know anything at all. Plato once again presents us with a problem of which he simply cannot have been unaware. Perhaps it is the same problem with which Socrates' personal example left him. In any case, I detect an interesting theme, implicit already in the Early Period dialogues. Socrates does *not* claim to know nothing; he consistently insists upon the fact that he knows one thing quite well: *ta erōtika*, the things associated with *erōs*. What we see happening in the Erotic Period dialogues now is Plato beginning to flesh out what it is more specifically that he thinks Socrates knew. The erotic seems to involve the intimate connection between pleasure and pain in every embodied life, such as we see in the *Phaedo*—a dialogue in which all those present find themselves laughing, laughing in pain (*Phaedo* 59a,60b,62a,84e,86d,115c,116d,117c). The erotic, in fact, involves all aspects of human relations and thus orders the ethical realm itself, as we see in the *Symposium*. The erotic involves the art of writing as well, as we are shown in the *Phaedrus*. And finally, the erotic involves us in an essential conflict with poetic understanding, as we see in the *Republic*. Concentration upon the idea of the erotic is Plato's way of beginning to resolve a problem that he has laid out quite clearly and systematically in the Early Period dialogues. It is a problem of knowledge, *moral* knowledge, and it implicates the problem of failure as well.

In the aftermath of these crucial dialogues (crucial for my purposes) come the more formally logical, the so-called *Dialectical Period dialogues*. These are less dramatic, somehow, than the Erotic Period dialogues were. Here the notions of true and false predication, logical categorization, the significance of negation in the construction of positive knowledge, and the essence of logical division are explored in all of their conceptual subtlety. To this group belong the *Theaetetus*, *Parmenides*, *Sophist*, and *Statesman*—dialogues that were presumably conceived, and written, as a group. They are among the most difficult works in an altogether lofty philosophical corpus.

The last group, the *Final Period dialogues* are also four in number. They are *Philebus*, *Timaeus*, the fragmentary *Critias*, and the massive *Laws*.[22] Several things are noteworthy about this group of dialogues, chief among them being that the ideas presented here are Platonic, abandoning at long last even the pretense of being Socratic in origin. Indeed, the first in the series, the *Philebus*, is the clearest explication of the Platonic, rather than the Socratic, conception of ethics. The next two both belong to precisely the kinds of cosmological investigation—cosmology as alternative myth-making—which Socrates had apparently, however partially, disowned. In any case, the myths they narrate are put in other persons' mouths, not Socrates'. Finally, the *Laws* represents a tacit giving over of the ideal project of the *Republic*. In the dialogue's own terms, the *Laws* is mere "prelude" (a *prooimion*, as opposed to an argument, or *logos* [*Laws* 723b]) to the formation of such an ideal republic. The *Laws*, which represents fully twenty percent of the entire Platonic corpus, also begins and ends "in the middle," an image I will emphasize in the next chapter. Three anonymous old men—one from Athens, one from Sparta, one from Crete—are on a pilgrimage, making their wandering way up to Mount Ida and the famous Cave of Zeus. They never get there. The dialogue begins with our pilgrims already underway, and it concludes with them apparently no closer to their goal, ten massive books later. It seems a final demonstration of Plato's dramatic and visual precocity and virtuosity, but it is a rather jarring metaphor for the philosophical life. One plays hunches, uses hypotheses as starting points. One undertakes a "second sailing" when the first sailing fails to produce results. One begins and ends in the middle.

Let us return then to the middle, to the so-called Middle Period that I am referring to as Plato's Erotic Period. It was in the *Republic* that the most hostile salvos were fired across the bow of the poetic tradition (*Republic* 377a–383c, 595a–608b). They constitute one of the best-known claims in the entire Platonic corpus; even those who appear not to have read them seem to know the arguments. These debates frequently recur; they figured prominently, for instance, in the period of Cromwellian reform in England. We tend not to remember that the very legitimacy of the theater as an institution was called into question, ironically enough, in its pre- and post-Shakespearean heyday. The theater's friends argued that the stage served a clearly *moral* and *pedagogical* purpose. Its Puritan detractors insisted that "pagan means pagan," and that in any case even the most perceptive pagans, like Plato, had themselves already condemned the theater as an institution.[23] The difficulty lies, of course, in the fact that Socrates hangs on to part of Homer and the tragedians, and dispenses only with a part. His is hardly a wholesale rejection of poetry (*Republic* 383a–c). Indeed, poetry of a peculiar sort reasserts itself in the later Platonic dialogues.[24] Not only is poetry allowed back into the city of the Magnesians, in the *Laws*, but Plato there describes the project of (re)founding this city in the most deliberately jarring language, jarring to anyone who has read the *Republic*:

> Most excellent stranger, we ourselves are the authors [*poiētai*] of a tragedy which is most excellent and lovely. For our whole society [*politeia*]²⁵ is constructed as the imitation [*mimēsis*]²⁶ of the most beautiful and best way of life, which we at least claim to be really the truest sort of tragedy [*tragōidia tēn alēthēn*]. Now you are poets [*poiētai*], and we are poets [*poiētai*] too, in the same way. We are your rivals as artists and performers of the most beautiful drama [*tou kallistou dramatos*], which true law [*nomos alēthēs*] alone can by its nature bring to perfection—that is what we hope. (*Laws* 817b–c)

Suddenly, the very project of *polis*-building, to which Plato has devoted so much of his philosophical life and labor, is called a "tragedy"—and not only *a* tragedy, but *the truest sort* of tragedy. The one who builds such a city is involved in *mimēsis*, an imitation, the selfsame practice that Plato had questioned in the *Republic*. And the one who builds such a city is also a "poet," a maker, precisely as were the makers who had been excluded from his previous version of "politics."

We are on difficult, and complex, ground. In order to venture a way to make some initial, however partial, sense of these apparently contradictory claims, I would like to reiterate the two assumptions that inform my approach here. The first is that Plato's dispute with poetry is animated by a *moral*, rather than an epistemological, concern. That may seem untrue to the text of the *Republic*, where "imitation" is condemned because it stands at three epistemic removes from the truth (*Republic* 602c). That seems to be an epistemological objection. But appearances are, as Plato never tires of telling us, deceiving. The way things seem is not necessarily the way things are. In the larger context of the *Republic* as a whole, the quarrel with poetry is a *moral* argument, a moral argument with a decidedly *erotic* resonance. Indeed, in this extraordinarily creative Erotic Period, Plato maintains a consistent, very nearly systematic, attention to the relation between erotics and moral philosophy. Epistemology, like geometry and number-theory, is a later development, a response to the time he spent among the Pythagoreans in Sicily. I will say a bit more about this in the third chapter.

My second assumption concerns the dating of the various dialogues. I submit that *Phaedo* and *Phaedrus*, *Symposium* and *Republic*, were all written at roughly the same time, in what is to my mind the most creative and fruitful Platonic period. By looking at these writings as a group, I think that some deeper sense of the apparent antipoetic arguments in the *Republic* may be made.

IV

What I would like to suggest is that there is a profound *structural* similarity between the *Symposium* and the *Republic*. I would like to use the *Symposium* as a lens through which to view the *Republic*'s arguments about poetry and the *polis*. Then, I think, we will be better able to read the *Symposium* in its own right—as a dramatic prose poem—which is my broader task in this book.

In the tenth book of the *Republic*—the final decrescendo in which we return again to poetry and it is condemned even more roundly than it was in the second book—we seem to be privy to a recurrent parallel or pattern. We have seen similar things in the *Symposium*. This is the *formal* similarity to which I have alluded and that I would like to develop here. Let me then sketch out the similarity in formal structure between the two dialogues. In doing so, I think that something altogether remarkable emerges in far sharper relief.

The *Symposium* begins at a festival, a tragic festival. In fact, it is a party celebrating the victory of Agathon's tetralogy at the Greater Dionysia. We begin with an interrogation of love, that which is called *erōs* by the various speakers. Many people speak of it in turn, articulating the sorts of stock beliefs of the many and the conventional wisdom of contemporary Athenian society. Indeed, we begin with the single greatest rival to, and temptation away from, the Socratic-Platonic vision: the distinction between the *erastēs* and the *erōmenos* (*Symposium* 180a–b),[27] that is, the formal notion that love necessarily involves us in pursuing and pursuit.

In the culminating statement of the *Symposium*, we get what we might easily expect of Plato in this period: an appeal to "the forms" which he has located as the fulcrum around which his maturing philosophical system allegedly has begun to turn. But it is the form of *Beauty*, not the form of *erōs*, that is described here (*Symposium* 210d–212a). There is no "form" of *erōs*. Rather, there is an understanding of genuine beauty that only a prior philosophical reflection upon the nature of human loving makes intelligible.

It is at this point that Alcibiades erupts onto the scene (*Symposium* 212d) and, in his attempt to subvert the whole program, he actually (however wittingly or unwittingly) confirms its most essential ingredient—by underscoring the inadequacies of the *erastēs-erōmenos* system in which his own erotic understanding continues to be trapped.

And so the *Symposium* concludes with two things: (1) a startling new appreciation of Socrates' wisdom as a lover; and (2) the tantalizing appeal for a new kind of poetry (already anticipated at *Symposium* 205c) that breaks the traditional, generic boundaries of Athenian society—that between "tragedy" and "comedy." The true poet, we are told, is equally at home in both realms (*Symposium* 223d). Already in Homer, we witness Andromache, "laughing in her tears."[28] Clearly, we are not done with the poets.

Now let us turn to the *Republic*. What we find here is, as I say, an astonishing formal similarity to the structure of the *Symposium*. The *Republic* also begins with a festival (*Republic* 327a), this time a newer festival devoted to a civic goddess only recently introduced into the Athenian pantheon, one whose festival is being celebrated for the first time. And we begin with an interrogation of justice, what is called *dikaiosunē* in Greek. Many people offer speeches on its behalf in the first book of the dialogue. And here, too, we begin with the greatest temptation to the Socratic-Platonic view: namely, Thrasymachus' notion that "justice" is defined by the interest of the stronger (*Republic* 338c). Might, it seems, may indeed make right.

In the discussions that follow, we get an interesting sort of an appeal to a form, but here in the *Republic* it is the form of the best city, the *politeia* of the best *polis*, not a form of justice. There *is* no "form" of justice.[29] Rather, there is an understanding of the *polis* (and perhaps also of the relative place for poetry within it) which only a prior philosophical reflection upon the nature of human justice makes intelligible. So it is that Socrates can conclude with the astonishing disclaimer that his political vision is not contradicted by the fact that such a city has never existed, and may never exist anywhere, save in heaven (*Republic* 592a–b).

It is at this point that poetry erupts onto the scene again, in a manner that deliberately recalls Alcibiades' intervention in the *Symposium*. In poetry's attempt to subvert the whole Platonic political program, it actually confirms essential aspects of it—by underscoring the complexity of concepts like rhetorical strength and weakness, by underscoring the danger, and the simultaneous high delight, of passionate involvements in political affairs.

And so the *Republic* concludes with two related points as well: (1) a new appreciation for Socrates as the very image of the just man; and (2) an appeal for a new kind of poetry, one that breaks out of the genres and boundaries which constrain its more traditional (Homeric? tragic?) forms, a sort of knowledge-poetry. Here we meet with an apologia for the dramatic-Platonic dialogue form itself, I think.

What I am suggesting is, unsurprisingly, based on the fundamental assumption that grounds the entire argument of the *Republic*: namely, that there is a meaningful comparison to be drawn between the city and the soul, the *polis* on the one hand, and the *psychē* on the other (*Republic* 368d–e). Political and spiritual matters are of a piece, and cannot be completely divorced from one another. Religion, despite Sagan's insistent denial, is not simply "oppressive" from a philosophical point of view. That is a tragic and lyric assumption with which Plato never did away entirely.

The suggestion seems to be something like the following: as Alcibiades is to Socrates, so poetry is to the *polis*; as the beloved is to a lover, so the theater is to a civic association and its citizens. Plato goes out of his way to make this connection for us, and the expected erotic vocabulary is once again prominent. Among the most remarkable passages in this most remarkable book is Socrates' concluding statement about the poets, his own conflicted and conflicting feelings for poetry. He is wondering what he will do if he cannot find a compelling reason to stay by poetry's side:

> If not, my dear friend, then we must be like men who fell in love [*erasthentes*] once, but who come to believe that this passion [*erōta*] is not good for them. Though it is hard, they hold back from such a love. So too do we, born to and raised on the love [*erōta*] of such poetry by this noble city of ours, happily wish to see her in her best and truest form. But if a defense [*apologēsasthai*] for such poetry is unavailable, then we shall sing the very argument we have just made to ourselves, as a sort of counter-poetry and love charm, to keep from backsliding into the passion [*erōta*] of children and of the majority of the people. For we now see more clearly that such poetry is not serious, that it does not seriously aspire to truthfulness; rather, it seizes hold of those who listen to it, putting the city [*politeia*] in their soul at risk, unless we keep in mind what we have just realized about poetry. (*Republic* 607e–608b)

We are witnessing nothing less than a break-up—in both the *Symposium*, and in the *Republic*—the break between Socrates and Alcibiades on the one hand (a break that is anticipated already at *Protagoras* 309a–d), the break between Platonic philosophy and poetry on the other. It is an *excruciating* break in both cases, presenting the endless possibility of backsliding into the very relationships, the very fears and vulnerabilities, and even the convictions, of which one wishes to be free. The end of the relationship does not mean that *erōs* itself has ended, anymore than life in an unjust city means that the notion of justice has ceased to be meaningful. Far from it. And for that very reason, there can be no doubt about the stakes involved. Socrates tells us what they are: "My dear Glaukon, we are engaged in a great contest [*agōn*], much greater than it seems. It is a contest to see whether we shall become good or bad" (*Republic* 608b). In the context of that struggle—passionate moral struggle—the *Republic* concludes its alleged argument *against* the poets.

V

In suggesting that there is a formal or structural similarity between the *Symposium* and the *Republic*, I am asserting a kind of philological judgment. My interests in so doing are not narrowly philological, however, and it will require the rest of this book to explain what they are. I share Socrates' pained awareness that there are indeed moral price tags attached to most knowledge-claims, that few forms of insight are really value-neutral or interest-free. And in any case, it seems to me that the similarities between the *Republic* and the *Symposium* run far deeper than matters of form and structure. The two dialogues are about much the same business, approached in strikingly different ways. For, in the final analysis, the line between the *polis* and the *psychē*, between the city and the self, *is* rather blurry. "Politics" can take us only so far. Spiritual matters—which is to say, the kind of "psychology" Socrates practiced, an *erotic* psychology—have a central place. Once noticed, it becomes clearer and clearer that erotic matters are never far from Plato's mind—at least not until the very end of his life[30] (and even then they tellingly resurface). Socrates is intimately involved in the daily life of his *polis*, appreciative of its variant beauties, tempted by its constant and many-splendored attractions. Alcibiades, in an interesting way, is never far from Socrates' thinking either (*Gorgias* 481b–c). That fact, introduced repeatedly in the Early Period, becomes one central focus in the dialogues of the Erotic Period, in the *Symposium* primarily. I will develop this point in the next chapter. Even in the much later Dialectical Period, "the problem of the one and the indeterminate two"[31] is a question fraught with erotic significance. I will develop this point in the third chapter. And even at the end of his long writerly career, in the *Laws*, Plato acknowledges that erotic attractions often govern the entire life of the *polis*. His goal, he tells us there, is to turn a natural passion (*emphyton erōta*, *Laws* 782e) into a divine one (*theios erōs*, *Laws* 711d). That is Plato's philosophical vision *in nuce*. For Plato—and this is the end of the matter—

there is no more political or philosophical act than that of *loving well*. It is to that same passionate conviction that this book is also dedicated.

An anti-poet who poeticizes, an anti-rhetorician who makes speeches, an anti-dramatist who writes dialogues . . . a *deeply divided soul*. Such is the Plato of the Erotic Period. Small wonder that his own doctrine of the divided soul, a tripartite soul, emerges in this same period. With matters erotic, how could it be otherwise?

Still, paradoxes persist. Earlier I asked, half in earnest, if Plato has gone mad. I will return many times to that question. It is another question with a profoundly erotic valence, as Plato himself tells us in still another of the Erotic Period dialogues. For *erōs* is, in the final analysis, a peculiar kind of madness. Sappho already suggested this. We are led by it; we do not lead.

> *Socrates:* We said that love [*erōta*] was a kind of madness [*mania*], didn't we?
>
> *Phaedrus:* Yes.
>
> *Socrates:* And that there are two sorts of madness [*mania*], one of which comes from human sickness, and the other of which comes from divine liberation, a liberation from normal customs and habits [*eiōthotōn nomimōn*].
>
> *Phaedrus:* Absolutely.
>
> *Socrates:* And we distinguished between four such divine liberations, assigning each one of them to a god. We said that prophetic [*mantikēn*] madness comes from Apollo, and that ecstatic [*telestikēn*] madness comes from Dionysus, and that poetic [*poiētikēn*] madness comes from the Muses, and that the fourth, erotic [*erōtikēn*] madness, comes from Aphrodite and Eros, and that this last one is the best. (*Phaedrus* 265a–b)

It is, in every way, a remarkable statement that nicely concludes our discussion up to this point. Note that *erōs* here is a two-edged sword, potentially a benediction, or a personal and political calamity. You do not gain something but that you lose something—that is *erōs*' tragic truth. As beneficent, madness is a gift of heaven that frees us from "normal customs and habits." Thus we meet here the plea with which both the *Symposium* and the *Republic* conclude: the plea for a new kind of poetry, free of the strictures and generic structures of the theater. Such beneficent and divinely inspired, liberatory madnesses are four in number. Third on the list is poetic inspiration, high praise, indeed, for a craft of which Socrates has elsewhere been so critical. But fourth, and higher still, on the list is *erōs*. Tempted by the very thing that threatens to undo us, drawn like moths to the flame of our own desiring, waxing lyrical about the sources of our deepest distress, we live and breathe *metaxu*, "in between." It would later become a crucial point for Romantic philosophy that, in the words of Friedrich Schlegel, "[l]ooked at subjectively, philosophy always begins in the middle, like an epic poem."[32] This book is intended as a brief meditation, Platonically inspired, on what that alternately bittersweet and magical—but always remarkable—fact of human life might mean.

The meditation begins, then, appropriately enough, in the middle—with the *Symposium*, to which I now turn.

Chapter Two

SYMPOSIUM, THE SECOND: THE EROTIC

or, Love in the Middle

THE FIST

The fist clenched round my heart
loosens a little, and I gasp
brightness; but it tightens
again. When have I ever not loved
the pain of love? But this has moved

past love to mania. This has the strong
clench of the madman, this is
gripping the ledge of unreason, before
plunging howling into the abyss.

Hold hard then, heart. This way at least you live.

—Derek Walcott

In the last chapter I sketched out the contours of Plato's writing career, focusing upon several intellectual developments that I think we can locate in what I am calling the "Erotic Period." I noted a formal, or structural, similarity between the *Symposium* and the *Republic*, and I suggested the presence of a common trajectory in their dramatic structure. I also underlined the equation that Socrates himself is alleged to have made between the Alcibiades we meet in the *Symposium* and the (erotic) poetry we meet in the *Republic*. Socrates anguishes over these relationships, as well as the obligations they place upon him, but he eventually breaks with both the man and the poetic tradition. Having touched briefly upon the question of poetry in the last chapter, I would like to turn now to the question of Alcibiades. His proves to be the far more complex relationship.

Socrates' rethinking of his relationship, both to the erotic tradition and to Alcibiades, does not imply that either relationship is at an end. Clearly, neither one is; they are the two most constant features of Socrates' life as Plato depicts it for us. I would like to offer a defense here of Socrates' decision to realign himself personally vis-à-vis Alcibiades. Their "break," if that is what it is, proves to be grounded in Socrates' dawning realization that they do not mean the same thing at all when they use an identical erotic vocabulary. They are not looking for the same thing when they are looking for "love." And neither Alcibiades nor the erotic tradition can finally help Socrates to find the language for what it is that *he* ultimately desires.

I

A symposium, as I have already suggested, is just a dinner party, or a little more specifically, a carefully choreographed drinking party.[1] This particular symposium, the one narrated by Plato, is a party replete with unique and startling paradoxes. It is ultimately a party *about* paradoxes. It is a party whose heavy emphasis upon ritual inebriation is inhibited by the fact that everyone is depleted by the festivities of the previous evening. Yet all save one at this party will eventually become drunk tonight, first on words and then on the very surfeit of wine they sought to avoid. It is a bittersweet story, tragedy and comedy by turns, and its "tone" is perhaps the hardest thing to render accurately in translation. For this was a society at war, an uncannily destructive war that had already raged for nearly twenty years when the party took place and that would soon conclude in disaster and defeat for the Athenians. Yet there is a time and a place, even and especially here, for the arts, for creativity, for celebratory self-creation, and even for love. The postwar years, in fact, will seem rather sterile by comparison, with Socrates and so many others gone.[2] *These* were the halcyon days of real promise and hope. The war looms over this party, just as Socrates' eventual execution looms over all the dialogues from Plato's Erotic Period, not just the *Phaedo*. There is a deep connection, between love and war to be sure— Sappho and Alcaeus had already played eloquently on this erotic trope—but there is also a relationship between *erōs* and death, which is never far from Plato's thinking in this period.

The party represents a collection of some of the most cultured and accomplished Athenian personalities of the day—yet they all defer to, and even stand in a sort of awe before, a rather uneducated, deceptively articulate stonecutter. They are, finally, an intimate group of "bisexual" men. Such a word is ours, not theirs, and probably would not have meant much to them. "Bisexual as opposed to what else?" would have been their most likely reply to the nomination. Each society has its own taxonomies, as well as its own buzzwords,[3] and this particular gendered taxonomy of ours was emphatically not a Greek one, I do not think.

The party is ultimately devoted to desire, these men's common desire to speak the truth about love and the meaning of their (largely, but not entirely) homoerotic longing. And yet—here is the tricky part— the most compelling portrait of the true nature of *erōs* will be vouchsafed to them by a woman.

The party is narrated entirely at second and third hand.[4] A young Athenian named Glaukon (Plato appears to have had a brother by that name who followed Socrates in these years), some years after the party and the respective death or exile of nearly all its participants, falls in stride with an older man named Apollodorus on the road from Phaleron, an outlying Athenian suburb. Apollodorus was, so Glaukon has been told, present at this symposium.[5] He had *not* been there, as it turns out, but he has heard the story from another man, Aristodemus, who was. And he is anxious for the opportunity to tell the story, too, in turn.

So too are the woman's words reported—at *fifth* hand. Plato tells us that Apollodorus (who was not there) heard from Aristodemus (who was) the words which Socrates spoke on this strangely sober occasion, yet would not, could not, claim as his own. They are not his words and thoughts at all, but a woman's—a woman named Diotima. The double entendre is unmistakable.[6] "I was her pupil," Socrates tells the assembled crowd, tongue firmly in cheek, "and *she* taught *me erōtika*."

This is a statement worth pausing over. The *Symposium*, which is structurally similar to other dialogues, especially to the *Republic*, is nearly unique in the Platonic corpus here. This is one of only two dialogues (the other being the rather curious *Menexenus*, which I mentioned with some confusion in the last chapter) in which Socrates does not tell us what he thinks, but rather tells us what *someone else* thinks, what someone else has told him. Here we are in the presence of a truth by which Socrates has himself become convinced—by Diotima. The passivity—which is to say, the receptivity—of that dynamic is an important factor as this dialogue presents to us its portrait of the appropriate manner of all human loving (and all human knowledge).

Three things are important about this foreign teacher, I suspect, and we are told all three at one stroke:

> ton de logon ton peri tou Erōtos, hon pot' ēkousa gynaikos Mantinikēs Diotimas, hē tauta te sophē ēn kai alla polla . . . kai eme ta erōtika edidaxen.

> An account of Eros which I heard from a Mantineian woman named Diotima, who was wise in this and in many other matters. . . . She taught me erōtika. (Symposium 201d)

Each of these factors, which Plato goes out of his way to enumerate—that she was a woman, that she was from Mantineia, and that she taught Socrates about erōs—is significant, especially so if Diotima is, as most scholars agree, a creation of Plato's artistic imagination. What I would like to do is to reflect upon the significance of the latter two invocations—of Mantineia, and of erōtika. By examining what these two names mean, I think that a great many of the central themes of this dialogue may be brought into better focus. Examining the significance of Diotima's gender would require a book in itself, and I reserve that task for subsequent work.[7]

What, then, is Plato trying to tell us about the teaching, the teacher, and her home? The invocation of "Mantineia" is an interesting, really a crucial detail, and yet it is *never* commented upon.[8] Where is Mantineia, and what do we know about it? It seems to me that the choice of locale is as deliberate, and as carefully crafted, as every other detail in this most artistic of Plato's Erotic Dialogues. Socrates (and Apollodorus, and Aristodemus, and Plato) mean to tell us something by including this detail. We are not told where anyone else in the party is from,[9] though they are all pretty clearly not from Athens, and in fact the man narrating the story is explicitly *not* from there. Why, then, are we really only told about Mantineia? What erotic wisdom might come from there?

I would like to begin with the question of what we know now about Mantineia.[10] We are fortunate to have an uncannily detailed account of the topography of the ancient Greek world left to us by Pausanias—himself, a frustrated Homerist from Asia Minor who finally gave up on the academic life and took to the road instead.[11] Word is that he never really stopped traveling, never stood still for very long—just wandered, and read, and listened, and wrote. It is important to mention, by way of reminding reader and writer alike, that Pausanias wrote his *Guide to Greece*[12] in the second century of the Common Era, some five centuries or more *after* our dinner party took place. Will his travelogue, so much later than the times we mean to discuss, say anything meaningful to our questions about Mantineia and about this curious Platonic dialogue? Indeed it will.

Pausanias went specifically looking for classical and preclassical Greek remains. His first questions at a site, virtually any site, are whether or not they sent a contingent to Troy in the Mycenaean period, and then how they lined up in the great battles between Persians and Greeks, in the generation prior to the one in which the *Symposium* took place. He seldom explores Greek history further than the Alexandrian conquests, except to comment negatively upon them. By then, he believed, the Greek wave had crested, and the classical Golden Age was at an end. Pausanias' literary effort was motivated by a profound sense of political and cultural nostalgia. He seems to have been interested in the contemporary Greeks (or Romans, for that matter) only insofar as they could tell him stories about the past, the past *before* the Romans came, with their decadent imperial courts and cults.

> Because of their justice [*dikaiosunē*] and their piety [*euse-beia*], the people of that time hosted the gods [*xenoi*] and shared a table with them [*homotrapezoi*]. The gods visibly rewarded their goodness and met their wickedness with wrath. . . .
>
> Some of them were even turned from human beings into gods. . . . But in my time when wickedness has increased to the last degree—populating the whole world and all of its cities—no human being is ever changed to a god, except in speech and in order to flatter authority, and the curse of the gods is a long time falling on the wicked [*adikois*], and is stored away for later, for those who have left the world behind.[13]

Clearly, Pausanias is not so interested in telling stories from the decadent times in which he thinks he lives. He wants heroic stories, from a distant past—the more heroic, and the more distant, the better. It is in this sense that Pausanias is looking for precisely the "Greece" we ourselves have in mind. What he finds in the course of his exploration is all the more telling for being so very old. If he has seen it himself, then the ruins must have been monumental, surely the dominant ones at the site. And if the locals recall these stories for him, then they must have been definitive in shaping the ethos of the place.

What, then, did Pausanias see and hear in Mantineia?

II

Mantineia is located in the region of Arkadia, allegedly the wildest and least developed region in the interior of the southern Peloponnese (the Mani, further to the south on the coast, is surely wilder still). Its inhabitants claimed to be the oldest in all of Greece. Arkadia as a whole was always loosely organized, and Mantineia seems to have been particularly independent. When you cross the isthmus of Corinth, coming south from Athens and the northern territories, you pass the major cities of Mykenai, Argos, and Tegea. Mantineia lies in the midst of

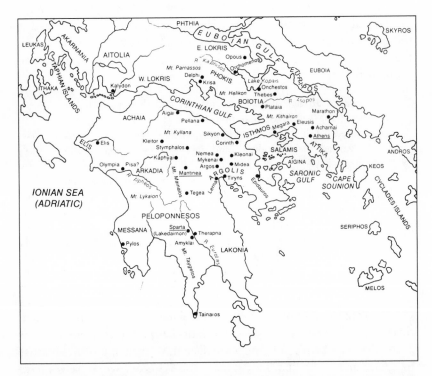

LOCATING MANTINEIA. Reprinted with permission of *Soundings, An Interdisciplinary Journal* (Knoxville, TN).

them all, closest to Argos, but farther west.[14] On the other side of the mountains, in the very heart of Arkadia, Mantineia is *metaxu*, "in the middle," a word that will prove to be crucial in this dialogue and in this book. I have already mentioned it, and will discuss it at length in this chapter. The Arkadian territories separate Attica, to the north, from Lakonia, to the south—which is to say, they find themselves caught in the middle of a long-drawn battle between Athens and Sparta for hegemony and spheres of influence. Wanting neither commitment, Mantineia seems to have been forced to choose first one and then the other power as an ally, when all she really wanted was independence, and *mutual* political relations.

Pausanias begins to tell the Mantineian story characteristically,[15] by noting that the Arkadians did send a contingent to Troy, under the command of a king named Agapenor. (It is worth noting that their leader's name already turns us to thoughts of love, deriving as it does from the word *agapē*.) They were later involved in the Messenian Wars (involving Messene and her allies against Sparta and hers), fighting on the losing side of the Messenians. Even then the Spartan threat to Mantineian autonomy seemed clear enough. And they fought, albeit unsuccessfully, for their independence.

In the first Persian invasion, Mantineia had five hundred men fighting alongside the three hundred Spartans who died at Thermopylae.[16] In the second Persian invasion some ten years later, the Mantineians sent groundtroops to Plateia, the site of the decisive final Greek land victory—and also the last great joint venture between northern and southern Greece, between Athens and Sparta.

Like so many cities in the Peloponnesian War (431–404 BCE), Mantineia wanted to remain neutral in this conflict, a political status that does seem to have been accorded some recognition in the ancient world,[17] but which was generally permitted only on the periphery. Arkadia was too central, too vitally *metaxu*, to be permitted its independence in this conflict, and she was slowly forced into the Spartan camp. She always found this an irritating political yoke, rebelling against Lakonia first with the Eleans,[18] and then later signing a one-hundred-year alliance with the cities of Athens, Argos, and Elis in 420 BCE.[19]

We ought, perhaps, briefly to recall the rough chronology of this last, and most destructive Greek domestic war in antiquity. It is particularly important to do so, since allusions to contemporary political affairs are sprinkled throughout the *Symposium*, and since Alcibiades figured so prominently both in the dialogue and in the war. The war, as I say, looms over this dramatic account of human loving, for reasons which will become clearer as we proceed.

The Peloponnesian conflict can be roughly divided into two periods. The first half, the so-called Archidamian War (named after Archidamus, who was the Spartan king at the time), was a period of intense political posturing, the playing off of alliances one against another, hostile diplomacy resulting in a good deal of skirmishing in contentious border territories, but seldom closer to home. Athens and Sparta seem at this time to have been unwilling combatants—much like the United States and Iraq, in those interminable months before *our* war began, when each was blustering at the other with the imagery of toxic gas, body-bags, and total annihilation, but was doing, precisely, nothing. What we see is less than total commitment . . . to the very idea of the war. Very little of permanent importance was accomplished in the Archidamian period. This is, moreover, the part of the war in which both Socrates and Alcibiades—who was still rather young at the time—fought, and these outlying campaigns at Potiaea and Delium are alluded to several times (*Symposium* 219e–221c). Since Greek cities were all being drawn into a war they did not really want, a peace was negotiated in 421 BCE, which was meant to last for fifty years.

This peace, the so-called Peace of Nikias, was named after a well-respected senior Athenian general who had always looked unfavorably on the war with Sparta, a city to which he was bound by ties of kinship and political sympathy. The anti-Spartan, hawkish party in Athens had been led by a man named Cleon, but Cleon had been killed in action in the year prior to the peace, and feeling for the war had died somewhat when he did.

It is interesting to note that there now existed a power vacuum in Athens, with no one to take the place of leader of the opposition to Nikias' overly pacific military policies. Whether by necessity or by cruel design, Alcibiades was destined to fill that role, however briefly. It was a disastrous role, for Athens now found itself trying to do what Mantineia and others had failed to do—attempting to play both roles, pacific and hostile by turns. *Metaxu*, caught between the accommodating policies of Nikias and the daring adventurism of Alcibiades, it was only a matter of time before Athens' military policies came undone.

That time was not far off; surprising no one, the Peace of Nikias did not last. All it had really done was to create the conditions in which all of the Peloponnesian cities were caught scrambling for cover, desperate to find protection in an alliance, any alliance, desperate not to be left alone. The Argive Alliance of 420 BCE was primarily Alcibiades' doing,[20] and it was a brilliant political coup. Still, like all things political, it was a mortal, all-too-mortal alliance. No sooner had the alliance been made than the new allies marched on Orchomenos and forced it into the alliance. They then decided to march on Tegea, but the Elean troops went home at this point, in protest. They saw the alliance as a defensive, not an aggressive, agreement. Terrified at what was happening now very close to home in Lakonia, the Spartans moved north and in the Battle of Mantineia in 418 BCE,[21] narrowly defeated the allies (Athenian and Elean reinforcements arriving just too late to save the day). The alliance temporarily dissolved, and each of the cities—Elis, Argos, and Mantineia—was forced to make a separate peace with its Spartan conquerors.

This conflict was instrumental in initiating the second half, the far more destructive half, of the Peloponnesian War. Both Sparta and Athens had by now taken off the boxing gloves, and were ready to fight in earnest. It was clear now, as it had not been before, that this would be a fight to the finish. No more tentative truces, no more half-peaces, no more semi-alliances, no more politics of the "in between." Battle lines were drawn, sides taken. Having finally taken the Athenian side, the Mantineians pursued it with a vengeance, sending a naval fleet with the Athenians on the disastrous Sicilian campaign—which left Athens in July of 415 BCE and was completely destroyed in the following year. The Mantineians were annihilated along with the Athenians there.[22]

The final Athenian capitulation in 404 BCE spelled the end of Mantineia even more profoundly—the city was dismantled and its population dispersed by her Spartan conquerors in 385 BCE,[23] not to be restored until the decisive Spartan defeat at Leuktra in 362 BCE. Within the *Symposium* itself—whose party is presumably meant to have taken place shortly *after* the Battle of Mantineia and shortly *before* the Sicilian expedition, probably in 416 BCE—mention of this is made in a stunning dramatic image. It takes its place within Aristophanes' wondrous myth of primal unity. "Now, on account of our crime [*adikian*]," he says, "we have been split by the gods, just as the Arkadians were by the Lakedaimonians" (*Symposium* 193a).[24] Having failed to defend her precious neutrality in this war, Mantineia was first coerced to the Spartan side, then later returned to the Athenian side, and was eventually toppled from the very political fence she sought to straddle. In war, it would seem, there is no middle ground.

When all is said and done, then, it would seem that "Mantineia" probably connoted bad political decisions to a Greek of the fourth century, not to mention the tendency always to choose the *wrong* side. The name quite simply connoted "in-between-ness," of a particularly dangerous political sort.[25]

I want to leave these issues to one side, however, and to pursue still another trajectory of Pausanias' description. He mentioned at the outset that the Arkadians under Agapenor went to Troy. Few, if any, made it home again. Agapenor himself did not. When the jealous gods broke up the victorious Greek fleet on its way home, scattering it all over the eastern Mediterranean, the surviving Arkadians wound up on the southwest coast of Cyprus. They came to the place where—so legend has it—Aphrodite was born, a place called Paphos, and they built her a sanctuary there.[26]

It is a pregnant detail, the very first story that Pausanias tells us about the Arkadians. It is a story that again turns our thoughts to passion. For Aphrodite and Eros are blood relations, twin sides of a common erotic coin. What I want to suggest is that the Arkadian region— and Mantineia in particular—was notable not only for its political instability and its uncanny habit of picking the losing side in a war, but also for the predominance of female deities in its local cults.[27] Two goddesses are worshipped here who are worshipped nowhere else: the Singing (*Hymnia*) Artemis;[28] and Alea, an unusual local goddess whose identity was later attached to that of Athena. The list of temples which Pausanias mentions in Mantineia is an impressive catalog of the profoundly *feminine* divine presence here.[29] The very first temple he mentions is a Hall of Dionysus,[30] that strangely androgynous god so well described by Euripides in *The Bacchae*. He is also the patron-god of the banquet the *Symposium* celebrates, a god of the theater as well as the god of wine. Demeter, the great earth mother and goddess of fertility, has *two* sanctuaries in Mantineia,[31] the second of which is dedicated both to her and to her daughter, Persephone (also called *Korē*, or "the Maiden"). Aphrodite also has two temples here: one dedicated to her as "Dark (*Melainidos*) Aphrodite" and the other dedicated to "Aphrodite of Alliance" (*Symmachias*)[32]—both titles thinly veiled allusions to the profound sensuality of the goddess.[33] We are also told of temples to Alean Athena, as already mentioned, and naturally enough, to Hera, Queen Mother of all the gods. Finally, and most peculiar, Pausanias mentions a "double temple, . . . divided pretty well in the middle by a wall," dedicated to both Asklepios and Leto.[34]

It is a fascinating idea for a temple, a sort of "in between" temple, divided in half, *metaxu*, and built to commemorate the lives of two "in between" sorts of beings—Asklepios, the great healer and son of Apollo, who eventually became divine himself;[35] and Leto, the paradigmatic long-suffering mother, who labored for nine days before giving birth to her Olympian offspring, Apollo and Artemis. Leto's own sexuality is also well attested—and profoundly ambiguous.

Now, Martha Nussbaum has written eloquently and at some length about the *Symposium*.[36] I will be turning to her interpretation of this dialogue in a moment. But she has also argued forcefully for the degree to which the stories our societies tell help to shape the way we look at, and even to experience, our own emotional lives. She has gone so far as to suggest that our emotions, our very capacity for deep feeling itself, "are not in fact personal or natural at all, [but] are, instead, contrivances, social constructs."[37] Our emotions are "constructed," so she says, by the stories we hear and choose to retell. Such a view suggests that a Greek temple, such as the ones we find in Mantineia, are actually quite complex social stories made architectural, sculptural, visible. The temple is a story we can *see*. We see the story of the erotic life here depicted just as surely as if we were sitting in a theater. And the way we think about love is in some profound ways determined by the erotic stories we see and hear every time we take to the road, into or out of town.

Taken together, then, the politics, the architecture, and the history of Mantineia tell an interesting story. Mantineia—even at the level of its name—seems to conjure up two sets of images, both of them *metaxu*, "in between." *Politically*, Mantineia represents a straddling of the fence long after a decision is called for; *erotically*, there are fascinating suggestions of androgyny,[38] and of erotic mutuality, which percolate just beneath the shimmering surface of sexual identities here. The two sets of imageries, the two sets of stories, are related in many ways, both being, in their way, states of radical "in-between-ness." The Greek word, *metaxu*, is also the grammatical term for the neuter case—again, neither masculine nor feminine, but something radically in-between.[39]

One of the points Pausanias emphasizes in his description of Mantineia is precisely this liminality, the "in-between-ness" of certain people, certain temples, and certain places. Clearly, in the political arena, "in-between" was a disastrous place for Mantineia to be. Yet I am put to wonder—Diotima's speech in the *Symposium* forces us to wonder—if perhaps in the erotic sphere "in between" isn't the singularly appropriate place to be.[40]

What is fascinating, in any case, is the manner in which these two forms of mediation—political and erotic, one of them an unparalleled disaster, the other a positive human good and a key source of human flourishing—coalesce in the dramatic figure of Alcibiades, the other key figure in this dialogue.

III

So much for Mantineia. Now, before turning to Alcibiades, I turn to the second of my initial questions. We have spent some time exploring the significance of Plato's invocation of Mantineia. And I have suggested that the word connoted *metaxu*, to a Greek ear, a kind of radical "in-between-ness." What did *erōs* mean, in Athens, in this same period? What did it mean to say that Diotima *taught* Socrates this? By answering these questions, we will be better able to see how Mantineia and Athens invite us to feel, and to love, rather differently . . . and how it is that Diotima's erotic vision will win the contest with its key rivals at this party. In Mantineia, one loves mutually and reciprocally, or not at all.

This is a significant claim, if only because the structures and stories of Greek homoeroticism in classical Athens were regimented and disciplined to such an extraordinary degree. There are actually *rules* about how to love and to be loved, if one is a free-born Athenian male. One may do one or the other—love, or be loved—but one cannot do both. A Greek male simply cannot love and be loved by the same person. Even their grammar works against such an erotic possibility.

Such *erōs* was, much as Nussbaum suggests, a *social* structure, and a social fact. It is, of course, not only that. The extremes of the social-constructionist account of human sexuality always founder on the shoals of our biology. For human sexuality, like gender itself, is a matter of nature as well as of culture. Sexuality—the entire bodily complex, in fact—is the place where "nature" and "culture" meet, an endless play of Apollinian and Dionysian forces which cannot be separated neatly or completely.[41] That is one reason why, for all of its *cultural* strangeness, the Platonic account of *erōs* continues to exercise its uncanny influence upon the literary and erotic imagination.

A younger boy is formally courted by an older man. Gifts are exchanged, interest is aroused, gradually confirmed, and erotic desire emerges. The relationship, once it has been made explicit and has been accepted on these terms, is intended to be a long one. How long is, as it always is, a more difficult question—Plato reminds us that love is neither immortal, nor merely transitory. Love is that desire which longs most achingly after permanence. It wants permanence, but such permanence is forever wanting. The older lover serves as teacher to the youth, introducing him into mature male society, teaching him about politics and the household, about economics and about warfare, perhaps even providing him with his first set of armor. He takes a boy and makes a man—which is to say a *politikos*, a *citizen*—of him. And yet it would seem that, once the boy has become a man, then the relationship would, of necessity and almost by definition, be at an end. We will return shortly to this problem.[42]

Sexuality both is and is not the point to such eroticism.[43] To be sure, a young boy *is* the source of a peculiar and long-standing attraction in classical Athenian art and society. Male bodies are carved in the nude; women are normally clothed in such elaborate costume that their form is only vaguely defined, if at all.[44] Women were not carved in the nude until some centuries later. The archaic and classical erotic poets are full of winsome remarks about the first blush of manhood—when the youthful face first begins to sport a beard, when beauty is freshest and most pure. It was one of the chief attractions of Alcibiades—the larger-than-life, disruptive force at the end of this symposium—so we are told, that his beauty lasted as long as it did, each season of life supplying additional character to his abundant physical charms.

> Euripides' saying that even the autumn of beauty possesses a loveliness of its own is not true of everyone. But even if it applies only to the few, it was certainly true of Alcibiades on account of his natural gifts and his physical excellence.[45]

On this latter point, the Greeks seem to have been profoundly ambivalent. While the poets are full of sensual sensitivity, there is an undeniable concern for choosing a lover well—and in this decision physical form does *not* precede function. A vase cannot take shape, nor be fired properly, if the clay is gritty and impure. A human character cannot be educated and shaped by the lover whose task this is if that character is egoistic, dissolute, oversexed. As Euripides should have said, in the autumn, physical beauty often does fade. And, as Voltaire once remarked, at the age of fifty each of us has the face we deserve. So much the more important, then, that the lover possess other more enduring charms, if the relationship is to run its natural and more-than-natural course.

This is all by way of making a point I have made several times already: *erōs* is not an easy idea to translate. Nor does the set of experiences it names admit of easy understanding. *Erōs* does not connote simple sexual desire. It connotes desire, to be sure, but desire in all the manifold forms it can have when human beings are at issue. Still, *erōs* always retains its nature *as desire*, and sexuality is never very far beneath the surface in human desiring.[46] Hence the ambivalence about sexuality in classical Greek thought, the way it was "problematized" in the antique world.[47] Practically speaking, we desire first and foremost in a physical fashion. But the gods help us if that be the limit beyond which our desire cannot go. We need to love souls as well as bodies, and ideally, we will come to love both in a single lover. The lover is, after all, an inseparable union of body and soul. This becomes an important insight in Socrates' own unfolding erotic life.

This is already abundantly clear in the way the Greeks try to talk about love. I have alluded already to the rather disciplined, even stultifying, character of upper-class Athenian eroticism—almost as though these men were desperately afraid of the madness, the sad mania of passion, that desire brings in its wake. In love, one is never so settled, nor so secure, again. The very words the Greeks use tell us a great deal about this. In a love-relationship, one is either *erastēs* or *erōmenos*, a lover or a beloved, a pursuer or a pursued.[48] Both words are constructed out of the same root—which is *erōs*—yet syntactically speaking, they possess an active and a passive meaning. The *erastēs* is "he who *erōs*-es," he who *does* the *erōs*. By contrast the *erōmenos* (the suffix-*menos* being simply the passive form in Greek) is "he who is *erōs*-ed," he who has the *erōs done to* him.

What remains to be said—and it will take this entire dialogue to say it properly—is that *erōs* does not work this way. *Erōs* is something which happens, not something which is merely, crassly, *done*. It is not merely a physical thing. Our love poets, ancient and modern alike, constantly remind us of this fact. Even in modern Greek, where it is far more common to say *s'agapō* when one wishes to say "I love you" (basing this on the root *agapē*, a rather different kind of love), there is a far richer, far more unnerving, and far more poetic way to communicate this bond. It invokes *erōs* explicitly. The demotic phrase, *eimai erateumenos mazi sou*, which is normally translated as "I am *in love* with you," actually says something much richer and more profound. It uses the same passive ending,-*menos*. But it names passivity of an entirely different kind. The phrase suggests that "I have been *erōs*-ed," or rather "*erōs* has happened to me—by being together with you." To say it again: *erōs* is something which *happens*, not something which can be *done*. We do not come to Love anymore than we come to thoughts; these things, contrastingly, come to us. Reclaiming the power of the passive voice has been a major preoccupation of western philosophy in this century.

Curiously, in this excessively masculine society and this exclusively masculine dinner party, the dualism between activity and passivity is also made a matter of masculine virtue. When *erōs* is "common" or pedestrian, it tends to be undiscriminating, warns Pausanias toward the beginning of this dialogue, indiscriminately attracted to women and to boys alike. A genuinely higher, spiritual love is possible only between men, he insists (*Symposium* 181c). When he argues this way, he seems to be asserting a widely held, if unrehearsed, Athenian orthodoxy—at least among the men. But his subsequent, tedious account of erotic roles and rules is meant to make us wonder, I think. Socrates wonders. And Diotima—both materially, because she is a woman, and formally for what she says about the nature of human desire—makes our implicit questions explicit.[49] It is interesting that Diotima consistently uses the word *erōtikoi* for the sorts of lovers she envisions, a word that connotes a kind of reciprocity and mutuality, one which is neither *erastēs* nor *erōmenos* at all.

Again, the issue both is and is not a sexual, somatic one. Sexually, only the young boy is penetrated by the "superior," the older male. He should not seek such sexuality out, nor should he enjoy it. There are in fact a host of disparaging, and graphic Greek idioms for the boy who prefers the role of *erōmenos*, which is also the role of women, and who can neither outgrow nor see beyond it.[50] Alcibiades is, in his way, such a boy. He himself admits that he is a slave to love (*katadedoulōmenos, Symposium* 219c). He plays the fool for it. But it is more than this. *Erastēs* and *erōmenos* are also pursuer and pursued. The *Symposium* is rich with fascinating and funny details—about lovers camped out in doorways (*Symposium* 183a), pining away for the boys (the love-objects, really) whom they desire. That can be the bittersweet agony of genuine longing. Yet it is also the *role* they are forced to play, as pursuer, as *erastēs*.

Such roles were seldom seriously questioned in the classical period.[51] They seem to be the very stuff of the classical Athenian erotic life, the buzzwords that most upper-class Athenian men used to describe their erotic self-understanding. It is surely not accidental, but really the very heart of the matter, that Phaedrus, in the very first speech of the *Symposium*, introduces these categories as a given, the undisputed material conditions of men's loving. Still more significant, the seeds for the eventual displacement of these terms are sown in this selfsame speech.

It is all couched in terms of an arcane debate about the *Iliad* (*Symposium* 180a–b). Phaedrus complains that Aeschylus has gotten the relationship between Achilles and Patroklus backwards. It is self-evident, Phaedrus alleges, that Achilles was himself the *erōmenos*, who must have been pursued by Patroklus—after all, as Homer tells us, Achilles was clearly the younger of the two. So much do these terms, and the roles they inscribe, set erotic conditions which allegedly cannot be altered, boundaries that cannot be crossed. If Achilles is the younger man, then he must de facto be the *erōmenos*; there is no other way for Phaedrus to think about the matter.

Or so it would appear at first glance. But two additional features of Phaedrus' speech, rarely noticed, qualify this oversimplified erotic picture. In the first place, Achilles is the third person, not the first, whom Phaedrus discusses. After arguing that erotic desire brings with it the capacity to feel genuine shame (a claim later confirmed by Alcibiades), Phaedrus suggests that an army of lovers could never be defeated, precisely because each soldier would prefer to die facing the enemy rather than be witnessed by a lover to be involved in some shameful action, like retreat. Phaedrus opts to "prove" his point mythically, by looking at three examples which link loving and dying in this way. But the first person he mentions is Alkestis, a *woman* who offered her own life in order to preserve the life of her husband. This example does not fit into the *erastēs-erōmenos* framework at all. Phaedrus' second example is Orpheus, who tried, unsuccessfully, to steal his wife back from Hades into the light of day. This example is even worse. It does not follow the erotic framework which Phaedrus is trying manfully to elevate either; moreover, Orpheus is ironically *un*willing to die for his wife. He tries, instead, to bring her back into the light of day with him. Now, both of these examples link love and death, which is Phaedrus' main point. Yet both involve heterosexual and marital relationships, those most commonly described in heroic and Homeric mythology. This seems important and odd, upon further reflection. Women are introduced here, at the very outset of this symposium, and they will return most dramatically at the end, in the guise of Diotima.

The second complicating factor comes with Phaedrus' third example, and it is still more serious. Achilles, we are told, must have been the *erōmenos* in this relationship because he was the younger man—*eti ageneios*, "still without a beard," as Phaedrus notes, "and therefore much younger" (*Symposium* 180a). But now comes a leap in logical argument that makes nonsense of the whole discussion.

The gods honor that virtue [*aretēn*] which is associated with love [*erōta*] best of all. But they are still more amazed and they reward it even more when the *erōmenos* loves his *erastēs* rather than when the *erastēs* simply loves his *paidika*. For the *erastēs* is more divine [*theioteron*] than the *paidika*. In fact, he is inspired [*entheos*]. That is why they honored Achilles even more than Alkestis and sent his soul to the Blessed Isles. (*Symposium* 180a–b)

Phaedrus has gotten himself into real difficulty here, precisely because of the rigidity of his erotic categories. Alkestis and Orpheus and Achilles all risked their lives for love. Achilles did so on behalf of his *erastēs*, Patroklus. We know that Achilles was the *erōmenos* in this relationship because he was younger, just barely bearded in fact. Yet Phaedrus also knows that Achilles was the greatest and most marvelous (and therefore the "most divine") of all the heroes at Troy. These things he tends to associate with the active agent, the *erastēs*, not the *erōmenos*. And so, almost without our being able to say when or how, Phaedrus slips into an argument where Achilles is turned into the active agent again. Finally, Phaedrus goes so far as virtually to call Achilles an *erastēs*, the "divinely inspired" one. So his argument collapses finally under its own dead weight. Either Aeschylus was not wrong about the relationship, or else there is something wrong with the crude categories of lover and beloved.

What is remarkable, then, is that most every subsequent speaker at this party accepts this erotic framework—the rhetoric of *erastēs* and *erōmenos*—without question,[52] reflecting on the why's and wherefore's of our longing—how love drives us to do what we would otherwise never do, all in the name of an overwhelming, an undeniably inspired, kind of longing. *Erastēs* and *erōmenos* are two Greek buzzwords that Socrates, for his part, intends to interrogate, and ultimately, to disown.

It is Socrates—or rather, to be fair, *Diotima* when she is with Socrates—who calls this entire framework into question. She is simply underlining questions which have already been elucidated by the speeches we have heard. In the playful banter that separates Agathon's ornamental speech from Socrates' more substantive one, Socrates means to do to Agathon precisely what Diotima did to him—namely, to bring his own assumptions into the light, to open up the too-narrow strictures in which his own erotic thinking had been trapped. It begins with a fairly subtle philosophical point. Most everyone eulogizes *Erōs* as beautiful and good, and yet we seem to desire only that which we ourselves do not possess. None of us loves, really loves, a mirror image of our self. We love the difference, the inescapable otherness, perhaps even the in-between-ness, of the lover. If *Erōs* desires beauty and goodness, Diotima notes, then he must not possess these things. Does it then follow that *Erōs, who is a god*, is ugly, or evil?

> "How can you say that, Diotima?" I demanded. "Can Love then be evil . . . or ugly?"
> But she said, "Be quiet! Do you think that whatever isn't beautiful must necessarily be ugly?"
> "Of course."
> "And that anyone who isn't wise is ignorant? Don't you realize that there is something *in between* [*metaxu*] wisdom and ignorance?"
> "What?"
> "Don't you see it yet?" she asked. "Having correct opinions without having the words for them. That isn't knowledge (for how can something without reasons be knowledge?), but it's not ignorance either (how can it be ignorance, if it happens to be true?). Correct opinions are just this way—*in between* [*metaxu*] understanding and ignorance."
> "What you've said is true," I admitted.
> "Then don't insist on the thing which isn't beautiful being ugly, or on the thing which isn't good being evil. And when you can bring yourself to agree that *Erōs* is neither good nor beautiful, it won't be necessary anymore for him to be ugly and evil. Rather he is something *in between* [*metaxu*] these two." (*Symposium* 201e-202b)[53]

This reference to a different kind of knowledge is one of the loveliest and most important in this dialogue, and perhaps in the entire Erotic Period. Love knows what it knows, although it cannot give "reasons," and cannot always "find the words" for what it knows. Philosophy of the Socratic sort normally aspires "to give an account" of the things it investigates. Yet no account can be given for whom one loves, nor for why. And this practical impossibility of giving an account does not render the love "untrue," nor does it render it insusceptible to philosophical scrutiny. Rather, such loving points out to us the limits of all such human knowing. I am coming closer to the suggestion now that the best translation of the Platonic account of *erōs* is our well-worn anglicism, "true love."

The impossibility of giving an account, a verbal account, is not necessarily a problem. If anything, Diotima seems to suggest that it is the very intuitive strength of this kind of knowledge that is so dramatic, so certain, and so disarming about it. (It is this same insight that makes Martha Nussbaum's book title, *Love's Knowledge*,[54] so singularly appropriate and instructive for my argument.) There are more things in heaven and in our hearts than are dreamt of in most modern philosophy.

Now, at this crucial stage in the argument of the *Symposium*, it doesn't take any great feat of moral imagination to extend this intuitive rationale to the central assumption of the entire dialogue. It is almost as though Diotima were really asking—as she surely is—"Surely you're not so naive as to assume that you must be either *erastēs* or *erōmenos*? Surely there is more to love than camping on doorsteps in the rain, or else staying locked up inside the house, waiting for someone to brave the storm on your behalf." In rejecting this extreme erotic framework, Socrates must necessarily reject Alcibiades, as well.

Indeed, almost every speaker thus far has relied on certain essential, and entirely unquestioned, dichotomies—between beauty and ugliness, between good and evil, between knowledge and ignorance, between *erastēs* and *erōmenos*. Diotima disowns all of these, arguing that things are never so simple, arguing that there is crucially important territory "in between" such extremes. Now we are invited to extend this question-posing to other essential dichotomous assumptions: that between heterosexual and homosexual relationships; that between men and women; that between mortality and immortality; and, most significant of all of them, that between the body and the soul. *Erōs* involves not one or the other, but a fascinating combination of both. We will meet this important Platonic claim again in the next chapter.

IV

With a winsomeness worthy of Socrates, and a circumlocution worthy of this, Plato's thrice-told tale, Martha Nussbaum says that I said that she failed to say some important things about *erōs*. "Now I have never before been accused by my professional peers of neglecting *erōs*," she smiles.[55] Nussbaum is saying that I said that she failed to say something. So I did. So, I think, did she.

Now, to be fair, it needs to be added that, with the eloquence and fairness that are her trademark, Nussbaum also admits that there is a point here, and that my claims, "while not exactly on target about the book," do "confront [her] with a valuable challenge." The challenge, such as it is, concerns a fuller, more fully human account of human desire, a recognition that love is, if *anything* human can be, a two-edged sword. In fleshing out this point, in giving love's knowledge a body, we are asked to wonder about the fleshiness of *erōs*, its ability to drive us down paths we know we ought not go. "It seems important to ask," Nussbaum concludes,

> whether erotic relationships in particular involve this risk more often and more intrinsically, and thus are especially linked with the possibility of anger and vindictiveness. In my current work on Stoic arguments against the passions I am looking at this question. It seems to me that the Stoics have powerful arguments that the removal of cruelty and murderous rage requires the removal of erotic love. I feel that it is particularly urgent for us to investigate these arguments, and I have tried to do this in some recent work on Seneca.[56]

It is this very "problem" that seems to give us grounds for a friendlier reading of the Socrates we meet in the *Symposium*, as well as the woman who taught him what he knows. Socrates may well be an answer, not a version of the problem in its crudest, hardest form.

As I understand Nussbaum's position, the "problem" with Socrates is that he fails to understand, and to live within the constraints of, the necessary *particularity* of *erōs*.[57] His love, his passion, is all bound up in an idea. And thus there is something cold, hard—nonhuman if not actually *in*human—about his erotic life. In the worst of all possible lights, he loves himself yet cannot really love another. He is in love with Love, but never lets himself love a person. "Socrates is weird," Nussbaum says with uncharacteristic bluntness. "We need to ask ourselves more clearly before we can say whether we would like to become this other sort of being, excellent and deaf."[58]

In an erotic translation of her philosophical Aristotelianism, Nussbaum calls us "back to the *phainomena*,"[59] insisting that love must not be turned into some heady and self-serving *idea*. Love is the very stuff of an *embodied* human life—messy and particular, uncanny and complex. The *dis*embodied philosopher tries to turn it into something else again. "The philosopher asks to be taken to the *agathon*, the respectable and universalizable Good. Alcibiades asks to be taken to Agathon, a not-very-good particular boy."[60] I appreciate the point, and nothing quite so well as Nussbaum's impassioned eloquence, yet these polarities seem overdrawn to me. The truth of the situation, like the truth of *erōs* itself, seems to me to lie in between, *metaxu*, where in the final analysis this whole dialogue wants to take place.

Doubtless there *are* problems with Socrates, and he may well have been precisely that kind of man one very rarely meets: an intimate friend, yet always keeping a certain distance, keeping something of himself in reserve; a man very easy to love, yet who grows maddeningly aloof the more one loves him; easy to like, but in the final analysis impossible to love. And no one sketches out these problems with greater sensitivity than Martha Nussbaum. Yet there are other issues at stake in her criticisms, it seems to me.

If I may be permitted to play a little shamelessly with Nussbaum's text, might we not retitle her discussion of Plato's middle dialogues as "the *frigidity* of goodness?" She makes more than a few casual remarks which strongly suggest that the problem with Socrates is that he is erotically frigid.[61] When he spends the entire evening in bed with the naked Alcibiades, and is not aroused, we have at least arguably moved outside the realm of philosophical discipline and into the realm of erotic insensitivity—insensitivity not just to the particularities of the given situation, but also the real emotional damage we may do to our infatuated and unrequited friends. Or so we are invited to believe.

> Socrates might conceivably have abstained from sexual relations while remaining attentive to the lover in his particularity. He might also have had a sexual relationship with Alcibiades while remaining inwardly aloof. But Socrates refuses in every way to be affected. He is stone; and he turns others to stone. Alcibiades is to his sight just one more of the beautifuls, a piece of the form, a pure thing like a jewel.[62]

Yet Socrates is always speaking in self-deprecating terms about his own "slavery" to love.[63] He is profoundly affected by male beauty. He is forever finding a way to get the unoccupied (or occupied) seat next to the beauties of Athens. And when he enters the room, no one else has a chance of making any erotic headway at all (*Symposium* 213c, 222b, 223a).

What, then, does he want? If he really is frigid, then a big part of what he wants is to be wanted. He *uses* beauty, drinks it to the dregs, then discards it when demands are made of his particular form of beauty, in turn. Nussbaum accuses him of just this kind of hardness—a sort of erotic brittleness and frigidity—and of being a heartbreaker to boot. He means to *use erōs*, to get himself where he really wants to go, alone—up the divine ladder toward the beatific vision of the Beautiful.

Perhaps. But there is another way to read Socrates. He is a simple man, a stonecutter by trade, a man uncomfortable with lofty language and lofty thoughts. A practical man, Socrates knows what he knows. And the one thing that he insists he knows, is *erōs*. I will make much of this essential Socratic paradox in the next chapter. He knows that "love's knowledge" is knowledge of a radically different sort, and he accepts it that way. To put it as simply—and as profoundly—as any human thing can be, Socrates has fallen in love. He has allowed himself to love, as no other participant in this dialogue seems to have done. He alone has been open to the risk, and the exasperation, and the sheer wonder, of an erotic experience. That is what makes Socrates "weird." What he wants is really what his own society—with its profoundly regimented, if not repressive, sexuality—will not allow him to have, will not even give him the words for: mutuality, the give-and-take of true erotic commitments, a world where the hopelessly simplistic (and really rather "frigid") categories of pursuer and pursued will have no place. He does not want an *erōmenos*; he wants an *erōtikos*. He wants his erotic and spiritual equal. Perhaps, just perhaps, what he wants is what he had with Diotima. That relationship broke all the rules: it was heterosexual;[64] the way it thought about masculinity and femininity was much too ambiguous; the way passivity and pursuit suddenly emerged into the clearer light of reciprocity was nothing short of astonishing. All this must have seemed a little weird to a fifth-century Athenian audience, at this drinking-party and afterwards.

According to Nussbaum, Alcibiades is the real unsung hero of this dialogue, not Diotima—Alcibiades the dissolute, the destroyer, the spurned and potentially violent lover. Why make a hero of *him*? For two reasons, I imagine. First, because it had not been done. Alcibiades has been marginalized by contemporary scholars, made so bad, in fact, that we fail to appreciate, even fail to discuss, his very real and abundant native gifts. If we know *anything* about Alcibiades (and few of us do), we know that he went around Athens late one night in some kind of drunken stupor, smashing the *phalloi* off the herms which lined the city streets.[65] It was this wanton act of impious violence that spelled the beginning of the end for him politically, lost him his promising career, and probably lost Athens the War. Perhaps. But isn't it fascinating that this one detail—a ritual castration, really—has captured the popular mind so thoroughly when it is far from the worst thing Alcibiades did,[66] and which is moreover probably something that he did not actually do at all.[67]

Alcibiades' real claim to a reevaluation, for Nussbaum at least, seems due to the fact that he alone understands the necessary and inescapable particularity of *erōs*. Love is love of some one, distinctive other person. In his drunken speech—an encomium, not of *Erōs*, but of *Socrates*—he is very clear about this.

> Now Socrates possesses many remarkable and amazing traits. And while he shares many of these things with other men, there is absolutely no one else like him—no man either ancient or contemporary—and that is the most amazing thing about him. (*Symposium* 221c–d)

Here would seem to be additional warrant for Nussbaum's contention that Alcibiades is in love with a man, while Socrates is in love with Love. Erotic idealism, again.

I cannot agree. Tempting as the claim no doubt is, it is finally too simple, too easy. In fact, it seems to me to be precisely and elegantly wrong. It raises the right question, but asks it of the wrong man. I want to suggest that Socrates, at a level far deeper than Alcibiades, understands the necessary particularity of *erōs*. It is Alcibiades who is in love with Love, or—what amounts to almost the same thing—is in love with himself. He wants a lover only until such a time as the lover wants him, too. Then he moves on, in search of new loves, passions, conquests. There is a whole world for Alcibiades to win; he is never still. Alcibiades' love is solipsistic; he wants to see his own reflection, made even lovelier in the admiring eyes of someone else.

Socrates knows this, knows him—knows him, in fact, better than anyone else,[68] perhaps because he shares more of this man's temperament than he would care to admit. And in any case it seems to me that Socrates' rejection of Alcibiades, far from being a case of frigidity, is in fact the final proof of his own erotic intelligence. Alcibiades, tempting and pretty as he no doubt is, is not the person for Socrates. Socrates was, whatever else he may have been, a perspicacious judge of human character, nowhere so well as here. Alcibiades would have been a disastrous lover—for Socrates, as he eventually proved to be for Athens. And Socrates, while he was willing to be a slave to Athens, and to philosophy—perhaps even a slave to *Erōs*—will not permit himself to be enslaved by Alcibiades' particular, and ultimately rather slavish, virtues.

From a *political* standpoint, Alcibiades is a lot like Mantineia—trying to play both sides, Athens and Sparta, off of one another, finding himself trapped finally in between, *metaxu*, destroyed by his own reckless political desire. But, unlike Mantineia, Alcibiades *never* learned his lesson. Mantineia decided, cast her lot with Athens, and was destroyed with her at the War's end. Alcibiades never decided, yet his destruction was even more complete. It is even possible that, if he had cast his lot—come what may—with Athens, she may not have been destroyed at all.

We should recall that Mantineia also symbolized an *erotic* and gendered "in-between-ness," and that this is an idea which Alcibiades clearly never understood at all. The kinds of stories that everyone told about the man tell the tale. In a fit of anger, Alcibiades beat a fellow citizen in public. Later, and privately, he goes to the man's house, and, by way of apology, stripped down and offered his body to be disposed of as the man, Hipponicus, pleased.[69] It pleased him, for reasons which are not clear, to give Alcibiades his daughter in marriage. A good and virtuous woman, Hipparete was finally so outraged by the quality and the quantity of Alcibiades' erotic indiscretions that she left him and sued for divorce.[70] Years later, the disastrous matter of the herms forcing him into exile, Alcibiades has intrigued his way over to the Spartan side and has exacted terrible revenge on his native city. When the Spartan king Agis is out on campaign, however, Alcibiades seduces his wife and has a child by her. Alcibiades, refusing to be cowed, and failing as always to appreciate the gravity of the grudges against him, mockingly says that he wanted to be sure his descendents would sit on the Spartan throne. Naturally enough, he is again forced to flee.[71] From Sparta, he flees to the Persian camp, where similar events unfold. In fact, the narrative of his death, with which Martha Nussbaum concludes her encomium to the man,[72] is actually the *penultimate* story Plutarch tells. On the night of his murder, Alcibiades dreams a dream—a dream in which a courtesan paints his face and clothes him as a woman. "It is a dream," Nussbaum suggests, "that expresses the wish for unmixed passivity."[73] It is no dream. It is a portrait of Alcibiades' truest self, the *erōmenos* who simply cannot live or love any differently. Poignantly, Nussbaum tells us, Alcibiades' lover at the time buried his corpse in her own clothing. So it is that Alcibiades found in death a passivity, even a femininity, that had always eluded him in life.

Alcibiades may not have died so pitiably. It was also rumored that, upon returning to Phrygia, Alcibiades seduced the daughter of a well-placed household, and that her brothers, outraged at his *hybris*,[74] killed him treacherously in the night.[75] A dissolute, impassioned, and excessive life, from beginning to end.

Where Alcibiades spends a lifetime chasing the wrong women (and men), invariably at tremendous personal and public cost, Socrates at least arguably held out for the "right" woman, learned enormously from her, has carried her memory and her stories with him ever since. Here, then, is another hint—if more were needed still—at the reasons behind Socrates' rejection of Alcibiades. He well understood that Alcibiades views love in terms of pursuit and domination. He desires to be desired. It is the very first thing Plutarch tells us about his character (*ēthos*), the fundamental reason for all his later troubles.

> In later life Alcibiades' character was to reveal great lawless-
> ness and inconsistency, as one might expect in a career such
> as his, which was spent in the midst of great enterprises and
> profound shifts of fortune. While there were surely many
> strong passions in his nature, strongest by far was the desire
> to be first among his friends and to win them over, as is cus-
> tomary among boys [*tois paidikois*].[76]

Alcibiades wants to be wanted, pure and simple. So much so that he will break *all* the rules, will even deign to become the pursuer himself—*until* he gets the attention he craves. Then, assured that you now love him, he is gone in the blink of an eye, a flash of light.

Love is like a bolt of lightning, Alcibiades believes.[77] The imagery is potent. When Semele, the human mother of Dionysus, demanded that she see her lover face to face—he was a god, after all, and came to her only in the night—a lightning bolt descended from heaven and killed her where she stood. Alcibiades' passion is like that—desperate in its inten- sity, hell-bent on its own destruction. Socrates' passion is equally intense, but it is not desperate. His knowledge, like his touch, is sure.

My point in going on so long about this? Only that Socrates cannot be written off as insensitive to the particularities of an erotic commitment. So sensitive is he to the complex, interactive dynamic of such a peculiar and magical relationship, that he chooses not to have it, though a part of his soul longs for it. He has, as he himself admits, been with Diotima—a diffi- cult love to follow. After the last of his failed erotic sallies, Alcibiades gives up in exasperation. Turning this erotic surrender to his own philosophical advantage, Socrates concludes their conversation with a smile: "Now you've got it right," he tells the still lovestruck Alcibiades. "From now on and in the future, we will deliberate together about what to do, by figuring out what seems to be the best thing to us both [*nōin*]" (*Symposium*, 219b).

V

The issue of mutuality, and of mediation, is absolutely central to the argument of the *Symposium*, just as it is to Martha Nussbaum's writing about these dialogues from Plato's Erotic Period. Nussbaum will admit this idea of mutuality to a later dialogue, the *Phaedrus*, but she will not allow it in the *Symposium*. She reads the *Phaedrus*, in fact, as Plato's explicit retraction of answers he gave to his own erotic questions in the *Symposium*—answers he now considers inadequate. In her reply to Christine Downing's defense of the mutuality apparent already in Diotima's speech, Nussbaum is quite clear:

> What is at issue, then, is how far this movement towards mutuality and reciprocity, and this endorsement of bodily sensuality as compatable with the best human life, are present in the *Symposium*. . . .
> I conclude that Downing should turn to the *Phaedrus*, rather than the *Symposium*, for the vindication of a virtuous sensuality and a temperate madness.[78]

Now, admittedly, Nussbaum has a really fascinating way of explaining this transformation: Plato himself, "this most intolerant of human beings [sic]," finally experienced the full force of *erōs*, and was dealing with the knowledge (*love's* knowledge) he had gained at tremendous personal cost, when he lost his own lover, Dion, and his self-sufficiency at the same time.[79]

There is something to what Nussbaum has seen in these comparative texts. Yet I suspect that there is something else here as well. Nussbaum is out to defend a fairly simple thesis, one which argues that the tragedies were attuned to the role of fortune and chance in the moral life in a way that Plato will not allow. Plato is, in the final analysis, afraid of such outrageous fortune. It is Aristotle who will, in the course of carefully correcting his teacher's excesses, rehabilitate this older, more authentically *tragic* vision. Aristotle, not Plato—save, perhaps, in one dialogue written toward the end of his career, well after he had made Aristotle's acquaintance. But why is this typology—tragedy, to Plato, to Aristotle—and this insistent polarity—Plato versus Aristotle—so important to her?

Sheldon Cohen has pointed to a possibility that seems to bear directly on the issue. It is not about Plato and Aristotle at all. "I suspect," he suggests,

> that Nussbaum, wanting to play off the Christian problem of evil against a pre-Christian alternative, somehow came to see Plato as standing in the former and Aristotle as representing the latter. Theoretically, there is something to this, but what is there is loose.[80]

Once highlighted, this crude polarity seems to run clearly throughout Nussbaum's erotic reflections. "Greek versus Christian" is at least as important a dichotomy to her as "Aristotle (and the Poets) versus Plato." This duality she has learned, as have we all perhaps, from Nietzsche. In a remarkable footnote at the outset of her massive study, Nussbaum candidly admits as much:

> I shall simply assert here my belief that Nietzsche was correct in thinking that a culture grappling with the widespread loss of Judeo-Christian religious faith could gain insight into its own persisting intuitions about value by turning to the Greeks. When we do not try to see them through the lens of Christian belief we can not only see them more truly; we can also see how true they are to us—that is, to a continuous historical tradition of human ethical experience that has not been either displaced or irreversibly altered by the supremacy of Christian (and Kantian) teaching.[81]

The invocation of Nietzsche is both telling and appropriate. Surely Nussbaum's work is a clarion call to a gayer moral science, as I have myself argued elsewhere.[82] But it is more than this. Nietzsche continues to haunt us, positively looming over contemporary philosophical conversation, with a question of which he will not permit us to let go—the same duality, really, that we have had before us all along: Paganism and Christianity. "Have I been understood?" he taunts, in his very last published remark. "*Dionysus against the Crucified!*"[83] If we are to take the "continuous historical tradition of human ethical experience" seriously, as Nussbaum does, then Christianity's crucial place within that continuous tradition may not be ignored. I suggested as much in the introduction. Nor may it be written off as the history of an error, a sad mistake, an uncanny lacuna in the tradition that would have passed more happily and easily from mature Hellenism to the later nineteenth century.[84]

The *Symposium* really is an essential text for tracing out the contours of this prejudice. Christianity is accused, perhaps more for this than for anything else, for having made *the body* a source of philosophical and spiritual embarrassment. We have been taught to think of ourselves, and our bodies, and certainly our sexuality, as somehow problematic and "unclean." And if we take such an attitude to the body, we are rather quickly turned into poor custodians of the souls that make a home there. Christianity has made us over in the image of the martyrs, made us all elite practitioners of self-abuse. As the body goes, so goes the soul—to perdition.[85]

Well and good, we are wont to say. We have all heard this a hundred times, and it is a fairly standard historical claim these days. Christianity did a happier, healthier, freer pagan antiquity to death. But there are signs that the veneer that protects this prejudice is beginning to wear a little thin. Michel Foucault has done much to correct this mistaken Nietzschean prejudice. The irony of the reception of his ideas,[86] Nussbaum's included,[87] is that he has been taken to task for not being critical, or radical, enough. He is certainly *not* offering a radical reappraisal of classical antiquity or Victorian prudishness in these studies of sexuality, but it was never his intention to do so. His point was a radical reappraisal of *modern* intellectual prejudices—"rationality" first and foremost—and in this work we have failed dismally to understand him.[88] If there is anything novel about our new Victorian age, Foucault notes, it is not our prudishness, but rather our need to turn sexuality into discourse, to talk it all to death.[89] Sexuality and the body—he is insistent on this point—had *already* been problematized in late classical and Hellenistic society, long before Christianity emerged on the scene. Christian moral thought inherited this problematic, perhaps took it to new and even regrettable extremes at times, yet hardly invented it. And in any case, it is not merely a "problem."

VI

In other areas, Martha Nussbaum has taken Nietzsche (and Foucault, for that matter) as well, and as far, and as eloquently, as anyone else writing about these matters today. She has made *sense* of it. She has done so, moreover, by focusing upon the very ideas that make the whole world and what had been a rather narrow academic debate about Greek moral thinking look profoundly and wonderfully different: contingency, tragedy, *fragility*. In conclusion, and in one of her loveliest insights, she observes:

> There is a beauty in the willingness to love someone in the
> face of love's instability and worldliness that is absent from
> a completely trustworthy love. There is a certain valuable
> quality in social virtue that is lost when social virtue is
> removed from the domain of uncontrolled happenings. And
> in general each salient Aristotelian virtue seems inseparable
> from a risk of harm.[90]

We are now returned to the point from which we began, the realization of just how *crucial* the idea of *erōs* (and the alleged Christian insensitivity to its importance) is to Nussbaum's whole program. *Erōs* is "fragility" objectified, fragility made viscerally and experientially real. *Erōs* teaches us how *not* to ask for control where control is impossible, teaches us how to open ourselves up to the pain, and the risk—and the high delight—that only one other person can embody for us. Such is the agony and the ecstasy of love's way of knowing.

Love is all of these things, and more. At the risk of making him sound hopelessly romantic, Socrates (or Plato) seems to be insisting that *erōs* is not what his friends have all made of it, precisely insofar as they wall themselves off from the attendant risks and fears which are the inescapable flip sides to the unparalleled joy of it all. *Erōs*, Sappho tells us, is *glykypikron*, "bittersweet."[91] And, Socrates insists that *erōs* is "true love." He is saying so, with Diotima's assistance, to a room full of men who have "settled" to one degree or another for a lover, or a beloved, and a view of the erotic relationship that has erected barriers—whether of rules or of roles or of expectations—that attempt to make the erotic more regular and safe. *Erōs* is not safe. To settle in this way is to buy into a world-weary vision of love as some form of crass social exchange.

Erōs also forces us, or at least Nussbaum's book has forced me—in ways by which I have been, slowly to be sure, convinced—to rethink what morality and moral value actually are, to recast the notion of what moral philosophy can and cannot be, where it does and does not have something to teach. In matters erotic, moral questions—if by this we mean questions about rules, roles, and duties—do not apply. Love is not exactly a moral category, in that way. There is no cartography of the human soul. Still less is there a moral science that speaks erotically. Love has not pitched his mansion at such a height. Ask too often, or rather too exclusively, about what the "right" thing to do is in a love-relationship, and you run the very real risk of making the lover an object, another kind of *erōmenos*, one who serves only as grist for your own moral mill. You create yourself, however beautifully, at another's expense. That is precisely Socrates' problem, according to Nussbaum. Yet still I wonder.

Human loving is as often as not an *aesthetic* matter, a *stylistic* matter. It is a matter of feeling as much as thinking, a matter of intuitions which cannot be completely grounded. To say this is not to say that there are no rules. Aesthetics has its own canons of right and wrong, of good taste and bad. Socrates was well aware of this. And his viewpoint is not really compatable with the prevailing attitudes of our own Alcibiades' or theirs. It is astonishing, in its own way, that Socrates should be criticized for "failing" to be responsive to Alcibiades' advances. To have such a man, naked before you, offering himself to you for your pleasure, as an *object* to be *used*—and not to take him—this is thought to be a sure sign of coldness, hardness, and frigidity. Christians and Platonists just say No, where the Greeks had once said Yes so eloquently and so well. That is what makes Socrates a premonition of Christianity, on Nietzsche's view, a renunciatory sign of things to come. Socrates is indeed attracted to Alcibiades, but he does not and cannot love him. He wants an *erōtikos*, not an *erōmenos*, not a boy-toy. To respond to Alcibiades' advances would be in poor taste and ultimately self-destructive. I am suggesting that the Socrates of the *Symposium* encourages us to think this way about erotic matters: that they are seldom as clear (and as boring) as the *erastēs-erōmenos* dichotomy makes them seem. There is a fine line, but a necessary line, to be drawn between asceticism, and practical good sense.

Socrates is no more an ascetic than he is a frigid intellectual. Socrates stands as a resolute reminder that we may not generalize outside of the erotic sphere. Love's knowledge is altogether singular, absolutely unique. *Erōs*—and this is the whole point of Diotima's constant hedging ("well, not exactly this, not exactly that either, but something *metaxu*")—is a reality *sui generis*. Nussbaum is surely right about the place that risk and fragility have in *most* of our moral commitments. Love can be lost, just as trust can be broken, irredeemably. But it is not always so. Socrates and the poets constantly remind us of this—that *erōs* names a limitless desire, the desire to make permanent that which cannot be permanent, the desire to make love stay.

It is misleading, dangerously misleading, to argue too quickly that what may have been an excellent example of practical Socratic wisdom was really frigidity cloaking itself in the drab colors of idealistic philosophy. *Metaxu* is a bad word in politics, and it is a bad word in Alcibiades' mouth. But it has a finer resonance in affairs of the heart. Hence the danger of facile comparisons. It would have been an undeniably good thing if Athens had been as resistent to Alcibiades' charms as Socrates was—or else if Alcibiades had been able to commit himself to something, anything, with his whole self.

A different *polis*, a different man, a different kind of desire. The fact that *erōs* is not exactly a moral category does not make the Platonic (or the Kantian) project obsolete or irrelevant. Nor would Nussbaum, if pressed, say that it does.[92] Yet such a feeling is there, resident in the text, as well as in her rather hostile reading of this dialogue, and of Socrates.

Socrates sees and says one thing more, as a new day dawns over the tattered remnants of this dinner-party. In Greek comedy, the erotic passions and their physical signs are caricatured, pilloried, laughed at, savored for the ribald pleasure that is in them. We should remember that it is only *the men* who fret and limp their hour across the stage and then are heard no more, enormous *phalloi* inflated and meant to indicate their exaggerated states of high erotic excitement.[93] Riotous in the extreme, literally satyric, these men are meant to be laughed at.[94] In the tragedies, we are stopped in mid-laugh. In tragedy, we are made to tremble at the destructive madness that love inspires— Clytaemnestra, Antigone, Medea, Helen, Hecuba, Phaedra, Megara, women all.[95] Socrates' last word as dawn spreads her rosy fingers over the remains of this day, is that both things are true, that both have their validity and their truth. Ripeness is all. *Erōs* is a god—albeit a middling sort of god—to be praised and feared. In fact, fear of this god is the beginning of wisdom—*love's* wisdom, love's knowledge. Masculine and feminine by turns, holding tightly then letting go, pursuing and pursued, *erōs* is the source of our laughter and our tears— surely the best, the most intense, of both. We cannot become beautiful, cannot really make ourselves either beautiful or good, until we recognize and accept this fundamental human truth. This Socrates teaches, tells, *embodies*.

To a further exploration of what this kind of embodiment might mean morally, I turn next.

Chapter Three

SYMPOSIUM, THE THIRD: MORAL VALUE

or, Counting, Being, and True Love

LOVE AFTER LOVE

The time will come
when, with elation,
you will greet yourself arriving
at your own door, in your own mirror
and each will smile at the other's welcome,

and say, sit here. Eat.
You will love again the stranger who was your self.
Give wine. Give bread. Give back your heart
to itself, to the stranger who has loved you

all your life, whom you ignored
for another, who knows you by heart.
Take down the love letters from the bookshelf,

the photographs, the desperate notes,
peel your own image from the mirror.
Sit. Feast on your life.

—Derek Walcott

In the first chapter, I examined the formal relationship between the *Symposium* and the *Republic*. What I noticed in both texts was a foregrounding of erotic language, especially evident in the fascinating comparison between Socrates' erotic relationship to poetry and to Alcibiades. It seems that Plato has latched on to the erotic as a way to resolve problems he left unresolved in the Early Dialogues. Virtue, Socrates insists, is a kind of knowledge. Yet Socrates himself, however disingenuously, claims to know nothing. In the Erotic Dialogues, by contrast, Socrates clearly emphasizes that he does in fact know one thing very well: *ta erōtika*. The erotic is the metaphor with which he orders his own moral life. Loving, in fact, lays claim to being a very particular kind of human knowing.

I defended Socrates' perspective in the last chapter, by making the case for his resistance to Alcibiades. It is a resistance—not a rejection, but a resistance—intimately related to the resistance he registers toward erotic poetry. Thus far, I have defended Socrates negatively, by defending his resistance. I want to try now to defend the Socratic position more positively—less by concentrating on what he has rejected, and more by examining what Socrates' view of erotic love claims positively about human life and moral value. What we discover in the *Symposium* is a carefully crafted "war of myths," or rather, a contest of erotic images. Aristophanes (and implicitly Alcibiades as well) offers a time-honored image of "the two become one," two lovers united to form a single primordial whole. Socrates, building upon the central image of pregnancy so prominent in Diotima's speech, argues contrastingly that, where love is "true," the two become three, not one. The argument is that two lovers, and the unique entity constituted by their (ethical) relation, *each* have legitimate moral claims to make. Erotics is fertile, productive of new relations, new knowledges, new perspectives. Love does not do individuality to death, so much as it creates newer and richer possibilities for individuality to flourish, a new kind of moral depth if you will. This Socrates alone seems to see and say.

I

It has seemed at times, as I have reflected upon the purposes of this book, a rather dark time to be a Platonist. It has, at times, seemed an even darker time to be in love. I would like to offer the tentative, simply intuitive, and perhaps even the *outlandish* suggestion that these two appearances are related.

It was Nietzsche, as I indicated in the introduction, who probably first popularized the outlandish idea that Plato was not all he had been made out to be. Nietzsche, still later in his career, went so far as to make Plato (and Socrates) the chief culprits in the story of the rise of a singularly "decadent" kind of western thinking. Martin Heidegger would popularize much the same idea, in reference to a kind of "metaphysical" thinking he associated with Plato. For fully a century now, modern philosophy has busied itself with demonstrating how and why "western" thought took a wrong turn—with Plato. The attempt to recover alternative, importantly *pre*-Socratic, philosophical resources has been a major preoccupation of Continental philosophy in this century.

More recently still, and in dialogue with this same Continental tradition, Emmanuel Levinas—whom some in this decade have already begun calling "the greatest ethical thinker of our century"[1]—positions himself against the Platonic tradition in ways that are suggestive of my larger concern. We should not be too easily deceived here; there are any number of "postmodern" points of view that are quite self-consciously engaged in a dialogue *with*, not *against*, the Platonic corpus,[2] and that are not nearly so dismissive of Plato himself. But it is the crude dismissal that is most dramatic, most memorable, and that seems to possess the most traction. Such accusations are, more often than not, as unfair to Plato's richly nuanced erotic views as they are predictable, these days.[3] Here, in any case, is what Levinas has to say about Plato, and about his own phenomenological response to the Platonic trajectory:

> Greek ontology, to be sure, expressed the strong sentiment that the last word is unity, the many becoming one, the truth as synthesis. Hence Plato defined love—*erōs*—as only *half*-divine, insofar as it lacks the full coincidence or unification of differences that he defined as divinity. The whole romantic tradition in European poetry tends to conform to this platonic ontology by inferring that love is perfect when two people become one. I am trying to work against this identification of the divine with unification or totality.[4]

"So was I!" is the fairest response to this nonsense charge that we might make on Plato's behalf. While Levinas' overgeneralization about "the problem" with Greek ontology seems virtually a statement of the obvious to the majority of philosophers working in a Heideggerian idiom today, it will be less obvious to anyone who has read the dialogues from the Erotic Period with some care. In recognizing this intimate connection, this *necessary* connection—between loving and knowing[5]—I think that we can begin to appreciate the real sensitivity and suppleness of Platonic thought afresh. Martha Nussbaum puts it this way, explicitly making the same connection between erotic passion, certain essential intuitions about human value, the possibilities, and the very real limits, of all human knowledge:

> How clear it is to me that there is no neutral position of reflection from which one can survey and catalogue the intuitions of one's heart on the subject of love, holding up the rival views to see how well they fit the intuitions—no activity of philosophizing that does not stand in some determinate relation to love.[6]

That is to say, the way we love, the manner of our loving—what we think has happened to us, *its* rhythms, and *its* rules—may well have everything to do with the way we claim to know, the very shape of our knowing, and even of what we think it humanly possible *to* know. In both cases, the loving and the knowing, there are a whole host of assumptions—about what it is to be human, about what the proper priorities in a properly ordered human life are like, about the realm and the role of poetry, and of mystery, even of a sort of magic in the intellectual life—which simply lay there, unstated, unreflected upon, unmoved and unmoving. Even Aristotle, the old encyclopediast, at the end of a rather lonely intellectual life, admitted to being powerfully drawn, only then, to the old myths.[7] If, in this third rumination on the relation of loving and knowing, I cannot make this all as precise or as clear as I might wish it to be, at least I may hope to enlighten and demystify some of the hidden assumptions which our own society has mystified to such a remarkable degree.

These are dark days to be a Platonist, I said. That is largely due to the fact that these are dark days for Socrates.[8] Ever since Nietzsche, it has been in vogue to pick his thinking apart, to show how he is not true, himself, to what he says[9]—if in fact we can figure out what he is saying in the first place. He has been called caustic, abrasive, egocentric, bombastic, intellectually dishonest, and still more recently, as I attempted to show in the last chapter, erotically frigid. He is "stoic" in all the worst ways—hard and glittering like a jewel, cold and unfeeling, perhaps very like a philosopher, unmoved by anyone or anything human, saving all of his passion for ideas and for forms. The Roman Stoics did, in fact, read Socrates very much this way,[10] although in doing so I suspect that they *mis*read him—just as surely as they *mis*read Medea,[11] and a host of other great Greek heroes, heroines, and speculative thinkers.

II

I would like to reflect a bit more fully on what this erotic connection means, and by way of doing so, we will need to be able to count—rather carefully and slowly, now—to three. The phenomenon of counting, and of representing such counting symbolically, as numbers, is a fascinating topic in its own right, nearly as fascinating as the phenomenon of human language. The first thing to be said about it is that there are surprisingly few base-systems for counting in all of human experience: all human beings, it seems, have counted on the bases of 2, 5, 10, 12, 20, or 60. No matter how "primitive" a counting system may be, *all* human beings, to the degree that they are counters, make at least this minimal distinction: between One, and Two, and Many.[12] And this distinction, while admittedly "minimal," proves to be of the utmost significance in conceptualizing our place in the cosmos. Counting to three, that is to say, is an essential moral task.

It would be difficult to overemphasize the importance that *numbers*, under the influence of the Pythagoreans perhaps, came to have for Plato in the Erotic Period. As he confesses much later, in the *Laws*, "a human being would fall far short of becoming divine if he could not learn about one and two and three" (*Laws* 818c). It is a little-noticed aspect of Plato's work that he plays so constantly and provocatively with numbers, especially with the complex relation of the number two to the number three. The trilogy (which would be a tetralogy)[13] of *Theaetetus*, *Sophist*, and *Statesman* perhaps illustrates this idea best. As the abortive attempt to discover "true knowledge" in the *Theaetetus* makes clear, the philosophical question requires *three* separate conversations, and hence three separate dialogues. We are promised three of them (*Sophist*, *Statesman*, and *Philosopher*), but we do not get them. The philosopher is missing. We are promised three dialogues, but we get only two. And what the Eleatic Stranger, who is the main speaker in these two dialogues, does is to attempt to divide the world into an endless series of dualisms. His method of *diairēsis*—philosophical discrimination—relies on this. But he cannot ultimately deliver, for the simple reason that there are more than two categories in the world.

So, we are promised a series of three dialogues, yet we only get two of them. In those two, we see the attempt to divide the world of appearance into twos, only to discover that the world lends itself to threes, not twos. Clearly, Plato is much concerned at this time with the transition from twoness to threeness. And this takes us to the heart of

Socrates' "science of *erōs*."[14] The end of the matter, then, in the *Statesman* at least, is that there are two sorts of people in the world: those who think the world can be divided in two, and those who do not. The Eleatic Stranger is one of those who does; perhaps Levinas is another. Socrates does not.

So I want to puzzle again over that age-old Platonic dilemma, the so-called problem of "the One and the Many," and I want to stop at each point along the way of getting from our selves to many selves: from One . . . to Two . . . to Three . . . and then beyond from Three, to Many. It is enormously difficult to appreciate the degree to which the Greek speculative mind—Pythagorean and Platonic, alike—was absorbed in reflection upon predication, defining the oneness in the one, the twoness in two, the threeness in three.[15] It was left to the Arabs (unless it was actually the Indians, far earlier) to contribute the number zero to our speculative lexicon, and thus, at a higher order of reflection, the notion of nothingness implicit in the number zero.[16] Among the preclassical and classical Greeks, numerically speaking, one (*hena, mia*) and ten thousand (*myria*) set the limits to the numbers for which they had words. And their limits, in some as yet poorly understood ways, remain with us (even the Modern Greek word for "million," *ekatommyrion*, literally means "one hundred ten thousands").

In a sense, I see Socrates, *both* emotionally *and* intellectually, now—that is the key—attempting to describe how the two become three, rather than how two are allegedly collapsed into one. Love and erotics—the human (and perhaps more-than-human) realm in which two become three, *never* one (*Symposium* 201e).[17] It seems to me that the *Symposium* is very much a dialogue constituted by the competing myths of Aristophanes (in which two become one) and of Diotima (in which two become three). It is a dispute between realms where sexuality is a pleasurable (however temporary) reunification of lost wholeness,[18] or else a miraculous and (pro)creative process that constantly overreaches itself. Now, this is admittedly a huge claim, perhaps the claim upon which my entire argument in this book hinges. Minimally, I want to argue that this really is a crucial metaphor in Platonic thought. But it is also, maximally, a profound truth of human experience, and I am simply assuming that here, not endeavoring to "prove" it. I do not know what the "proof" of such a claim would look like.

As we know, Plato was a profoundly imagistic thinker, in addition to being a marvelous dialectician. He knows well what language can and cannot do. It is *penultimately* valuable, but never, nowhere, ultimate.[19]

The dialectic gives way to poetry, to new myths, in the sort of divine madness that may occasionally sweep over the lover and the philosopher, alike (*Phaedrus* 244a–245c). As Socrates seems never to tire of telling us, he feels this *erōs* for two things: for philosophy, and for Alcibiades. "Callicles," he says,

> if there was not a kind of feeling [*pathos*] common to most human beings—even if it varies a bit from person to person—and if instead we each experienced feelings unique to ourselves [*pathos idion*], the it would not be easy to explain our own experiences [*pathēma*] to one another. I say this because I realize that both you and I happen to be experiencing [*peponthotes*] much the same thing right now—namely, each of the two of us happens to be in love [*erōnte*] with two different things. I am in love with Alcibiades, son of Cleinias, as well as with philosophy, whereas you are in love with these two: the democracy of Athens, as well as with Demos, the son of Pyrilampes. (*Gorgias* 481d)[20]

Now, on the one hand, this is part of a much larger argument about "certain feelings" that human beings have, roughly speaking, "in common." We might best think of them as moral and erotic intuitions, as I have suggested at several key points in this book, and as we shall shortly see again.

Socrates knows well that these feelings will "vary a bit" from person to person. He is not so insensitive to the particularities of personal feeling or personal taste as is normally alleged. He does not try to compress the erotic life crassly or oversimply into a single mold. He lets the Many *be* manifold. But he does not rest there. Socrates' broader point is that these are inescapably *erotic* phenomena. Different people, or different practices, may inspire us with passion. To that degree we are, and we will ever remain, different. You and I will only rarely experience this inspiration from the same person or practice (although certain practices, like philosophy, will hopefully be attractive to more of us). Our eroticism is *materially* different. And yet—this is Socrates' whole point, I believe—our eroticism is *formally* the same.

In the case of the Greeks, whose erotic lives have been the subject of my concern throughout this book, I do not think that we will ever fully understand their eroticism, materially. Even our curious notion of "bisexuality,"[21] so central a topic of discussion these days, does not seem quite to fit them. Surely they had no word for such a thing. The taxonomy is ours, not theirs. Yet their reflections upon the peculiar dynamics of human eroticism continue to be powerfully relevant in our own day and age. I, for my part, take this kind of intuitive, and rather chastened, universalism very seriously indeed. I will speak briefly in its defense in conclusion.

Whether one is in love with wisdom or with some one irreplacable other human being, language needs to be bent, manipulated, pressed into the attempt to make it speak what the heart, and language itself, cannot otherwise say. Meaning must be squeezed, poetically, from language that is bent without being entirely broken. So essential is this connection that Socrates' discussion of *erōs* in the *Phaedrus* leads necessarily to a myth, first, and then to a discussion of discourse in the second half of the dialogue. (See the appendix for further analysis of this dramatic movement.) Poetic imagery, symbols, and metaphors become not only important, but actually crucial, to the ultimate goals of Socratic interrogation and Platonic thought. This book is meant to underscore the centrality of one crucial Platonic craft, erotic loving, and this one crucially Platonic image: the Two becoming Three, rather than being reduced to One.[22]

A good way to illustrate what is at stake here might be to examine that notorious and, too often, interminable debate about the relation of the mind, or of the soul, to the body. The accusation of participating in a crass "mind-body dualism"—and, at least implicitly, of taking the mind too seriously and the body not seriously enough—is surely one of the great throwaway arguments in all of philosophy. It is too often used as a weapon to dispense with thought one finds uncongenial, rather than inadequate. Any athlete who is wrestling with a nagging injury will already know what I am talking about. A runner with a twisted ankle will tape it, because the ankle is both a pulley and a lever, which is unable to do the work that he or she needs done at that moment. The mind stands "outside" of the body in such a moment, metaphorically speaking, presiding over its functioning and using it like a tool. The long-standing Greek fascination with athletics was, in part, a fascination with this precise possibility. Such behavior does *not* mean that the athlete is suffering from a crass mind-body dualism. It means rather, in all likelihood, that he or she is a good athlete.

What is not said nearly often enough, although Socrates himself says it quite clearly and unambiguously (in *Phaedrus* 246a), is that these words—'body' on the one hand, and 'soul' on the other—are *metaphors*. Modern thought (or *post*-modern, if you prefer that metaphor, as I do not), to the degree that it is in dialogue with Descartes and his own alleged mind-body dualism, is attempting to unmask the limits of such dualistic metaphors, in order to illuminate those aspects of human life that are not best described in quite so "heady" a manner. And there has proven to be some special confusion as to whether human sexuality is best thought of in these, or else in other, fresher metaphors. Erotic experiences, properly so called, seem to involve us in bodily phenomena that seem to transcend bodiliness in their finest expressions.

What has not been confessed is that these metaphors—of "mind," and of "soul," and of "body"—work extremely *well*, with stunning and compelling descriptive power, in a wide range of human experiences: from athletics (*Phaedrus* 256b), to the experience of physical disabilities and their overcoming (*Symposium* 174d, 219e–221c), to the experience of disease and the sheer advance of age (*Republic* 329a–d), and finally, perhaps paradigmatically, to the experience of death itself (*Phaedo* 64c). To that august list of definitively "spiritual" experiences, Plato is so bold as to add the power of the erotic.[23] The body dies, yet many persons continue to hope that some aspect of the selves they have been so long in becoming survive that experience. The Platonic myths of metempsychosis, another product of the Erotic Period, surely name this aspiration quite well. The metaphor of the soul, as distinct from, perhaps detachable from, the body, is the metaphor that names a powerful aspiration toward a kind of human transcendence. Dame Rebecca West puts the point mightily in her magnum opus, devoted to the experience of Yugoslavia between the wars. While meditating on some Serbo-Byzantine frescoes and their depiction of the psychophysical constitution of their religious subjects, West confronts what she calls "that separateness of the flesh"

> which Proust once noted, in a passage which describes how we think in our youth that our bodies are identical with ourselves, and have the same interests, but discover later in life that they are heartless companions who have been accidentally yoked with us, and who are as likely as not in our extreme sickness or old age to treat us with less mercy than we would have received at the hands of the worst bandits.[24]

The body as friend, and alternately, as heartless taskmaster: these metaphors, too, may be apt ones when the talk turns, as it so often does in Plato's Erotic Period, to love.

We are *embodied* beings, to be sure. This Socrates, who is presented in these Erotic Period dialogues as a creature of some considerable bodily appetite, freely admits. It is not only Aquinas' doctrine of *hylomor-phism*[25]—namely, the metaphor which suggests that we *are* a body, not that we merely *have* one—that underscores the essential bodiliness of human life. I mean, as Plato does, to underscore the essential bodiliness of human love while raising important questions about this somatic connection at the same time. Plato himself will speak of "ensouled" (*empsy-cha*) bodies still later in his philosophical career (*Statesman* 261b, 288e).

Yet erotics are not "merely" bodily. This society has lost, it seems to me, a fairly essential distinction between sexuality and sensuality, or rather between what we call "sexuality" and what Plato calls "the erotic." This is why I have suggested that a better translation of the Greek term, *erōs*, might be "true love," this rather than "sex." *Erōs* involves far more than bodies, although it clearly, and *necessarily*, and inescapably involves them. To a Greek ear, *erōs* connoted the soul in the grip of pain every bit as much as it did the body in the grip of pleasure. The most cursory glance at the lyric poetic tradition makes this clear. Failing to see or say this, our discussions of love become fairly thin, and fairly self-serving. Such a crass mind-body dualism actually, and ironically, condemns the charge *against* Socrates that I outlined in the last chapter. To the degree that he is thought to be erotically frigid, he is deemed so because he did not respond *physically* to Alcibiades, even when he found himself naked in bed with the man. He slept with me like a brother, not a lover, Alcibiades tells us, with mingled anguish and astonishment (*Symposium* 218c–219d). Recall the question that Martha Nussbaum puts to Socrates' apparent lack of responsiveness:

> Socrates might conceivably have abstained from sexual rela-
> tions while remaining attentive to the lover in his particular-
> ity. He might also have had a sexual relationship with Alcib-
> iades while remaining inwardly aloof.[26]

The latter would presumably be a case of inappropriate inattention to the lover in his particularity, and in his own very distinctive erotic need-iness. But the former is *precisely* what Socrates does. He remains atten-tive to Alcibiades throughout their long lives together. He simply chooses not to become *sexually* involved with him. Even Alcibiades, in narrating the tragicomic stops and starts of this abortive seduction, admits that it was a case of remarkable self-control and practical wis-dom on Socrates' part, and even a kind of courage, not frigidity. Nuss-baum disagrees; she insists that "Socrates refuses in every way to be affected. He is stone; and he turns others to stone."[27] This is the common charge, despite the fact that Plato shows us Socrates, not in stony silence, but powerfully affected, in dialogue after dialogue. He does not get drunk on wine, admittedly; yet he is always on the verge of emotional dissolution, whenever Alcibiades is in the room.

While the text may not be authentically Platonic, it is nonetheless quite telling and appropriate that the first dialogue named after the man, *Alcibiades I*, is the text that raises this question of the relation between the body and the soul in an explicitly erotic context. It begins with a portrait of Socrates' romantic constancy, and Alcibiades' amazement that, of all his many lovers, only Socrates is still around (*Alcibiades I* 103a–104c, building on *Protagoras* 309a). All his other lovers have left him, now that he is grown, Alcibiades muses, off in pursuit of younger, as yet beardless loves. Socrates, who was never interested in his body alone, cannot leave Alcibiades quite so simply (*Alcibiades I* 131c–d). And so this dialogue concludes its erotic self-examination with the conclusion we have been arguing for: "A human being must be one of three things: a soul [*psychē*], or a body [*sōma*], or both together in one whole" (*Alcibiades I* 130a). It may not be Socrates who suffers from a misleading mind-body dualism, but rather some of his chief detractors.[28] It is they who are collapsing the two into one. Socrates knows that, in the miraculous affairs of the heart at least, one plus one equals three.

I want to underscore this essential Platonic image of twos and threes. I also mean to defend some rather traditional poetic terms (which are also metaphorical images, of course) along the way: like the "soul," and the "spirit," and "true love." Despite what Levinas says of the Greeks, it is we, in *this* society, who seem insistent on reducing two terms—mind and body, or body and soul, if you will—to one. Mental processes are reduced to biochemical contingencies; love itself is made a matter of considerable physical contingency, a meeting of bodies, where it is not made a matter of subtle psychic forces, the endless replaying of old family romances in new forms. I prefer the infinitely richer metaphor of two becoming three: a mind and a body, constituting a mysterious third entity,[29] which is what all of us are, human beings, reducible neither to a body nor a soul, alone.[30]

Let me say just one word more about why this is so crucial to a proper understanding of what Socrates and Plato are about. The Socratic revolution, as I noted in the first chapter,[31] hinged upon his casting a philosophic eye upon the human heart, rather than upon an impersonal universe. Gone are the cosmological speculations of the pre-Socratic Ionian Greeks. Indeed, we call them *pre*-Socratic precisely because Socrates is the pivot around which most later philosophical thought revolves. He managed the transition from cosmology to moral philosophy—in a manner not so very different from what Levinas was attempting to do with phenomenology in this day and age.

Now, moral philosophy requires us to get some clarity on what twentieth-century philosophers have grown accustomed to calling "the other." Simply put, we would not need something called "ethics," whatever that is, if we lived alone. In solitude, or on a desert island, "Libertarian" is the sole political option, radical freedom and autonomy the only moral possibility. Ethics, that is to say, *presupposes* the existence of others. Other people are a large part of what constrains us. And the way one thinks about "the other" may indeed have everything to do with how one envisions the ethical enterprise itself. Loving well has everything to do with living morally, on this view.

The phenomenologists make this connection explicit—and here I think that Sartre is a good, if somewhat confusing, example. Sartre is building upon the earlier work of Hegel, Husserl, and Heidegger in displaying his philosophical vision of life-with-others.[32] Levinas, for his part, is dialoguing explicitly with these same thinkers, especially with Heidegger, and his objection to Platonic thought has everything to do with his allegedly variant beliefs about the ethical status of the Other. What I find impressive in *Sartre's* phenomenology of "being with others" is, first and foremost, his concept of *negation*: the Other is that real human agent, or lover, who remains always and inescapably "not me," who resists every one of my erotic or ethical attempts to collapse him or her into me. The Other, that is to say, *resists* me.[33]

Equally rich is Sartre's very clear, and really rather sharp, distinction between being two together, and then being three.[34] Sitting alone or walking about my room, I act as I do in no other environment.[35] When a friend, or lover, or even a stranger, enters the room, I am no longer myself in quite the same way. And, with the introduction of a third person—what has recently been called "the earthquake of the Third"[36]—the whole game changes yet again.[37] Each of these modes—singular, dual, and tripartite—are ontologically and experientially distinct. In Archaic Greek, in fact, the dual voice is even a separate grammatical modality.[38] This is the grammatical mode, incidentally, with which Plato plays throughout that fascinating passage from the *Gorgias*, in which each of us is supposed to have two erotic centers, not one.

Sartre's play *No Exit* is a stunning and disturbing display of this same dynamic. When we are three together, alliances constantly form and reform, two against one in endless permutations. Many have been extremely critical of the "social" vision we see in *Being and Nothingness*. There seems to be no place for love in his social ontology. Sartre was himself critical of that work for similar reasons, in *The Critique of Dialectical Reason*.[39] But the larger point stands. The way we interact with a single other person is radically—and, *philosophically*—distinct from the way we interact with two others, or more than two. That is precisely the existential "earthquake" that the introduction of a third party represents.

Quite simply (though there is nothing simple about the matter), "the other" becomes "others." "You" becomes "they." And ethics, properly speaking, can begin. Being two defines the realm of the erotic, not ethics—which is one reason, I have long suspected, why "sexual ethics" are such confusing and hapless fields in which to labor. Sexuality, the new communitarians and Aristotelians aside, for now, is not precisely "political" activity.[40] It is confined to the relative privacy (a privacy that is neither solitude nor solipsism)[41] of dual spaces, not the *polis*. Erotics, unlike politics, even if only at the outset, is a realm of twos, not threes. In love, again unlike the realm of the *polis*, three is a crowd. And yet— here is the Socratic contribution, which might be especially worth recovering in this day and age—the manner of our loving might well have *everything* to do with the way we are able to conceive of being with two or more people, ethically.[42] Erotics *precedes* ethics and politics. Love and knowledge are primordially linked. The question, "What is knowledge?" is unanswerable in theory (*Theaetetus*). But it may be answerable in practice—in political action (*Republic, Statesman*), in death (*Phaedo*), and in love (*Symposium, Phaedrus*).

III

Perhaps now we are better positioned to discuss Socrates, and to understand better why he has fallen so far from philosophic grace in this century. He has, I am arguing, in large measure because this absolutely essential connection—between *erōs* and *epistēmē*, love and knowledge— has been missed. It is presented as what I take to be the pivotal moment in the *Symposium*, that lovely initial exchange between Socrates and Diotima that I discussed in the last chapter. Socrates has agreed that we love what we ourselves lack, that *erōs* is itself (in Sartre's fine phrasing) the desire for an "absence." And yet, if *erōs desires* beauty and goodness, why then, surprisingly, it must lack these very things. Such a thought is well nigh unbearable to him.

> "How can you say that, Diotima?" I demanded. "Can
> Love then be evil . . . or ugly?"
>
> But she said, "Be quiet! Do you think that whatever isn't
> beautiful must necessarily be ugly?"
>
> "Of course."
>
> "And that anyone who isn't wise is ignorant? Don't you
> realize that there is something *in between* [*metaxu*] wisdom
> and ignorance?"
>
> "What?"
>
> "Don't you see it yet?" she asked. "Having correct opin-
> ions [*ta ortha doxazein*] without having the words for them.
> That isn't knowledge [*epistasthai*] (for how can something with-
> out reasons [*alogon*] be knowledge [*epistēmē*]?), but it's not
> ignorance [*amathia*] either (how can it be ignorance [*amathia*] if
> it happens to be true?). Correct opinions [*orthē doxa*] are just
> this way—*in between* understanding and ignorance [*metaxu
> phronēseōs kai amathias*]." (*Symposium* 201e–202a)[43]

Diotima goes on to underscore this idea of knowing, and loving,
metaxu, "in between." The reference, to a different kind of knowledge,
a different *way* of knowing, is among the loveliest and most suggestive
in the Platonic corpus. It recalls Proclus' commentary on the *Republic* to
which I referred in the first chapter. Intuitions are often, perhaps even
always, the starting point for any meaningful philosophical reflection.[44]
When *Erōs*' arrow strikes home—a haunted, mortal image, if ever there
were one—we simply know it to be so. Love has an accidental quality
about it, which "just so happens to be true." Yet love is the *accident* that
mysteriously becomes *necessary* to us and to our self-understanding. An
intuitive opinion that just so happens to lay claim to truth, our love
seeks out its own peculiar, and deeply compelling, level of knowing. The
relationship between accident and necessity was a source of enormous
concern to the Greek erotic and lyric tradition, long before Aristotle
made it a matter of first philosophy.

Now, Socrates, on the most favorable reading, is a compelling character because of his lack of pretense, his surprising contentment with
such moral intuitions. Masked by no obscure philosophical jargon, no
soaring flights of rhetorical fancy, he is a "straight-line" thinker. He is
compelling, and absolutely unique (so Alcibiades tells us), because he
knows what he does not know (*Apology* 21d).

I want to point out the obvious alternative—which should not need
saying, yet which clearly *does* need saying, in this day and age—namely,
that Socratic matters are never as simple as all that. There is one thing

(at least one) that Socrates repeatedly insists that he *does* know: *ta erōtika*, the things associated with *erōs*.[45] In an early dialogue on friendship, Socrates tells us something quite surprising. His uniqueness, like his wisdom, is directly tied to this erotic sensitivity:

> In most matters I am a fool, or at best rather useless, but I have been given this one gift from the god: I am able to recognize almost immediately when someone is in love [*erōnta*] as well as who it is that they want [*erōmenon*]. (*Lysis* 204c)

In another early discussion of moderation and human wisdom, Socrates recalls the fateful day in the gymnasium, when he first met Charmides. It is, incidentally, the time when Socrates has just returned from the battlefield of Potidaea, where his courage in retreat so impressed Alcibiades and the enemy. Clearly, the turmoil of war disrupts this philosopher's soul far less than the erotic does.

> [W]hen everyone in the palaestra pressed in on us in a tight circle—then, just then, my noble friend—I saw inside his robes. I caught fire [*ephlegomēn*] and could not control myself. And I believed that no one was wiser about *erōtika* than Cydias, who, when speaking of a beautiful boy, warns against "wandering as a fawn before the lion, lest you be seized as a portion of his meal." That is precisely how I seemed to myself, a helpless creature seized upon by such a force. (*Charmides* 155d)

Socrates tells his friend immediately prior to this tremor—"the earthquake of the third," again—that he is completely indiscriminate in the matter of *erōs*: "I am as useless as a white line on marble when it comes to measuring beauty," he grins. "Absolutely every boy who is on the verge of manhood [*en tēi hēlikiai*] seems beautiful to me" (*Charmides* 154b). We have already looked at the important transitional dialogue, the *Gorgias*, transitional precisely from the Early to the Erotic Periods, the dialogue in which Socrates makes clear his own convictions about human nature and what we have at least vaguely in common, again with explicit reference to the power of *erōs*.

It is in the Erotic Period that Plato begins to ask these intriguing character-sketches to do real work for him. In the *Phaedrus*, we meet again the portrait of a man who is astonishingly capable of letting himself go. Socrates' passion is galactic, and Phaedrus knows it to be so:

> Well, Socrates, the talk was very much worth your hearing. The issue [*logos*] about which we conversed was in fact rather

erotic [*erōtikos*]. Lysias had written a speech designed to seduce some young beauty—but the speech was not for his lover [*erastou*], and that is what's so clever about it. He claims that it is better to have a lover who is not in love [*mē erōnti*], rather than one who is! (*Phaedrus* 227c)

Later, Socrates will invoke his own peculiar erotic gifts again, by way of meeting the challenge represented by Lysias' speech, as well as by way of repenting for his own flirtation with the same sad seducer's art:

This, dear God of Love [*Erōs*], is the best and noblest song I can offer you, the best that my limited powers will allow, especially given the poetic niceties I was forced to use on Phaedrus' account. Please forgive me my first speech, be gracious, and do not take away that erotic skill [*erōtikēn technēn*] which you yourself have given me. (*Phaedrus* 257a)

The point was emphatic in the *Symposium* as well. When Eryximachus first suggests that the party-goers offer speeches in praise of *Erōs*, Socrates is the first who leaps to agreement to the proposal:

"No one will vote against you, Eryximachus," Socrates said. "I could never refuse you, since I claim that there is nothing I understand except for *ta erōtika*." (*Symposium* 177e)

Later, in turning Agathon's ornate speech ironically upside-down, Socrates sounds the same theme again:

Then I realized how laughable it was to have agreed to take my turn along with you in singing *Erōs*' praises, and to have claimed great skill in the erotic life [*deinos ta erōtika*], without even knowing how to sing praises in the first place. I, in my foolishness, thought that you should simply speak the truth. (*Symposium* 198c–d)

And even later, in the *Theaetetus*, Socrates is still playfully putting the same point, even where "the erotic" is not explicitly invoked. He confesses to a deep commitment to his city, and therefore especially to the young beauties who live there:

If I cared about the people of Cyrene, Theodorus, then I would ask [*erōtōn*] you about them, especially whether any of their young men are concerning themselves with geometry or any other kind of philosophy. But since I care far less for them than I do for the boys right here, I worry [*epithymō*] far more about our own young men, and about which of them are likely to become notable [*epidoxoi*] in the future. These are

> the things I look after myself, as well as I am able, and I
> inquire of [*erōtō*] all the others I see who are following these
> young men most closely. (*Theaetetus* 143d)

Philosophy, that is to say, *is* a seducer's art. Already in the *Protagoras*, we are presented with a picture of philosophy as a contest, a contest for the affections and attentions of the city's most promising young men. And Socrates is the seducer par excellence. Curiously enough, the most constant of his many affairs is the one with Alcibiades.

If anything, this same point is made even more explicit in the post-Platonic literature about Socrates. There were any number of dialogues written in the Platonic style, boasting Socrates as their main character, composed in the centuries after Plato's death. Some of these were included in the first critical editions of the "complete works of Plato," compiled in Alexandria (in North Africa) already in the first century. Several of the dialogues so included probably were not written by Plato. Yet they are deliberate attempts to imitate his style, thus making it all the more notable that the one thing on which they all agree is Socrates' status as *erōtikos*.

So, in the *Theages*, we hear the most astonishing claim yet made on Socrates' philosophic and erotic behalf:

> I am not blessed with any of the higher learning. Would that
> I were. But I always say, you know, that I happen to know
> nothing except one little subject, *ta erōtika*. But in this little
> subject, I claim to be better skilled [*deinos*] than any person
> who has ever lived. (*Theages* 128b)

In addition, we get an entire dialogue called "The Lovers" [*Erastai*], which is explicitly labeled by Theophrastus as a dialogue "on moral [*ēthikos*] philosophy." Finally, there are *two* dialogues which bear the name of *Alcibiades*, one of which I have already mentioned. The second, and shorter, of the two is a rather crude attempt at Platonic imitation. But it concludes with Socrates' telling wish to Alcibiades to "win out as the victor [*kallinikos*] over all your other lovers [*erastōn*]" (*Alcibiades II* 151c).

Socrates claims a nearly outrageous erotic expertise for himself, in dialogue after dialogue. Socrates claims to be the only *true lover* Alcibiades has ever had. He loves his soul, as well as his body. Recognizing the inseparability of that attachment is what seems most unusual about Socrates as a lover. I am arguing that this is the source of his singular genius.

I will go even further by suggesting that Socrates knows what he knows precisely *because* he has been reflective about the power and the mystery of *erōs*. He knows what he knows for one very simple reason: he has been there, he has *felt* it. He has been open to the risks, the vulnerabilities, the essential mutuality and essential nonsolitariness that the erotic life demands. Through that experience, he has learned about the nature of the philosophical life as well. Even Nietzsche grudgingly admits that "Socrates was also a fabulous *erotic*,"[46] although I'm not sure he intended it as a compliment.[47] For my purposes, it is enough to say that Socrates has studied One intensely: himself. He has studied Two at least as well: he and his *daimōn*; he and Diotima; he and Alcibiades. And, through this deep philosophical introspection, he claims to have gained some knowledge of the peculiar dynamics of human selves, and of human love—not to mention the complexity of human groups in Three or more, the dynamic out of which all political and ethical life emerges. It all began with an erotic intuition.[48]

> As Sokrates tells it, your story begins the moment Eros enters you. That incursion is the biggest risk of your life. How you handle it is an index of the quality, wisdom and decorum of the things inside you. As you handle it you come into contact with what is inside you, in a sudden and startling way. You perceive what you are, what you lack, what you could be. What is this mode of perception, so different from ordinary perception that it is well described as madness? How is it that when you fall in love you feel as if suddenly you are seeing the world as it really is? A mood of knowledge floats over your life. . . . This mood is no delusion, in Sokrates' belief. It is a glance down into time, at realities you once knew, as staggeringly beautiful as the glance of your beloved. . . . Sokrates says it is a glimpse of a god.[49]

In a word, Socrates loves, therefore he knows.

The superficially simple portrait of this allegedly simple man is one that we all probably received in freshman lectures on "Western Civilization," and it persists in far too many twentieth-century caricatures of Platonic philosophy. It misses the essence of the man, in all of his erotic particulars:

He knows that he does not know—until the talk turns to *erōs* (*Symposium* 177d–e). He uses no obscure philosophical jargon—until he speaks of the things that lie closest to his heart and mind.[50] He participates in no soaring flights of rhetorical fancy—until he is driven outside of his own mind by Alcibiades', or Phaedrus', or someone else's moral and physical beauty (*Phaedrus* 234d, 237a, 238c–d; *Protagoras* 309a–d; *Charmides* 154e, 155d; *Gorgias* 481d). He thinks in a straight line—until *erōs* draws him into the softer, subtler contours of a circle.[51] He knows that he does not know many things. But he also knows what he knows. And what he knows is *erōtika*. To say it again: He loves, *therefore* he knows.

IV

I want to risk an oversimplification, now, by summarizing the cases to be made for and against Socrates—in the realm of knowledge, and in the realm of love. It turns out that they are mirror images of much the same case. This is not simply because, for Plato in the Erotic Period, the realms of knowledge and of love are linked, but rather because this same essential pattern—of twos and threes—animates his best intuitions in both realms.

First, then, to knowledge. On the kindest view, Socrates is characterized—he is absolutely unique in this—by the fundamental assumption that he, alone of all the pundits and sophists in Athens, knows what he does not know. He listens, long and well, before he ever speaks. He allows others to provide him with a starting point. He may finally run dialectical circles around an interlocutor, may even seem hell-bent on proving how little they actually know, but he is building upon what they themselves offer up to him, what they have said first, what they have audaciously claimed to "know." He lets them begin. He listens. Then he responds.

That is the kindest view. It is hardly the prominent view of Socrates, these days. Much more frequently we are told that Socrates never really listened to *anyone*. So far is he from being open to dialogue with—to his mind being changed by—other people that most Socratic dialogues end with everyone else talking just like him. He never listens, really, precisely because he always knows, before a dialogue even begins, what he thinks and where it will eventually be going.

To evaluate such widely divergent views of Socrates much depends, it seems to me, upon this essential Platonic oscillation between twos and threes. How many terms are there, finally, in a dialogue? Two? Or three? For those who are inclined to disbelieve Socrates when he speaks on his own behalf, there are only two people in a dialogue—two people, one of whom is not really listening. The Other ever and always remains radically "other." In a dialogue, the difference stays. Failing to see this, or having conveniently forgotten it too well, Socrates tries to collapse the many (in this case, the other) into one—namely, into himself. He doesn't listen, he merely spins rhetorical circles around everyone else, and then leaves them all thinking and talking just like him.

Yet Socrates insists that the only thing that matters in a dialogue is the truth. There are, finally, three terms in a dialogue, not two: the self, and the other, and the truth which both conversation-partners are ideally pursuing.[52] No one possesses it; it is not a commodity in that way, not a singular possession. That is why one cannot *write* the truth in any simple way, Plato insists—precisely because writing takes place in solitude (*Seventh Letter* 341c–345d). Truth is an *event*, a horizon that comes gradually into view when two come together—or more specifically, when two persons come together in the interest of giving birth to a third.

This same pattern is apparent in erotic matters, on the Socratic view. The only kind of love affair we ever actually see in the Platonic corpus is Socrates' relationship with Alcibiades. We hear about others, but never really see them.[53] It is *not* a mutual relationship. And that presents a real problem for my defense of the Platonic vision. Again, on the kindest reading, we seem able to say only that Socrates knows that he does not love Alcibiades, even though he is powerfully attracted to him (as a great many in Athens, and elsewhere, were). He does not love him, precisely *because* he has been "attentive to the lover in his particularity,"[54] and he now sees that they do not want the same things from love. Alcibiades, in fact, is in love with Socrates in a way that Socrates cannot be in love with him. So, for this reason and for no other, Socrates resists being erotically bound to him.

That is, again, the kind view. I attempted to trace out this defense of Socratic erotics in the last chapter. But this view has been superseded by the much more common account of the *frigidity* of Socrates and of the equally barren philosophic life he prescribes. Socrates never really loves anyone, we are told, because his life is an extended exercise in solipsism.[55] He never really loves because he never really listens, never really lets himself feel. Everything is an idea with him, even love itself. He may be in love with *the idea* of love, yet his thrills come from the cold heart of logic and the dead realm of ideal forms, never the messy, hot, flesh-and-blood reality of lived human experience. Socrates *consumes* people. He makes love inhuman, somehow, an elaborate shadow-play designed to elevate his soul, to get underway on a journey toward a goal that he must finally achieve *alone*.

Here again, I think, everything depends upon this same persistent Platonic back-and-forth between twos and threes. How many terms are there, finally, in a love affair? Two? Or three? Two people, but three terms. Socrates is accused of trying to turn a love affair into a monologue, of consuming, digesting, then finally expelling the other whom he will not allow to remain "other." He is trying to collapse the many (or at least the two) into one. He is trying to make his lover just like him. His behavior may indeed be read in this way. *Any* lover may be read in this way, if he or she is worthy of such a name. That danger—the danger of loss and mortal disappearance into another—comes *necessarily* with such intimacy, with such emotional vulnerability. Socrates seems to me to be marvelously clear about all of this. The only thing that *ultimately* matters in a love affair is love. You and I are penultimate entities, deeply significiant and relevant in our ways, indispensible in fact, yet subservient to a third term that takes the form of a we, the love that we, in some mysterious way, have become. In love, if anywhere in a rightly ordered human life, the two become three: you, and me, and we. *Erastēs* and *erōmenos* cast in the finer, and infinitely harder, form of *erōtikoi*.

Now, obviously, loving in this way—just like knowing in the Socratic manner—is not as easy as counting to three. It is as difficult as any other *spiritual* discipline, as difficult as any other thing really worth having. Just as we do not come to thoughts—*they* come to *us*, as Heidegger so often insisted[56]—we do not come to love. It is not precisely a volitional act. Love happens, love comes to us. We stand in the role of grateful erotic recipients, if we are so fortunate, grateful to be receptacles for that overwhelming, maddening, disconcerting range of emotions which is also the source of our highest delight. "It is bigger than both of us," Socrates seems to say.[57]

This lovely image of what I am calling "erotic mutuality"—of being truly and completely attentive to the lover, in his or her inescapable otherness—lies at the heart of the *Symposium*, as I read it. It is the image, the ideal, around which the whole dialogue—and much of Platonic thought—revolves. It is an image that refuses and undercuts the elaborate role-play—of pursuer and pursued, *erastēs* and *erōmenos*—in which every other character in the dialogue remains trapped. Yet we rightly puzzle over the speech that Diotima makes right on the heels of her extraordinary exchange with Socrates. She has been speaking about attempting to live, and love *metaxu*, "in between" the you and the me. She has been grasping after a language of erotic mutuality, a rhetoric of "we's." She speaks of pregnancy, of the two giving birth to a third. Yet her speech, the apparent crescendo of the entire dialogue prior to the Alcibiadean denouement, sounds as if it undercuts everything she has said. Hierarchies reappear. Men seem to stand over women, again—this, despite the fact that Diotima is a woman herself. And the body, it seems, is to be superseded or outgrown—as we move from an appreciation of one body, to many bodies, then finally to the form of Beauty itself. Suddenly, erotic things look again for all the world to be as solipsistic and lonely as Socrates' many detractors insist that they are. *Erōs* is an emotion, a powerful and even slightly mad emotion, that equips us for contemplation of eternal forms—alone, and in a vacuum.

Fair enough, as far as it goes; there *do* seem to be deep contradictions in Diotima's final speech. Yet it is perhaps not so completely discontinuous with the dialogue she has just had with Socrates as is normally allowed. She is still a woman. The image of *pregnancy*—so telling and so appropriate—is the central metaphor of her entire speech (*Symposium* 206b–209a). What is pregnancy, if it is not the miraculous moment in which two beings create a third, in love? It is a bloody and bodily experience, none more so, the moment in which excruciating physical pain brings new life into being. As such, it is one of the most "spiritual" moments in a life. Self and other give birth to that which is both self and other, together, and yet neither of these selves at all—all of this in the same singular moment. Parenting must rank as another of the most radically vulnerable moments in a properly constituted human life. Just as we do not come to knowledge or to *erōs*, so we do not come to our children. They also come to us. We *receive* them, if we are so fortunate. We do not *choose* them. We do not know exactly where they come from. We can only open up our home to them, accept them, nurture them. We cannot even teach them, finally, only help them to learn, accompanying them on the vast journey. The two become three—in a manner that seems completely out of our own limited control. A more fitting image for the risk, the vulnerability, the mutuality, and the spiritual ecstasy of an erotic bond is scarcely imaginable.

Now I know, as Socrates does, the problems and the implicit dangers in such a view. The invocation of "the truth" can be an extremely aggressive move to make. I "have" it, somehow, as you do not. The *Symposium*, for its part, begins with just such an admission, a portrayal of just how aggressive the philosophical life can be (*Symposium* 173a). But it is no less aggressive—only more subtle—to undercut any and every claim to truthfulness with the crass claim of relativism.[58] The knowing pat on the head with which my every claim to knowledge is met—"well, that's an interesting interpretation"—is ultimately no less aggressive, and probably a good deal moreso, than Socrates' truth-toward aspirations.

Here again, the parallel with erotics is, I hope, clear enough. It is potentially self-indulgent, naive, or simply bombastic for "me" to speak of "our" love, for one person to wax poetic about the magical, mysterious constellations that revolve around our being two persons together. That, too, can be an aggressive move, especially when the other has his or her doubts. All it takes is a denial on the part of one lover—a simple No will do it—to bring the whole affair to a crashing, and crushing, halt. Yet here is the paradox, *love's* essential paradox: What if it is *true*? We are back to Diotima's essential defense of erotic intuition: Love knows what it knows, even if it cannot give a rational account of itself. It may not be *epistēmē*, a sure kind of knowledge, but that does not necessarily make it ignorance, or self-deception. It is sure knowledge indeed, *love's* knowledge. What if we are each running, in our own peculiar ways, from the radical vulnerability of the erotic bond, from the open wound in my otherwise independent life that comes from *your* presence, from *our* presence, in it? What if it is love's place, quietly and simply, to ask *us* to stand still for a moment, beyond the you and the me, to dwell appreciatively with the mysterious connection that so eloquently and movingly comes, all unbidden, to us? What, that is to say, if it is simply "true?"

V

A fascinating phrase: "true love." Truth? Love? A connection. A *necessary* connection.

Most theater—and much of human life, I suspect—is unthinkable apart from the idea. In thinning, and ultimately losing, the language of *erōs* and of erotics, we have traded in much of our poetic birthright.[59] Consider the paradigmatic love-story in the English language. What is *Romeo and Juliet*, if not an attempt to defend the intuitive fact that there *is* such a thing as love, that it is rather difficult to understand, *and* that it turns your universe upside down?[60] Romeo, when first we meet him, is pining away for love—love of a young girl, *not* Juliet. He will never love again, he insists, and he does not miss an opportunity to poeticize his grief. It is wretched poetry, *buffo*, overdrawn.[61] This is a man who is very much in love with the idea of being in love, *a man in love with love*, the way Socrates was alleged to have been. Complaining of the day's interminable length—when actually it is his poetry which is too long—how idle the hours are when Love is idle, Romeo opines:

> Here's much to do with hate but more with love,
> Why then, o brawling love, o loving hate
> O anything of nothing first created
> O heavy lightness, serious vanity
> Misshapen Chaos of well-seeming forms,
> Feather of lead, bright smoke, cold fire, sick health
> Still-waking sleep that is not what it is—
> This love feel I that feel no love in this.[62]

Romeo's abrupt question, "Dost thou not laugh?" is answered, for all of us, by Benvolio: "No coz, I rather weep."[63] We weep at the agony of poetry so tendentious and overdrawn. Like Plato, Shakespeare is such a craftsman with the written word that he can write in many different styles. He can write bad poetry as well as good, when it suits his dramatic purposes. Read these lines aloud, and hear how flatly they fall upon the ear. It all sounds too studied, too crafted, all artificial. It plays on the rhetorical ploy of paradox for paradox' sake. This poetry *speaks* love, does not feel it. It does not feel anything. It is all too wordy, somehow, as if there is always one syllable, or one image, too many. It plays on the kind of stuff you might presumably buy on any streetcorner for Valentine's Day in Elizabethan England. This man who pines away so dramatically, who poeticizes so wretchedly, reads books, but cannot "read anything [he] sees."[64] Or anything he feels, for that matter. His love is childish, solipsistic, and rude.

When he spies Juliet at a party he originally had no heart for, everything—even his poetry—changes.

> O she doth teach the torches to burn bright.
> It seems she hangs upon the cheek of night
> As a rich jewel in an Ethiop's ear—
> Beauty too rich for use, for earth too dear. . . .
> Did my heart love till now? forswear it, Sight!
> For I ne'er saw true beauty till this night.[65]

Cupid's arrow has flown true, this time—an image that suggests precisely how intertwined love and danger can be, the way erotics and emotional violence *really are* joined. Romeo is now *in* love. His poetry is suddenly as rich, as heartfelt, as it was stale and bookish before.

Romeo does not change completely, now. Stealing a kiss from the girl he so suddenly adores, it is she who calls his bluff: "you kiss by th' book."[66] The paradox—and here neither of these children (for such they are) quite knows it yet—is that the rich and traumatic connections that love inspires draw the soul near to its individual, personal death. *Erōs* and *thanatos* are linked in ways which both of them will learn, disastrously. Alcibiades will die for the mistaken commitment to passion for passion's sake. Socrates will die for his lover, *philosophia*. Romeo and Juliet will die, in turn, for one another. True love—a genuine kind of erotic mutuality—is thus ecstatic, wonderful and dangerous, "a little death." There is a parable in the populations of our prisons, statistics which tell us that the vast majority of women imprisoned for murder have killed a lover or spouse. Abuse, both emotional and physical, is often one cause, but so too is jealousy. Men kill for other reasons, as well, but the erotic story their statistics tell is also astonishing. True love is a dangerous, volatile thing, nearer to death than our Hallmark poets know. This Romeo has learned, in perhaps his best, and final, poem. It is love which has taught it to him.

> O my love, my wife!
> Death that hath suck'd the honey of thy breath
> Hath had no power yet upon thy beauty.
> Thou art not conquered—Beauty's ensign yet
> Is crimson in thy lips and in thy cheeks
> And Death's pale flag is not advanced there. . . .

> Ah dear Juliet,
> Why art thou yet so fair? shall I believe
> That unsubstantial Death is amorous
> And that the lean abhorred monster keeps
> Thee here in dark to be his paramour?
> For fear of that I still will stay with thee
> And never from this pallet of dim Night
> Depart again, here will I remain
> With worms that are thy chambermaids, O here
> Will I set up my everlasting rest
> And shake the yoke of inauspicious stars
> From this world-wearied flesh. Eyes look your last,
> Arms take your last embrace, and lips (O you
> The doors of breath) seal with a righteous kiss
> A dateless bargain to engrossing Death![67]

Romeo and Juliet—and hardly this play alone—is impossible apart from the assumption, the intuition of something called "true love." Its truth is inseparable from its danger, from the risks of harm, dissolution, even of death. Yet the play goes on to examine love's essentially nonbookish character as well. Love, like truth, cannot finally be written down. And yet—we all sense this, Plato says (*Symposium* 215d–217a)—it seems as though it were finally the only philosophy worth doing, the only thing really worth talking, or writing, about. Why in the world do poets speak of love more than of any other thing—death being its only serious rival—if it is so unspeakable, so private, and so unknowable? We find ourselves, once again, on complex ground.

It was ground well-trod by the Hellenistic—that is to say, the *post*-Socratic—Greeks. *Both* the Epicureans *and* the Stoics who invoked Socrates as an example of the properly ordered human life, did so largely on the basis of how he loved. The Stoics finally conclude that he did not really love at all. Their imitative desire is thus the extirpation of the erotic passions.[68] The Epicureans counter that Socrates did not love passionately. Their goal is thus the acquisition of a pain-free, muted kind of erotic pleasure.[69] Recognizing, as both schools do, the heady danger and disarray of loving in an erotic way—of desiring, and wanting, and needing—the Stoics refuse to do so. The Epicureans counsel a different approach, which is not so very different as was alleged in antiquity. Stoics and Epicureans share a common question and concern—the problem of *erōs*—and they turn to the same complex figure to answer their question: Socrates. They differ more due to a difference in emphasis and tone. Epicureans counsel the pursuit of pain-free loves, since the goal of the sage's life is the minimizing of pain and perturbation. Their resolve is to have erotic relationships in which *erōs* is not present—Lysias' position in the *Phaedrus* (230e–234c), as we may recall. We should love, or else be loved, by those who do not passionately love us.

Socrates himself *was* deeply tempted to such a view, in the *Phaedrus*, yet he ultimately denies it as blasphemous (*Phaedrus* 237a–242e). I suspect that the same temptation helps to explain Socrates' lifelong fascination with Alcibiades. So clear is his awareness of love's darker and more dangerous face. Yet so sure is his touch, so clear are his convictions about the *necessary* relation between love and any sort of practical human knowledge worth having, that he embraces the erotic life in spite of, indeed *because* of, its inherent risks.

VI

In contrast to the cultural standpoint just examined, we seem to be living in a rather Stoic culture,[70] nowhere more so than in the erotic realm. We embody unstated assumptions which may have more sympathy and continuity with the Senecan view of life than they do with the Socratic. Some contemporary philosophers have even rewritten Socrates' sexual persona in the light of such Stoic antieroticism. Nietzsche, as I suggested, may have started this trend, but it has accelerated in this century. The contemporary emphasis upon life's quality rather than life's quantity—to say nothing of its inherent mystery—owes much to later Stoic conceptions. Our debates about euthanasia, and now about assisted suicide, might be helpfully compared to Seneca's writing on suicide,[71] as well as to the broader Stoic idea that all of life's a stage,[72] a rather short production in which each of us has a relatively brief role to play.

The therapeutic paradigm, which has become so essential an ingredient of "our Emotivist culture,"[73] may owe a great deal to the Stoa as well. The soul—which lies, after all, at the very heart of any *psychē-logia* or "soul-study"—is sick, and can be made well through the proper sort of *therapeia*. Stoic literature is extremely rich in medicinal imagery and language, much of it deriving from Socrates' own foregrounding of the metaphor.[74] Popular culture is steeped in therapeutic imagery, nowhere more so than when it speaks of love. The culture seems at times to be very nearly obsessed with the twinned notions of "healthy" relationships on the one hand, and of something else called "safe" sexuality on the other. The two are often confused, such that healthy relationships are virtually defined as those that are sexually healthy, a crude enough somatic reductionism. Now, I want to be sure to offer a word of caution—although it is a measure of the perversity of our own cultural moment that this even needs saying[75]—namely, that I do not mean to be overly dismissive of such important concerns. Surely there *are* relationships that can become unhealthy, even ones that need finally to be ended or escaped. And surely sexual promiscuity can be physically calamitous in this day and age.

Yet the culture's very obsession with health seems to be deeply and ironically unhealthy; its fixation upon safety seems, at times, to be an exercise in illusion, if not emotional retreat.[76] I want to begin to reflect, near the end of these self-styled Platonic symposia, upon how hollow much of the therapeutic language which so saturates North American popular culture can sound. Here, if anywhere, the many are being collapsed into one—as though there were only one way of being, one way of thinking, one way of loving. We have forgotten how to count to three. Therapeutic language is designed to be discrepant with itself in much the same way that a great deal of other "ethical" discourse seems to be. I spoke to this dilemma in the introduction. We aspire to be tolerant as well as normative, individualistic and public-minded, all in a single breath. If "health" is defined as *self*-realization, *self*-actualization, and *self*-promotion, then it is difficult to see how we might meaningfully aspire to be in "relationship." Romeo and Juliet's relationship, for its part, was unhealthy and unsafe. Socrates' was as well. The self is too much with us, Plato seems to suggest in the Erotic Period; we should aspire to the Other, and through him, or her, to that third thing we allegedly all desire to bring into being. Loving and knowing are both inherently risky, chancy, and radically un-selfish affairs. Philosophy can be a brutish taskmaster, as well as a ravenous lover. She got Socrates killed, in the end, yet he went to his death *willingly*.

A similar confusion appears in the contemporary rhetoric of "safe" sexuality. It may be misleading to seek "safety" in such affairs. The poetic-erotic image of nudity—of being disarmed, and in some profound sense vulnerable and unprotected in a lover's presence—is a potent metaphor speaking to the risk and vulnerability that is an indelible component of the erotic bond. There is an equally potent—if alternative—set of metaphors in this society's concern for sheathing itself, its citizens protecting themselves from one another, all in the name of an inadequate prophylaxis—the headlong pursuit of a kind of "safety" that frustratingly eludes them. The more intense this rhetoric of "safety" becomes, the further it strays from a Platonic philosophy that encourages reflective risk-taking,[77] the exceptional daring to be just a little bit unsafe, erotically and knowingly so.

Now, there may appear to be a question of consistency in what I have just suggested, and I will develop the dilemma in the conclusion. On the one hand, in criticizing our "cultural stoicism," I seem to be arguing that our culture is too stoic, that it excessively valorizes rationalism and emotional detachment. But now, in reference to the triumph of therapeutic language, I seem to be accusing this same society of being too emotive and nonrational. Moreover, I seem to be claiming that *both* phenomena—the "stoicism" and the "emotivism"—share a common source of moral confusion. In brief, I am trying to come to terms with contemporary North American culture, and I am trying to use Plato's very different assumptions about the good life as a way to get purchase on what I do not yet fully comprehend about my own.

There are several points to be made by way of addressing this important conceptual dilemma. First, 'stoic' and 'emotive' are not necessarily antithetical terms. A society in its "mainstream" can be both; I think that ours *is* both. To the degree that stoicism valorizes detachment—detachment not only from our emotions, but also a certain detachment from one another—then the emotivism of many of our own moral appeals ("That's just the way I feel," or "That's just the way I am") is emphatically "detached." What we are demonstrating is our own profound moral isolation, the fact that we are uncertain how best to care for one another. What I have discovered in the course of these symposia is that "erotic mutuality" is a powerful Platonic idea, the full force of which continues to elude us.

A second point begging to be made here is that "rational" is not a bad word. Properly understood, in a Platonic register at least, "rationality" names a complex capacity of human perceptions, dispositions, and reflections. In a sense, both stoics and emotivists, as I intend the terms, share the same false assumption—namely, that "rational" and "emotional" are antithetical, that there is nothing "in between" the two. The stoics privilege the rational; emotivists privilege the emotional. What neither position, taken to its extreme, can allow is that the emotional life is *a part of* the rational life, and that "rationality" represents an extraordinary capacity for becoming reflective even about things as near and dear to us as our ownmost emotions. Martha Nussbaum has made this point eloquently, in a great deal of her more recent work. She is building upon the Socratic model in so doing. What the Greeks called "practical wisdom" (*phronēsis*), as well as what they called "skill at being human" (*sōphrosunē*), name precisely this middle ground, somewhere in between (*metaxu*) stoicism and emotivism. What they ask us to do is to examine reflectively our deepest intuitions about moral and erotic value—why it is that diamonds and flowers are singularly appropriate erotic gifts, why it is that a heart with an arrow through it might be the most appropriate symbol for the eruptive quality of the erotic life, what it is that we mean to affirm, and desire, in the guise of a singularly other human being. In a word, our intuitions are meant to become more intentional, more deliberative and deliberate.

A third and final point may be registered about the nature of moral argument today. Both stoics and emotivists seem to share the mistaken assumption that the erotic life can be completely moralized. Our moral judgments seem most deeply distorted, precisely when we do not reflect sufficiently upon what we have asserted in making them. The stoic obeys a moral commandment against erotic loving: "Thou shalt not become attached." One may think here of the lover who stubbornly refuses to admit to a jealous feeling, who thinks it would be unfair or unjust to lay such an emotional need at the foot of a lover. Agonizing inside, he or she says nothing, admits to nothing—because it would be morally wrong, somehow, to do so. One may think of Martha Nussbaum's portrait of the stoic Socrates (with which I have been in dialogue throughout this book), as a man who abstains from Alcibiades in every way, refusing to be affected by him because he is consumed with the moral point to be made at Alcibiades' expense. Ironically enough, when we worry too much about the right thing to do in an erotic situation, then "the lover in his or her particularity" is in very real danger of disappearing. *Attentiveness* is a supremely difficult virtue, one we perhaps are not entirely sure we want.

At the other extreme, the emotivist extreme, our culture recognizes a precious few erotic issues which it has decided are all right to moralize. Spend a week at random watching any one of the astonishing permutations of the morning talk show, and what you will find is a stunning portrayal of a culture in erotic (and perhaps in moral) disarray. In the name of sensitivity and, alas, of relevance, these shows actually do little more than titillate with nauseously repetitive stories that always end up being about sex—sexuality endlessly unmasked, in public and on-stage. What we unmask here is, ultimately, the deep confusion in the culture, well attested by the current scandal at the presidential level—a schizophrenic interest-and-disinterest in all matters sexual, and a widespread "tolerance" of things, except for that varying handful of moral-sexual matters that we have intuitively decided *not* to tolerate in any way. I mentioned this paradox in the introduction; it seems to have an especially powerful erotic dimension.

What is missing from both the stoic and the emotive (loosely so-called) positions is some more careful reflection about the important *limits* of moral language, about contemporary conceptions of duty, and about the relative virtues of our intuitive judgments. I spoke about this matter in the introduction as well; clearly, moral reflection is an essential matter for any society that wishes to have a constructive political life. I do not mean to be dismissive of such concerns. I have simply become better aware, with Plato's help, of moral *limits*, of arenas in human life that cannot be so easily moralized; I have been made better aware of the *fact* of moral failure as well. The erotic life, I am suggesting, is a crucial arena for thinking about all of this. That is why Plato returned to it so often in this period. For *erōs* is not, ultimately, a *moral* category in quite so simple a way.

What this suggests is the simultaneously disturbing and thrilling idea that the so-called classical tradition is not best read for its *moral* insights. Nietzsche suggested as much in his own classicizing revolution. The categories of the *tragic* and the *erotic* are, he suggested, representative of the Greeks' most enduring contributions to our own thinking about the constitution of the self and of moral value. They underline precisely the categories that neither stoics nor emotivists ever fully understand: ideas of control, receptivity, and risk.

It may be that the contemporary fixation upon *control*—ours, and not the Greeks—is the clearest indicator of everything that our control can never achieve, of the fact that our control will never be as total as we feel we need it to be. It seems essential to recollect at this point, as I suggested in the introduction, that Greek thought was concerned less with ethical knowledge, and hence the regulation of ethical behavior, than it was with the enduring problem of moral failure. That is to say, Greek moral thinking presupposes some intuitive knowledge of the good, and worries precisely about our failure to do that which we already know we should do. In Martha Nussbaum's terms, the Greeks' moral and erotic concern was with *fragility*, first and last. We live in an age which seems to aspire to control, and certainly to autonomy, more perhaps than to any other thing. Insofar as that is the case, some essentially Greek moral insights slip illegibly over the horizon of our comprehension.

We may trust the therapist to make us better—and by "better" we seem to mean more whole, more complete in ourselves, more independent, and self-secure. The moral life is still conceived within the metaphor of a journey, but now it is framed as an adventure in *self*-discovery, not the discovery of another, not even that "stranger who was yourself." To be made "well" is to be rendered more independent and self-contained—and perhaps also a little self-involved. Such wellness seldom encompasses the admission that we are incomplete, each and every one of us, that it is all right to say to someone you love, "I am *not* complete, without you." Perhaps even when that someone is (a) god.

We also inhabit a world that increasingly invites us into a tempting bond of trust to our *technology*, another suggestive form of illusory control. The "better" our technology becomes, the better, and thus the more certain, our control will be. Who of us has not daydreamed, if only in a private moment, that our age will be the one whose technology finally cheats death itself?

That is one reason, I suspect, why the explosion of the *Challenger* was so devastating,[78] and probably why we experience such a uniquely visceral horror at the fall of an airplane. It all spins so suddenly and horribly out of our control. We *trust* technology, we *depend* on it, and no one likes to see his or her trust violated in this way. Our whole worldview blew up when that rocket did. The culture confronted that technology virtually like a lover who had failed it.

Ours is an age where the dead body lying in its casket "looks just like he (or she) always did," even though *it* is not what he or she always was until now—namely, a sentient being who breathed, and laughed, and cried, and loved. Here, in death, the mind-body dualism powerfully reasserts itself. The corpse is *just* a body, now. Socrates faced up to this truth unblinkingly (*Phaedo* 115b–116b). So perhaps should we.[79]

Ours is an age in which computers are making everything in our lives "better" all the time—so we think, so we trust, so we say—and yet we all pull out more hair over terminal disc failures and demagnetization than we ever did over frayed typewriter ribbons or broken pencils. Computers were intended to save a lot of paper. They do the opposite, of course, maximizing waste instead. Electronic mail was intended to save us time. Paradoxically, it devours as much time as one chooses to sacrifice to it. The frantic spectacle of unintended consequences is the uniquely modern drama of contemporary technology.

In such a curious and confused age as ours, it is the drama of *technological* failure, more than moral failure, that shocks us. Nothing else seems to shock us quite so thoroughly, nor quite so well. Perhaps this is akin to the shock that *erōs*, once upon a time, provided. It shocks us with a much-needed dose of reality. War will always be a dangerous thing. That is why the Gulf conflict, with its outrageously lopsided casualties, was not, precisely speaking, a war. Space travel will always be a dangerous thing; that is an inescapable part of what space travel, by its very nature, is. Love will always be a dangerous thing; that is an essential part of what love—the love of *another* person, not the love of ourselves—demands. And life will always be a mortal thing, emphatically bodily and therefore tremendously uncertain, susceptible to dissolution. That is just the nature of embodied life.

Love and death are deeply related in ways the poets, as well as Plato, seem to sense. Think of it: If you love someone enough, enough to commit yourself to him or to her, "for better and for worse" as the poets have it, then you commit yourself to an *inevitable* loss—short of dying together in some sort of accident, one of two persons will outlive the other. To love is thus to open oneself to the eruption of an *inevitable* parting, and to the enormity of debilitating loss. Our bodies, these lovely mortal coils, are suffering and salvation combined.[80] Feminist and other contemporary discourses which have so dramatically and often eloquently rediscovered "the body" as a site for significant moral reflection, and which celebrate the so-called "dance of the body," simply are not looking at the body with open eyes—as disabled, or in pain, or even in death. We simply do not ever get the one without the other, no dance without the dismay, no delight without dissolution. So it can seem at times the most subversive kind of faith to love, erotically, in a culture whose idea of love has been so deeply deformed through the de-eroticizing of stoics or the false moralizing of emotivists.

Such loving can be a lonely endeavor—the open-eyed and astonishingly frank Platonic perspective insists that it will be.[81] When I say that we seem to be living in a stoic culture, I mean to suggest that we seem to inhabit an *unloving* culture. In an unloving society, one that cannot bear the terrible burden which the passions lay upon the human soul, erotics always gives way to ethics, and to politics.[82] That is, after all, precisely what "stoics" preach: politics, ethical engagement, mingled at times with a curious brand of emotional apathy. At its best, stoicism entails a public philosophy of ethical engagement; at its worst, it de-eroticizes the public and political spheres altogether.

Philosophia is a Greek word, a word that Socrates deeply loved (*Phaedrus* 278d). It connotes "the love of wisdom." He might almost have called it *erōsophia*, a veritable *passion* for wisdom. Socrates often speaks of it in these terms. Hegel was so bold as to claim that the "modern" age is best conceived as the age in which, at long last, the love of wisdom is supposed to give way to wisdom itself, to the vast labor of actually becoming wise.[83]

Might it be better to say that *our* task, in these perplexing days at the millennium's end, is to be certain that the love of wisdom remains passionately engaged, and that our knowing becomes a better reflection of our loving? I can think of no metaphor more fitting, nor any more courageous, nor any more potentially healing, in these peculiarly stoic days.

ON ENDING GRACIOUSLY

or, The Greek Legacy Today

BYPASSING RUE DESCARTES

Bypassing rue Descartes
I descended toward the Seine, shy, a traveller,
A young barbarian just come to the capitol of the world.

We were many, from Jassy and Koloshvar, Wilno and Bucharest,
Saigon and Marrakesh,
Ashamed to remember the customs of our homes,
About which nobody here should ever be told:
The clapping for servants, barefooted girls hurry in,
Dividing food with incantations,
Choral prayers recited by master and household together.

I had left the cloudy provinces behind,
I entered the universal, dazzled and desiring.

Soon enough, many from Jassy and Koloshvar, or Saigon or Marrakesh
Would be killed because they wanted to abolish the customs of their homes.

Soon enough, their peers were seizing power
In order to kill in the name of the universal, beautiful ideas.

Meanwhile the city behaved in accordance with its nature,
Rustling with throaty laughter in the dark,
Baking long breads and pouring wine into clay pitchers,
Buying fish, lemons, and garlic at street markets,
Indifferent as it was to honor and shame and greatness and glory,
Because that had been done already and had transformed itself

Into monuments representing nobody knows whom,
Into arias hardly audible and into turns of speech.

Again I lean on the rough granite of the embankment,
As if I had returned from travels through the underworlds
And suddenly saw in the light the reeling wheel of the seasons
Where empires have fallen and those once living are now dead.

There is no capitol of the world, neither here nor anywhere else,
And the abolished customs are restored to their small fame
And now I know that the time of human generations is not like the
      time of the earth.

As to my heavy sins, I remember one most vividly:
How, one day, walking on a forest path along a stream
I pushed a rock down onto a water snake coiled in the grass.

And what I have met with in life was the just punishment
Which reaches, sooner or later, the breaker of a taboo.

—Czeslaw Milosz

Socrates spent his entire life philosophizing, which turns out to be another way of saying that he spent his life entire erotically. He also spent his entire life, figuratively speaking, with Alcibiades. He was, whatever else one may say, a remarkably constant lover. We meet him with Alcibiades in dialogue after dialogue, and their relationship, for all that changed in it, was lifelong. Alcibiades himself proved to be a short-lived character, as we saw in the second chapter, but Socrates was not. It is fitting, then, that it is in conversation with Alcibiades that Socrates unwittingly stumbles upon another essential factor of Greek conversation, and of human loving. He begins, as Socrates seems always to begin, with a question.

> Do you consider it troublesome [*chalepon*] to answer
> things which are asked of you [*ta erōtōmena*]?
>   No trouble at all.
>   Well, then answer me.
>   So, ask [*erōta*]. (*Alcibiades I* 106b)

Socrates begins with a question, but the question ends in *erōta*. *The question*, we suddenly realize, is the premier erotic gesture. Those whom we love truly are those most fit to question. Socrates claims to know only one thing: *ta erōtika*, the things associated with *erōs*. But he knows something else, we now discover. He knows how to ask good questions.

He knows *ta erōtōmena*. Is Plato merely punning, or is he trying to tell us something (*Cratylus* 398d–e)? Is the pun itself perhaps the point?[1]

The word for a question becomes identical with the word about which questions are being asked. Alcibiades invites Socrates to "ask." The word is *erōta*. Accented on the antepenult, *erōta*, it is the word for love. Accented on the penultimate syllable, *erōta*, as it is here, it becomes a curious sort of command: "Ask!" The Socratic dialogue, we suddenly realize, is more than a seducer's craft; it is an *erotologue*. It brings things to birth. To submit to the back and forth, the Socratic question and answer, no matter how apparently innocent, seems now to initiate an erotic exchange. This Alcibiades knew better than most. He spent most of his life, after all, answering Socratic *erōtōmena*—so well, we suspect, that he taught Socrates a thing or two about the process. For teaching and learning are not only "subversive" acts; they are *erotic* ones.[2] There is no other way to learn, no other way really to know. Small wonder that some early Christian communities worried so about the image of Jesus as a teacher, after the Socratic model. *Erōs*, after all, allegedly had no place in the world of the New Testament.[3]

I

For all of the complexities and contradictions I have mentioned, we live in an interesting cultural moment, one in which we may be better able to appreciate the particular fineness, the romantic rightness, of this central Platonic image—the image of two becoming three.[4] Modern science, which contributes so profoundly to our contemporary self-understanding, witnessed courageously for centuries to a resistant Church hierarchy, witnessed to the fact that the Earth was *not* the center of the universe. The Sun was, so they thought for a while. Cosmology has progressed far beyond that insight, naturally. Modern science has, in the words of Carl Sagan, contributed crucially to "the great demotions" of the modern self.[5] We now know that the Sun is not the center of the universe, either. There is no center of the universe—a fact that carries with it the odd implication that any point is potentially a center, of sorts. Perspective, like the readiness, is all. So the Church fathers were not quite so wrong as the cosmologists once believed them to be.

The Sun does not orbit the Earth, the early modern astronomers went on to say. Rather, the Earth orbits the Sun. Or, to put it a bit more precisely, neither body orbits the other. The two bodies form a larger gravitational system; they orbit one another. Two bodies, that is to say, combine to form a third entity, a system. The vastly superior mass of the Sun simply makes it appear that the Sun is stationary; still, the earth's comparatively weaker gravitational pull *does* effect it. *All* matter so attracts.

Such astronomic musings led to epistemological developments, in the era of high modernity. Kant began his writerly career writing about optics on the one hand and the heavenly bodies on the other. As Hegel made clear, brilliantly so in the next generation, subjectivism and objectivism are both one-sided philosophical positions. The subject does not simply create objects. Nor does an object simply reveal itself to a passive subject. Reality is constituted rather of the fascinating manner in which an I and an It interact.

> When modern thought distinguished the real as it is in itself from the real as it exists for itself, it initiated a new epoch in being as much as a new stage of reflection. Indeed, it opened a gap in the very nature of the real that will never be closed again. Despite the erroneous assumption that the meaning of the former depends entirely upon the latter, implied by the modern distinction between object and subject, the more fundamental view that mind stands in a creative relation to that physical reality on which it in other respects depends, is definitive. All Greek thinkers from Plato to Plotinus had declared mind a reality in its own right. But the spiritual discovery of the moderns consisted in understanding the active relationship of mind to cosmos as one that changes the nature of the real. . . .
>
> The rethinking of the idea of transcendence, even as that of self and cosmos began in the fifteenth century, has not come to rest in our time.[6]

And I and an It interact, and a world is born. A distinctively human sort of reality emerges, then, when there are interactions betwen two or more I's (Hegel puns shamelessly with the language of doubling throughout *The Phenomenology of Spirit* when he first turns to this subject).[7] Perhaps it would be fairer to say that a world is born first (through the intercourse of an I and an It), and that *erōs* emerges next (as intercourse between an I and another I), then to be followed by a collective entity called "society" (an I and a They). We are still counting whole numbers—from one, to two, to three.

Hegel's *Phenomenology* was ultimately devoted to a moral vision. His was a deeply *erotic* moral philosophy, grounded in what I have elsewhere referred to as his "tragic vision."[8] Hegel's vision was ultimately aimed at something not so very different from what I was arguing for in the introduction—namely, a new and different vision of what "ethics" entails. Hegel had little interest, it seems to me, in weighing in on the rather tiresome controversy concerning the relative universality of moral judgments. He was deeply informed, however, by the Greek interest in moral failure—his technical term for this idea is 'negation' [*Vernichtung, der Negativ*], the one permanent fixture on which he hung his system—and in what these moral deformations do to the ethical subject. Such an exploration—of the evolving constitution of something called "ethical subjectivity," the coming to be of moral selfhood—appears to be what Hegel meant by "phenomenology."

So I conclude this book, in a sense, where Hegel began his. I began, in the introduction, by taking note of the curiously modern interest in universalizing (or else relativizing) moral judgments. "Ethics" is commonly thought to be in the business of laying claim to universality or else in proving that ethical rules cannot be so grounded. Such an obsession is modern, I suggested, not the Greeks'; it always makes for an odd fit when we try to cram the Greek tradition of tragic and erotic literature into this Procrustean moral framework. The Greeks had their own deeply interesting debates and questions. I would like to think more attentively about them. We will find this tradition of moral enquiry excitingly different, bracingly different, and profoundly instructive, for that very reason. I am trying to describe something of the way in which Plato's sheer different-ness has instructed me about my own times and their primary ethical interests.

Now, I do not mean to suggest that the Greek-speaking tradition of philosophical reflection was entirely innocent of, or unconcerned with, questions of universality. To be sure, the Greeks were well aware of the fact that justice-at-Athens was not the same thing as justice-at-Sparta, much less justice-in-Persia or justice-in-Egypt. Moral diversity was a fact with which they were well acquainted, especially in the matter of sexual mores (*Symposium* 181e–184a). This observation provides the starting point for Plato's *Republic*, an extended and rather heated argument about competing definitions of justice. Clearly, the Greek tradition of moral enquiry was not unaware of the problem of universalizability; it simply was not obsessed with the question, as so much modern moral theory seems to be. "That," Nietzsche quipped, "is *English* consistency for you."

Here, as elsewhere, the preferred Greek starting-point was a fairly noncontroversial set of intuitions and observations about widely shared human values. They are grounded in the fact of *embodiment*, as much as anything else. Given the universal fact of the human body, Greek travelers and colonials were much impressed by how many meaningful social transactions can indeed take place across the great divide of cultural and linguistic difference. First, and arguably foremost, physical pain and the threat of bodily death translate almost immediately: all human beings may wage war with one another; all human beings may kill or be killed. (Of course, Homer assumes that his Trojans spoke Greek [*Cratylus* 393a]—the *Iliad* would not have been much of a poem if they did not—but the larger point stands.) Secondly, and in a related vein, generations of notorious Greek sailors doubtless knew well that one might be sexually involved with anyone from anywhere in the world, regardless of one's linguistic or cultural background. Polemics and erotics meet, later, in the Hellenistic era, in a third distinctively Greek arena: the *athletic* arena. Presumably athletics, to the degree that it is conceived as an exploration of the meaning of embodiment and of bodily limits,[9] is accessible to anyone from anywhere in the world, once they learn the rules of the game in question. Panhellenic games which had once been only for Greek-speakers, were significantly expanded to include Romans and Jews[10] by the second century BCE.

To that fascinating list of alleged human universals—mortality, bodily pain, sexual pleasure, athletic competition, and bodily limit—other categories were added by the philosophers. The tradition of "wisdom-loving" (*philosophia*) included intensive study of music and of mathematics— "languages" both, if you will, which are theoretically accessible to anyone, anywhere. Finally, the philosophers of the Hellenistic era intensively examined the role of "rationality" in the complex process of cultural exchange and human development. Our modern philosophers are still engaged in this task—with however uneasy a conscience, *after* Nietzsche.

The rather surprising thesis toward which I have been moving, albeit tentatively and between the lines in this book, has something to do with the deeply divisive debates about human sexuality which have so polarized our campuses and our culture. What Plato has to contribute to such a debate is the deceptively simple observation of an odd, yet compelling, paradox. Sexuality is without question the most culturally *over*laden, the most culturally encoded, the most "socially constructed" phenomenon in our lifeworld.[11] "Sexuality" also constitutes one of this society's premier buzzwords. "The body" is another. I would like to make the case for "the erotic" as an important supplement.

Now, this would *seem* to make the erotic life the most culturally relative fact in the world. And so it is. Even more perplexing, it is a *personally* relative fact: no two people love in precisely the same way. We never know, when a lover says "I love you," what they actually mean to say (they may not even know, themselves). We are lost, it would seem, in a sea of subjectivity.

While freely acknowledging this, Plato seems simultaneously to be arguing the reverse. *Erōs* is also, and at the same time, arguably the most universal of human phenomena. Human sexuality is precisely the place where "nature" and "culture," as the Greek speculative tradition began to construe these ideas, meet. Human eroticism, loving in a distinctly human way, is precisely that third thing which emerges from the positively hybrid synthesis of "nature" and "culture." *Erōs* is one name we give to the shattering experiences of transgression, of emotional excess, of disruption, of the exceeding of every social, and cultural, and even personal boundary or taboo. Romeo and Juliet are destined to falling in love with the very person to whom they are forbidden. That is a root-metaphor for the erotic life. *Erōs* always has something forbidding and forbidden about it. In love, it becomes impossible to say where the "I" ends, and where the "you" begins. Words set boundaries. So do social and cultural norms. So do you and I.[12] But love does not have a clear boundary. That dialectic—of boundary and boundlessness—is one of the marvelous and awful negotiations in which each of us is fated to live out our erotic, if not our moral, lives. There is a parable in the Valentine's image of a heart transfixed by an arrow, of a winsome *Erōs* drawing back his not-so-innocent little bow. This is a picture of erotic love, we say. It is also a mortal wound. What is astonishing is just how universal such an image, such a subjective experience, proves itself poetically to be.

A second paradox grows out of this first. Loving in an appropriately human way is, so I have been suggesting, one of the most decisively moral facts in the world. Yet it is for this very reason impossible to moralize. It often seems to be the attempt to implement a crudely normative erotic vision that consistently gets human societies into trouble in the first place. There are precious few laws relevant to the erotic arena. Living with that kind of moral complexity is the task of a maturing and complete human life.

How else is it that *erōs* is the thing about which we never tire of speaking? Since language never "gets it right," since *erōs* precisely transgresses every linguistic boundary with which we attempt to circumscribe it, there is always something left to say. Plato's *Phaedrus*, which begins where the *Symposium* left off (with a complex debate about the meaning of *erōs*), ends as a piece of philosophical reflection on the nature of rhetoric and of writing (*Phaedrus* 259e). I take this matter up in the appendix. With *ta erōtika*, it would seem, there is simply no end to words. There is always something left to say.

II

I have not yet delivered upon certain promises which I may seem to have made in my introduction. Let me conclude these wide-ranging Platonically-inspired erotic symposia by attempting to do so, in what is still an admittedly sketchy way. These are tentative thoughts still very much in process. And there is always something left to say.

One of the big questions that has been implicit in this book, one that has become a matter of explicit scholarly attention in the study of Greek sexual mores evident in such charter texts as Plato's *Symposium*, is whether human beings *need* taxonomies, however arbitrary and socially constructed they may appear to be, in the making of meaning, especially of moral meaning. That is one implicit dimension to this long debate about human universals. And it is one of the central issues around which a new curricular phenomenon called "multiculturalism" has established itself at many of our major universities. I have been trying to use the tradition of Greek moral reflection—as we see it crystallized in Platonic thought, and as the early Nietzsche sought to reconstitute it—to assess some of these questions. It seems that the three arenas in which we are now most hotly contesting "the taxonomies of modernity" (a far too grandiose terminology that has probably contributed to the intensity and vehemence of the debate) involve gender, and race, and sexual identity. I will not speak of a fourth essential category (arguably the *essential* question in this society), that of *class*—that is to say, the question of distributive justice and of economic fairness—not because the question is unimportant, but rather because it is not a taxonomic question in the same way. Class is a purely *cultural* question, having nothing "natural" about it, since cultures define what "counts"—as money, as value, and as status. Nonetheless, a fuller account of what is happening in our society today, especially the intensive taxonomic debates at our major universities, would need to attend closely to economic matters, and to the gross distortion of so many social relations which comes with the increasing disparity between riches and impoverishment. As Aristotle argued at length, the death of the middle class presages the death of a moral community[13]—that was, for him, the most axiomatic political truism. Suffice it to say here that, some self-congratulatory Anglo-American rhetoric aside, I do not think that the era of Marxist theory is over, nor that Marx is "dead." His criticism of capital, and of countless capitalist practices— practices that generate their own divisive internal contradictions—has enduring value especially in an environment like North America, where such contradictions are, if anything, accelerating.[14] Money, Marx knew well, too often makes the university, and the rest of the world, go 'round.[15] Marx also recognized money's essentially *symbolic* value; that was arguably the single greatest achievement of the *1844 Manuscripts*.

What many find frustrating about the rhetoric one meets in these self-styled "culture wars"—on *both* sides (can there really be only two?)—is that it so quickly loses touch with some rather important, and really rather obvious, realities. We seem not to have moved very far beyond that great sophistic imponderable: the question of nature's rela- tionship to culture. These, too, are metaphors, metaphors I find helpful as I try to think about these questions. Gender and race and sexuality are all arguably *biological* facts, essential aspects of "human nature," albeit to varying degrees. Now, we must immediately add that none of the lines we draw in North America—between men and women, between black and white, between homosexual and heterosexual—are as clear as all that. There are interesting interstices where our taxonomies fail us, and those borderlands are, sometimes (not always), very interesting places in which to begin to do serious work and important moral reflection. *Erōs* is a boundary-crosser, a god of the borderland, a middling sort of god, as Plato insisted in his Erotic Period for this very reason.

Race has been, in the United States at least, probably the clearest example of this.[16] For myself, it took a trip to Central America in December of 1994 to instruct me in just how arbitrary, and how thin, our own culture's language of "black and white" actually is.[17] There, in Panama, I witnessed faces which had all of Iberia, West Africa, and the indigenous Central Americas in them. Various "races" have been having children together for a *very* long time in Panama, magnifying a process of which Greek sailors and colonists of the seventh century BCE must already have been well aware.[18] Race itself, in such a "multicultural" environment, is an extraordinarily fluid category. It suffers no tax- onomies, allows no cartographies, denies any simplistic description. The phenomenon of the *mestizo*, the person of mixed racial identity, is a por- trait of the racial future, especially in the so-called New World. I used to be suspicious of this term—this world was not "new," after all, to those already living in it—but now the term seems to name an important pos- sibility, the possibility of creating something new. Derek Walcott, whose

poetry has provided such a fine lyric accompaniment to this book—
makes the point elegantly with regard to his own Caribbean context. It
comes in the form of his address to the Nobel Committee in 1992.

> And here they are, all in a single Caribbean city, Port of Spain,
> the sum of history, Froude's "non-people." A downtown
> babel of shop signs and streets, mongrelized, polyglot, a fer-
> ment without a history, like heaven. Because that is what such
> a city is, in the New World, a writer's heaven.
>   A culture, we all know, is made by its cities. . . .
>   This is Port of Spain to me, a city ideal in its commercial
> and human proportions, where a citizen is a walker and not
> a pedestrian, and this is how Athens may have been before it
> became a cultural echo.[19]

I think Walcott is right about the Athenian connection here; this same
phenomenon has characterized the eastern Mediterranean basin, at least
in its great coastal cities, from Iberia to Palestine, for millennia.

A similar point might be ventured about what we are now in the
habit of calling a "sexual identity" (a terminology that looks to be less
than one hundred fifty years old).[20] Certain people may be more erotically inclined to one sex than to another, and many seem to be very
nearly exclusive in their gender preferences. Still others are not at all. I
will have more to say about this in a moment, since it so clearly relates
to the apparently homoerotic presuppositions of all Plato's dialogues in
the Erotic Period.

Even gender, far the surest of the three taxonomies I have mentioned, biologically speaking (*Statesman* 262e), allows for some ambi-
guity. Chromosomally (*chromo-soma* is a telling Greek coinage that
means, roughly speaking, "body-color," indicative of the primarily
racial attentions of those geneticists who invented these terms in the
nineteenth century), we know that there are people who have an extra
X or Y chromosome, and that this occasionally blurs the sharp line that
we otherwise labor to draw between the sexes. Still and all, sex difference is a pretty hard fact to argue with, a far surer taxonomy than either
race or sexual identity. We see this when we attempt to be more "inclusive" in our speech and in our thinking. What we call "inclusive language" attends specifically to gender, as it must. But we have no need to
reform our language on matters of race or of sexual identity, if for no
other reason than because language does not make these sorts of distinctions. These categories are already blurred by our grammar. Gender
seems somehow more primordial.

Black and white, homosexual and heterosexual, male and female: these ideas establish categories which enable us to think about ourselves, all the while being far-from-perfect categories, and we should probably attend to their fluidity more than we normally do. Such taxonomies exist, in a sense, on an ascending scale of certainty. Gender is the most "natural" of the three (indeed, there are so-called Eastern religious traditions which found their entire cosmology on such principles). Race, while still a biological "fact," is the least clear, and a far more fluid construction. It certainly allows for a profound and elegant range of "in-between-ness." Sexual identity seems somehow to lie in the middle here, appropriately enough.

Here is one arena in which the example of Greek antiquity is especially interesting and instructive. And here is still another arena in which Nietzsche was both profound and premonitory:

> Education is first and foremost the teaching from *necessities*, and then from *transitions and changes*. We send our youth out into Nature, generally show them the rule of laws, and then the laws of Civil Society. Here the question already emerges: does it *have to* be so? Generally speaking, the student needs History, in order to see how this came to be. But at the same time he learns that it can also be quite different.
>
> How much power does man have over things?—that is the question that lies behind all education. *Now, to demonstrate how completely different it all can be, point to the Greeks, as an example. We needs the Romans to see how things* came to be *the way they now are.*[21]

To be sure, the Greeks were well aware of the fact of ethnic and racial diversity—we see it clearly rendered in their art, in their pictures of themselves, and in their pictures of other peoples. But they did not attach the sorts of cultural or moral valence to the "natural" facts of racial variety that some northern Europeans did in the nineteenth century and earlier.[22] The Greeks' foundational identity concepts seem rather obviously "cultural" in this regard: who had a good Greek education, who spoke Greek without too bad an accent, and the like. The Greek word 'barbarian' [barbaros] did not originally possess a moral valence at all; it was simply an onomotapoetic description of the way people who could not speak Greek sounded to them (bar-bar-bar, is presumably the way foreign speech sounded to a Greek ear). Any person from anywhere in the world could presumably acquire the Greek language and a Greek education. Homer potentially belonged to everyone, an astonishing and extraordinarily liberating cultural claim, if ever there were one.

It is we, especially in the New World, who have an enormous and largely unresolved problem with race—and that is not at all difficult to understand, historically. The peculiarly New World institution of plantation slavery was also an indelibly racial phenomenon, a sad chapter in the history of colonial politics, emerging global markets, and late-European racialist attitudes. The Greeks and Romans had slaves, of course, but there was not the same racial rationale for the practice in antiquity. Our own English word comes from a name—Slav—and thus indirectly, if unconsciously, invokes the Byzantine and Ottoman periods, when there was a thriving slav-trade, if you will.[23]

The Greeks also were obviously aware of gender as a natural fact. Here, they seem by and large to have attached tremendous moral valence to the idea. In matters of gender, the Greeks are often far less progressive and emancipatory than we consider them to have been elsewhere. The sexes were essentially segregated, and women's orbit—at least in Athens, in the classical period—was quite small, confined as it was, with notable exceptions, to the extended household. Other periods and other places in Greek antiquity probably did a little better—archaic Lesbos has become an intriguing site for more contemporary scholarly enquiry—but it was still far from ideal. Marriage in such a setting was thus a complex social process of ritual celebration *and* ritual mourning for women, as it marked the beginning of the rest of a hard life of labor and childbearing (also called "labor" in English, tellingly enough) for most of them. That natural necessity has only really changed in the last one hundred years or so, as child-survival rates in the industrialized nations have improved so dramatically, and as women, with comparative suddenness, were no longer required to be about their labor so narrowly in the household, that is to say, to be pregnant constantly for fifteen years or more. In any case, the matter of gender-equality seems to be the area where Greek antiquity will be of least assistance to us in envisioning—or revisioning, in Nietzsche's own idiom, "how different it all might be." No amount of nostalgia for "the glory that was Greece" will assist in these, our own halting kinds of intellectual and moral reforms. Sappho is an extraordinarily interesting (however tantalizing) personality and poet, but she is hardly a proof of gender-equality in antiquity. Here, in matters of gender relations, we are trying to reinvent the wheel, to dream a reality we have arguably never yet experienced. Nostalgia, especialy nostalgia for "the glory that was Greece," will be of no assistance to us in this work. This is just one of the many things that makes modern feminism very *un*like its intellectual neighbors in racial and cultural and sexual studies across the curriculum. Feminism's real historical novelty is the source both of its promise, *and* of its difficulty. Far too often, the multicultural trinity of "gender, race, and sexual orientation" is invoked—everywhere from department meetings, to college brochures, to commencement addresses. It is a deeply misleading constellation. Each of these matters is dramatically different, fraught with unique challenges and altogether singular. We need to learn again to count to three. Greek antiquity has a very different message for us in each arena. It does not help matters to collapse such important intellectual and moral distinctions; doing so has led to some very fuzzy-headed thinking about the most divisive moral debates in this society.

Sexual matters are, in the period of Greek antiquity (a vast period, temporally and geographically, I know), the most complex. The Greeks were, throughout the eastern Mediterranean and across several centuries, as nearly as we seem able to tell, "bisexual."[24] One problem, of course, is terminology: that word itself would have made little sense to them. In other words, our modern taxonomy—the categorizing of sexual matters in accordance with the same-sex-ness or opposite-sex-ness of your erotic attachments—seems *not* to have been a distinction made with any precision in Greek antiquity. It seems to have become one in later Roman antiquity, according to John Boswell.[25] The Greeks—men and women alike, if their vase-painting is any indication[26]—were erotically inclined toward men in some settings and toward women in others. There were, I expect, cultural invitations to respond in certain ways at certain times. When the men at Plato's *Symposium* dismissed the flute-girls (*Symposium* 176e), I suspect that they were also deliberately reconstituting their environment in such a way as to invite reflection upon the nature of their *homo*erotic desire. This is an area where Greek taxonomies are so unlike our own that we have trouble wrapping our minds around them, trouble knowing how to put them into words, much less in knowing how to use them for our own moral reflection. And here is where some find Greek thought—their *erotic* thought—the most liberating, for that very reason. The Greeks help demonstrate "how different it all might be."

The intellectual challenge before us lies in knowing how not to deny utterly the facts of "nature." It is strange that Camille Paglia acquired such an astonishing, however short-lived, publicity by making this rather uncontroversial point: that sexual matters are complex precisely *because* eroticism is the human arena in which "nature" and "culture" are inextricably bound.[27] *The body* is, itself, such a site, I have been suggesting. What Paglia does not say with sufficient attention is that "nature" and "culture" meet here in ways which are impossible to disentangle. The human body is a natural-cultural complex, especially in an erotic state. No sooner do we establish this polarity—nature and culture, man and woman, gay and straight, black and white—than it begins to melt away between our fingers. Such is the mirror-play of *erōs*.

III

The fact of the matter, the supremely human fact of the matter, is that people can be, and often are, consumed by eroticism. People can be stupid[28] about sex. That superficially simple claim tends to push all matters of sexual morality subtly into the realm of the *super*-natural; it is not only religious persons who appeal to the "supernatural" in the construction of moral selfhood. Biblical lawgivers, prophets, and others had a notoriously hard time getting riled up about their followers' sexual transgressions, if only because they seem to have known—as I do, alas, as an "ethicist"—that people *are* stupid about sex. Passion is not orderly. Disorder and disruption are in its nature. Sexuality is also extraordinarily regulated activity, lending itself to values and to rule-making. Yet Erōs is the quicksilver, changeling deity, the one who respects no rules. That fact raises an acute moral dilemma.

The dilemma intensifies when you live in a society where "power," that other modern intellectual imponderable, is not evenly distributed across the lines of gender and of race—as it still is not in the Americas. Then sexual transgressions also tend to be lopsided. White men have been doing most of the workplace harassing in this society until quite recently. Regrettably, however, I do not expect ever to live in a world where we are entirely *free* of such harassment. Sexual transgressions probably come with the human territory. As women and minorities move into positions of greater power, some of them will be harassers as well, in their turn. We are already becoming familiar at first hand with this fact. Sexual harrassers may be white, black, or otherwise. They may be male or female. They may be gay, bisexual, or straight. *Erōs* brooks no such distinctions. Such a claim may seem sexually anti-utopian, and so I suppose it is, but there is another word for it. That word is 'Romantic'.

I certainly am attracted intellectually to some aspects of Romanticism,[29] as I suggested in the introduction, for this as well as for other reasons. The Romantics knew well that the overwhelming force of the erotic almost necessarily implied that *erōs* could not be legislated or moralized. In the playfully ironic words of Lord Byron, when confronting one of the more fascinating characters to have been created in the modern era in Europe,[30] Don Juan:

> Happy the nations of the moral North!
>   Where all is virtue, and the winter season
> Sends sin, without a rag on, shivering forth
>   ('Twas snow that brought St. Anthony to reason);
> Where juries cast up what a wife is worth,
>   By laying whate'er sum, in mulct, they please on
> The lover, who must pay a handsome price,
> Because it is a marketable vice.[31]

Where does this leave us, then? Groping in half-darkness, lanterns lit, in search of a single honest man or woman, I suppose. Such is the Socratic portrait Plato goes out of his way to paint. The natural facts of gender will not go away. Some of us can carry a fetus to term and then nurse that child from our own flesh if we so desire; the theory of womb-envy has always seemed to me at least as credible as the more notorious and culturally-laden notion of penis-envy. Now, how our society has chosen to interpret that extraordinary biological fact—telling me that I can't write poetry, or that my women friends can't do math—seems silly enough, today. We seem to be in the presence of a natural taxonomy that is beyond serious disputing—man and woman—yet we want to blur the *cultural* (and thus the moral) lines which this society draws around them, presuming to interpret them, to tell us what these natural taxonomies mean. Male and female can mean other things than what we have said that they mean. We need classical models from the past, Nietzsche suggests, as well as undreamt of futurist models, to show us "how different it all can be." But the natural fact of sex difference is not going to go away, despite the emerging contemporary technologies of bodily management, as well as our still more jarring contemporary fascination with androgyny. I take the essential linguistic reform of "inclusive language" to be necessary for that very reason. Inclusiveness is a noble moral goal, deeply indebted to the cosmopolitan ethos of the major Hellenistic schools. Such may even be read as one of the moral roots of modern feminism.

There is also a natural fact of race. It is far less clear and far more mutable than gender, yet it does exist. It came to mean astonishing, and astonishingly toxic, things in this society. We still labor under the lingering burden of that great cultural weight. It surely does not mean that whites are smarter than blacks,[32] nor that Asians (defined regionally rather than racially, be sure to note) are smarter than the rest of us. The biological fact of race probably means very little, ultimately—far less, it seems clear, than gender does. As the paleoanthropologists remind us, viewed in one way—"naturally," if you will—then "we are all Africans." There seems a lovely parable in that image, and the moral vision it attempts to communicate.

There are, arguably, some "natural" roots to human sexual identity as well. Central to the Freudian revolution was his insistence that children already are sexual beings in infancy, and that they are very nearly pansexual. The process of acculturation is thus also partly a process of channeling such libidinal energies into certain prescribed objects and arenas. The implication would seem to be that most of us inhabit some place on a spectrum of bisexuality—beginning with the much-touted polymorphous perversity that may characterize the pansexuality of earliest childhood—and that various cultures tend to encourage or discourage any, or all, of these erotic inclinations.[33] Precisely because it does exist on a continuum, Freud suggests, human eroticism avails itself of no easy definition. One cannot really draw a line around human sexuality, except on the extremes—those being exclusive heterosexuality on the one hand, and exclusive homosexuality on the other.

Where, then, does this leave us, as Platonists, as ethicists, or what have you? And what is the enduring value of the Greek legacy to contemporary moral debate? We are trying to reinvent the wheel, in some significant ways, as I have already suggested. Some of our deepest moral concerns take us rather far from the abortion clinic or death camp, far from the nuclear abyss that we may have just managed to escape, at least for half a generation or so. It leaves us in the midst of rather heated, and intensely personal, controversies about *identity*, and about the enduring constitution of our personal selves. It is striking how much moral energy is devoted to such debate in this culture. I am uneasy with the way the language of "tolerance" is being used in current debates about curricular "multiculturalism,"[34] precisely because I do not think the university's mission has ever been to "tolerate" things. We do not tolerate intolerance, as I noted in the introduction—a profound inconsistency that is still lost on too many colleagues and administrators. The contemporary buzzword of "tolerance" breeds a view of mutual toleration that seems, in its turn, to suggest that "multiculturalism" names the perfectly sophomoric North American principle that all persons—regardless of gender, race, or sexual orientation—can eat at MacDonald's together in peace.

That alleged peace is too often purchased at the price of *mono*cultural-
ism, American style. Insofar as that is the case, this is probably *not* a
credible model for the kinds of globalism to which we should have
learned to aspire from the Hellenistic Stoic tradition, a cosmopolitanism
upon which the modern liberal university may in fact be built.[35]

What, then, should we be trying to achieve in the new-yet-not-so-
new university environment we are envisioning, however haltingly and
imperfectly? And what does Plato's Erotic Period have to contribute to
our ongoing search for new moral metaphors? Difficult questions. In
most departments of religious studies at secular universities with which I
am familiar, we seem to be committed to the project of acknowledging
and accepting gay sexuality as an intrinsic part of the remarkably wide
spectrum of human eroticism. But we are also institutionally obliged to
recognize our Orthodox colleagues' beliefs, whether Jewish or Christian,
that homosexual practice is a violation of several Levitical restrictions
that quite clearly prohibit it.[36] How may we mediate, not to say resolve,
such apparently intractable moral positions? Not simply, and not easily,
to be sure. But at least we can admit, frankly and at the outset, that some
of our personal moral perplexity, like some of our most divisive social
problems, may not be easily resolved—and then to roll up our sleeves and
have at it, working toward their suppler and more sensitive mediation. It
is one of the sulkier pronouncements of modernism to claim that the existence of such ethical intractibilities is itself a sign of the disease of modern times.[37] There has never been a society which was not riven by certain fairly essential moral questions. Mediation of simple problems is no
challenge: societies devote their better energies to their most challenging
and persistent debates. Now, the first challenge before us in this case is
translational. The biblical mandate(s) must be taken seriously, and must
be translated into a non-doctrinaire idiom that can be made intelligible to
some degree to a non-confessing audience. Then, arguments for "the
other side," if you will, with its competing account(s) of the purpose and
place of sexual practices in the construction of the good life, must receive
a fair hearing. Only when this vast labor of mutual translation has been
done can the infinitely harder task of interpreting and negotiating
between these "rival traditions" begin.[38] Here is work for which com-
parativists and religionists are especially well-suited. Minimally, we can
begin to display what reasoned argument about some difficult and challenging moral material might in fact look like.

One meets a similar dilemma when the question of monotheism
comes up. There is no easy way to resolve the dispute between monothe-

ists and polytheists—unless the practical *"tritheism"* of Christian practices is a compromise one can live with. Yet we *do* live with it: Orthodox Jews, liberal Protestants, Muslims, Hindus, and at least one Greco-pagan, all inhabiting a single department—if not as practitioners, then at least as sympathetic students—all engaged in a common practice, doing something together called "religious studies."

Erōs seems to lie metaphorically at the heart of this matter, too—and not only in the polytheistic traditions of Greece, or of India, where the erotic was ritualized in explicitly *religious* settings. As the Hebrew scriptures make abundantly clear, especially the tumultuous and long-suffering book of *Judges*, in the great war with polytheism, it was the *fertility cults* which simply would not go away. And as Juliet tells it, the lover always threatens to become "the god of [her] idolatry." Yet this seems to be an idolatry—the comparative idolizing of the lover—we can live with, an idolatry we all do live with, and even celebrate poetically, at times.

We cannot undo "nature," whatever it would mean to try. Sex difference, like gender, are facts of human life, although they may clearly be revisioned in ways that are not so toxic to our sense of ourselves and our relations as men and women to one another. Sexual identity seems to inhabit more of a naturalist continuum; it is, as I have reflected on the matter, the most "middling" of all such modern moral matters, decidedly *metaxu*. This much have I learned from Plato's Erotic Dialogues. Race will be a still blurrier natural fact in the coming millennium, one which nevertheless continues to have some meaning, although the lines mapping out the vast terrain of human ethnicity are probably the blurriest and least tractable. Here again, I am less interested in questions of nature per se than in the question of how our culture has interpreted such natural human realities. "Nature," after all, may be invoked to justify, or to condemn, very nearly anything.[39] And here—in those places where nature and culture meet—is where we have some hard thinking still to do. The human being is an embodied soul. The human body is itself a fascinating complex, the place where nature and culture mingle. We are marvelous, miraculous, complex creatures. Plato in the Erotic Period seems singularly attentive to the mystery.

This was another one of Nietzsche's fundamentally classical insights. He, too, speaks of "nature," knowing that he cannot entirely do away with so entrenched a moral buzzword. Still, Nietzsche was clear enough, eloquently so, about what he did *not* mean when he invoked the term:

Nature, evaluated artistically, is no model. It exaggerates, it
distorts, it leaves gaps. Nature is *chance*. Study "in accordance with nature" seems to me to be a bad sign: it betrays
submission, weakness, fatalism.

This fawning in the dust before *petit faits* is unworthy of
a *complete* artist.[40]

Nietzsche was also fairly clear about what he *did* mean:

I too speak of a "return to nature," not as a going back, but
as an *ascent*—up into the higher, freer, terrible heights of
nature and of naturalness, an ascent where great tasks are
things one plays with, things one *may* play with. . . . To put
it *metaphorically*, Napolean was a piece of this "return to
nature," as I understand the phrase. . . .

But Rousseau—to what did he really wish to return?[41]

This *antinostalgic* perspective—the metaphor of ascent rather than of going
back—is essential to a proper understanding of what Nietzsche was trying
to do with his own idiosyncratic brand of classicism already in the early-
to-mid-1870s.[42] It is also what I find most congenial about him as a thinker
and as a social critic. The insight grew initially out of his own philological
commitments, his radical reappraisal of the pre-classical Greeks. They were
not available to be recovered through rank imitation, Nietzsche insisted;
they exist, if at all, as competitive models, models to be *surpassed*.

To surpass Greek culture with action—that should be the
task. But to do that one must know it first!

There is a kind of profundity which is only a pretext for
inactivity. One thinks of what Goethe understood about
antiquity—certainly not as much as a philologist, but more
than enough to inspire him, to make him prolific. One *should
not* know more about a thing than one can embody. This is
the only way to *know* something truly: by striving to *create*
it. One strives to live classically—and in this way one comes
a hundred miles closer to classical antiquity than through any
amount of learning.

Our philologists show no evidence of *emulating* antiquity—thus their version of antiquity has no impact on their
students at all.[43]

"Classical studies"—the sort of thing I have been trying to *display*,
rather than to argue for, in this book—will help us to do some of this
thinking and striving, surpassing difficult though it will be. It helps us
more clearly to name some very laudable modern aspirations. And it
renders them problematic, too. The Greeks are very liberating, in terms

of sexuality—*if* the frank acknowledgment of sexual diversity is your
goal. They are pretty good on race. They are pretty bad on gender. So,
we are left very much where we have always been—as *bricoleurs*,[44] picking and choosing, looking forward rather than backward where history
does not provide precise enough models relevant to our experience and
to our perceived moral needs. That kind of moral pluralism (if not prag-
matism) is not a crass version of moral relativism, and that is what the
proponents of multiculturalism have yet to explain with sufficient clarity. Many do not see it as a problem. Here, too, Nietzsche's criticisms
have been premonitory: The English, he noted with a resigned sigh, do
not even see morality as a *problem*, yet.

To repeat: multiculturalism does not preach the tolerance of the
intolerable. It never did. The fact that truth is complex does not mean
that there are no lies. We all still draw lines; we continue to live in
bounded moral spaces, and likely always will. Societies cannot do without taxonomies altogether, least of all in the sexual arena. This, too,
Nietzsche knew: "Reason in language—what a deceptive old woman she
is! I am afraid we are not yet rid of God because we still believe in grammar."[45] It is a caricature of "multiculturalism" to claim that it wishes to
do away with line-drawing, norms, or taxonomies altogether (some multicultural rhetoric has invited the caricature). We are simply trying to
draw our lines better, and this will sometimes mean drawing them blurrier—more lovingly, more graciously, and in ways more attentive to the
astonishing diversity of cultural responses to certain natural human facts.

Plato's erotic vision seems to me to provide us with a better sense of
the full complexity of matters that *are* complex—human sexuality, most of
all, and especially a sexuality that plays out across the great divide of gender, as it does heterosexually. The much-touted "war between the sexes" is
made infinitely more complex, because it is an essentially erotic war. This
is one thing that renders the making of a lasting peace so difficult.

What I have been underlining in this book is a point already amply
made by Martha Nussbaum: that risk, vulnerability, and even harm
(emotional as well as physical harm) are inescapable components, even
if only potentially, of a well-lived life. Erotic pleasure cannot be
detached from erotic pain. Plato seems to suggest in the Erotic Period
that, while every society has its taxonomies, the power of *erōs* in a
human life names the eruptive force of boundary-crossing, the blurring
of lines we wish to draw with better clarity. What I want to suggest here
at the end, as I did also at the beginning of this book, is the one thing
which has as large a claim as any to being an *unchanging* constant in

human affairs is precisely this profound experience of disruption we call "true love," and which the Greeks named for us as *erōs*.

Every society has its taxonomies; every society has its members who disrupt them. Some of these persons we incarcerate, or even execute; others we celebrate. It is not always easy to say why we do one rather than the other—especially when they have been women.[46] Joan of Arc was burned as a heretic; less than fifty years later, the Church admitted its error, and eventually canonized her.[47] Socrates' life and death map out a similarly ironic trajectory.

Think now of a rather structured and traditional society in which marriages are, by and large, arranged.[48] The marriage ceremony is thus a sort of social ritual, and the marriage commitment is a sort of social duty—a duty with often terrifying implications for young women. Sappho hymned some of these complex social transactions for us.[49] What I am struck by is how often *erōs* is described in precisely such a society's epic and dramatic literature as a deeply disruptive force.

Erōs is a madness. *Erōs* is the human phenomenon that breaks all social boundaries and taboos, shatters them really. On this view, *Romeo and Juliet* (much like Lorca's *Blood Wedding*)[50] is a charter text of such erotic disruption. Heinrich von Kleist's "Penthesileia"[51] is another classic Romantic example, and one of my personal favorites. This play has had an interesting afterlife in the twentieth century on the Continent, and again more recently in North America. The image of the star-crossed lover is a cultural as well as a natural phenomenon. This disruption cuts *both* ways.

Here at the end, I wish to conclude with what has proven to be a deep, and perhaps insoluble, dilemma: How is it that the most subjective of *all* human experiences—erotic love—is, when looked at another way, the most objectively constant fact of human life? That seems a paradox well worth pondering. Plato ponders it richly. Becoming sensitive to this paradox is one essential principle which animates our halting curricular reforms on the one hand, and aspirations toward a well-lived, morally reflective, human life on the other.

As I suggested in the introduction, and repeat now, here at the end, Socrates presents us with a fascinating sort of philosophical challenge: show me what kind of lover you aspire to be, and I will tell you a great many things about what you consider ultimately worthwhile, worthy of emulation, and possessing real value. I may even be able to say something essential about your religious convictions. Love encompasses all of this.

And *erōs* is the metaphor we live by.

ON LANGUAGE AND LITERACY

> To reproach mystics with loving God by means of the faculty of sexual
> love is as though one were to reproach a painter with making pictures
> by means of colours composed of material substances. We haven't any-
> thing else with which to love. . . .
>
> —Simone Weil, *The Notebooks* II

The question of the so-called "origin of languages" was one of the
most vexed and vexing questions among European philosophers in the
1700s. It was unclear to social theorists of the time which came first,
language or society? And it was unclear to them how "natural" such an
impulse toward human socialness was, to begin with. Rousseau composed an essay devoted to this topic in 1749, but it was published
posthumously.[1] The question of the origin of languages culminates, in
Rousseau's case, with the intriguing suggestion that language is essentially related to music, to what he sees as "natural" rhythms and
cadences.[2] In fact, the subtitle of the essay reads "In Which Something
Is Said about Melody and Musical Imitation." Rousseau's conclusion
involves what we might call "the priority of poetry." The earliest human
speech was poetry, a speaking in meter, a kind of speaking that made
memorization and repetition allegedly easier. Most all of the pre-
Socratic philosophers spoke and wrote in verse. This was simply an article of faith in the late eighteenth century—the idea of the priority of
poetry—that would be advanced significantly in the next century by the
Romantics, in Germany, in France, and in England. It is an idea that,
largely thanks to Heidegger, has not yet come to rest in our own century.

The intellectual scene has changed, if not seismically then at least
significantly, in the past thirty years. Attention has been paid, increasingly, to the essential difference between oral and written communica-

tion, between orality and literacy, between speech and writing.[3] One learns to speak simply by being born into a human society, after all. But writing . . . writing is a *technology*, and, like most technologies, one accesses it (in this society, at least) by going to school. I will have more to say about this distinction.

There is a Platonic precedent to this study of language, which Plato himself called *grammata*, and which Jacques Derrida has popularized more recently as "grammatology."[4] The precedent comes in the form of Plato's *Cratylus*, one of the more unusual dialogues in the corpus, and the first full-length philosophical treatment of the origin of human language. It is an aporetic dialogue, significantly enough, one that leaves its fundamental question unanswered in the end.

The question hinges on whether there is something "natural" about language (a variety of phrases are used for this idea, among them, *kata tēn orthēn, kata physin, orthōs pephyke*), or whether words and names have a merely "conventional" value (again various words and phases appear, among them *nomos, ethos, xynthēkēs, xynthemenoi*). Hermogenes, the chief interlocutor, inclines to the conventional view, but Socrates is committed to the belief—it is, he freely admits, no more than that—that there is more meaning in our words than the arbitrariness of social convention will allow. He does not prove the case, naturally enough, since it is not clear what "proof" would look like in such an endeavor. Most of the dialogue consists of an ever more dizzying, and only half-serious, list of hypothetical etymologies, all of them Socratically inspired. And inspired he is, Hermogenes notes, whether by the Muses or by some other god (*Cratylus* 396d). This is one of the telling details that links this dialogue on language to the far more central and significant Platonic dialogue, the *Phaedrus*.

Etymologies aside (there is even a curiously doubled analysis of the word *erōs*, linking it both to the word for "hero" as well as the verbal ideas of "flux" and "flow," [*Cratylus* 398c, 420a]), Socrates makes several important observations about human language. First and foremost, the origins of language are unknown. Words have come either from some superhuman force (*Cratylus* 438c), or else from the first namers (*Cratylus* 397d, 425a) and lawgivers (consistently called *nomothetai, Cratylus* 390d, 429a) whose own names are lost in prehistory. Human language also exists in time, and in the havoc of cross-cultural exchange: pronunciations and spellings have evolved, or devolved, with time, and the Greek language has itself been transformed through frequent lexical borrowing from barbarian tongues (*Cratylus* 409e).

Language, Socrates concludes, is an *imitative* art, a kind of *mimēsis* (*Cratylus* 423a–424c, 430b–431e)—the very thing, we will recall, that made poetry problematic in the *Republic*. Now, Socrates is no more willing to give up on language than he is to give up on poetry, or on Alcibiades. Instead, he prefers his commitment to language, to its nature and its meaning, to be tentative. The gods have access to the essence (*ousia*) of things, Socrates repeatedly insists in this dialogue. Insofar as we inhabit the realm of mutable, human language, we can only say what things are like, never what they are in themselves (*Cratylus* 400c–401a, 425c, 439b). This is a crucial Platonic point in the Erotic Period: if there are indeed "forms," then we do not have any simple access to them. Such *gnōsis* escapes us (*Cratylus* 440b). The same point is central to the *Phaedrus* as well: as human beings, we inhabit the realm of metaphor, the matter in the middle, in between (*metaxu*) "reality" and the mere shadow-play of "appearance."

Now, the *Phaedrus* is one of the richest and most challenging of all the Platonic dialogues. So fundamental are the questions it raises that Schleiermacher concluded it to have been the first dialogue Plato ever wrote. The seeds for everything he says later are sown here, in the *Phaedrus*, Schleiermacher believed. His dating is suspect, of course, but there is no denying the central importance of this dialogue, which I assume to have been the last one written in the Erotic Period (I shall date this period to somewhere between, say, 380 and 365 BCE). I want now to walk briefly through the *Phaedrus*, in order to reiterate some of the larger Platonic points I have been trying to rehabilitate in this book. It is, in any event, always worth casting a glance backward at the end of a journey, if only to remind oneself of the terrain one has been over, as well as of the high points which still remain visible, even now at a significant temporal or spatial remove.

PRELIMINARIES

The *Phaedrus* begins where the *Symposium* left off, in the midst of an apparently never-ending discussion of *erōs*. In the *Republic*, Socrates cautioned us that we might need to make a break with poetry if a fitting defense of poetry could not be made. The *Phaedrus* offers something very like that defense, as well as an intriguing body of alternative myths, each of them Socratically inspired. They are every bit as creative, and a good deal moreso, than the often strange-sounding etymologies that inhabit the *Cratylus*.

Socrates and Phaedrus are walking outside of the city walls, where Socrates himself, significantly enough, rarely goes unless he has to. (We will recall that the *Republic* also took place outside of town, in the Athenian port of the Piraeus.) In this case, Socrates has been tempted outside of the city and to a secluded river grove, led there by Phaedrus. They turn to talking, talking about a talk prepared by someone else, a famous orator named Lysias who is currently visiting Athens. (It is interesting to notice how many of the notable Greek-speaking intellects of the day make a point of visiting Athens. The *Protagoras* is a lovely sketch of this thriving intellectual cosmopolis.) Phaedrus tells Socrates that he has heard Lysias' speech himself, and would like now to share it. He seems inclined to deliver the speech from memory, but Socrates stops him. If I know you, Socrates smiles, then you've surely managed to get away with a written copy of the speech, so that you can pore over it time and again (*Phaedrus* 228a–e). He identifies Phaedrus as "sick" (*nosounti*, 228b) with a fascination for speeches, and also as being a "lover" (*erastou*, 228c) of speech making. Phaedrus confesses to having a written copy of the speech, and produces it—from within his cloak, no less (*Phaedrus* 228d)—a gesture that caused Socrates no little dismay when Charmides was the young man in his presence (*Charmides* 155d). And then he commences to read.

Here, at the outset of this strange dialogue, Plato is underlining the difference between written and oral communication. We are presented with the opposite condition from that which initiated the *Symposium*. In the former, we heard people relate speeches they had heard at third and fourth hand, some years previously. Here, we are in the alleged immediacy of the written word. It cannot help but seem strange to us, once Plato has underlined this issue in this way, that the Platonic (not Socratic) dialogues also take the form of written speeches, things which are written *in imitation of* spoken speech.

All of these Socratic-Platonic speeches, that is to say, are speeches that are written to be heard. This makes them, ironically enough, very like the Homeric poems and hymns, the Pindaric odes, Sappho's lyrics, and even the great tragedies and comedies of the classical Athenian renaissance. All of these materials are books to us, written words, but all of them lived and breathed as oral performance in antiquity. There is thus a powerful irony in the very act of reading a Platonic dialogue, an irony that is not lost on Plato himself.

Lysias' is a curious kind of speech, as we have already seen. It creates a dilemma very much like a scene out of a situation-comedy, in which a good writer is hired to compose a love speech, or a love letter, for some-one else who cannot write so well. Lysias' is a *contracted* love-speech, one that he has presumably been *paid* to write. It is all quite strange.

Then the speech turns still stranger. For the strategy Lysias selects is nothing short of erotically bizarre (*Phaedrus* 231a–234c). He attempts to talk this anonymous *erōmenos* into a love affair by insisting that he (the equally anonymous speaker of the speech, but clearly *not* the writer of the speech) is not really "in love" with the would-be *erōmenos*. That fact will make the whole relationship safer, more in control, and generally easier to bear, the speaker promises. In the absence of *erōs*, he suggests, there will not be the threat of those deforming emotions—of jealousy, of anger, not to mention all of the other emotional perturbations that make "true love" so difficult and so trying. That, Phaedrus grins, positively delighted by it all, "is what's so clever about it" (*Phaedrus* 227c). Lysias, so it would seem, has already seduced one member of his audience. It is left to Socrates to offer the sort of counter-charm (*Republic* 608a) that is his trademark.

Socrates admits that it was a pretty good speech, but that he has heard better. It is interesting that Lysias' speech seems to break off rather abruptly at the end: "if you want [*potheis*] more, or think I've left some-thing out, then ask [*erōta*]" (*Phaedrus* 234c). Unimpressed, Socrates means to ask. Surely "the lovely [*tēs kalēs*] Sappho," or else "the wise [*tou sophou*] Anacreon" (*Phaedrus* 235c), has spoken at least as elo-quently about the power of the erotic, he notes. Then he brashly suggests that he himself could offer a speech that would rival Lysias' offering. The *agōn* commences. Socrates delivers, and offers a speech that sur-passes even Lysias' carefully crafted oratory (*Phaedrus* 237a–241d). He begins the speech by invoking the Muses. And he ends it with what Phaedrus mistakenly took to be "the middle" (*mesoun*, *Phaedrus* 241d). Socrates' speech shares two essential assumptions with Lysias' speech. First, he assumes that *erōs* is a madness, and that this is a *bad* thing. Sec-ondly, he assumes that erotic pleasure can be *detached from* erotic pain. He is badly wrong on both counts (*Phaedrus* 244a).

Having concluded his speech, Socrates gets up to leave the grove in which they are luxuriating, and so to return to the city where he feels more at home. Caught in the act, as it were, he is visited by his infamous *daimōn*, that private voice (*phonē*) or sign (*sēmeion*, *Phaedrus* 242c) that speaks to him in strictly negative fashion, informing him when he has done something wrong, or else is about to do so. Socrates' *daimōn* informs him that, in the interest of impressing Phaedrus (and probably of seducing him as well), Socrates has been both foolish (*euēthē*) and impious (*asebēs*, *Phaedrus* 242d). He has actually sinned against a god, the god Erōs (*Phaedrus* 242e). Socrates then offers a second speech, as we have already seen, in order to repent, in order to correct his error, and in order to keep this god from taking away his own erotic skill (*erōtikēn technēn*, *Phaedrus* 257a). In Lysias' and Socrates' first speeches, the language of *erastēs* and *erōmenos* are prominent. In the second speech, they disappear. And it is here, in this second speech (*Phaedrus* 244a–257b), that the famous claim is made about the four sorts of madness, each of them a gift of the gods, not mere symptoms of human illness. *Erōs*, as we have already seen, is the last and best of these four.

There are many things to be said about this curious, second Socratic speech. Socrates is speaking in a manner to which we are unaccustomed. He himself keeps telling Phaedrus that he feels funny, that his muse, and his mania, is running away with him. He is inspired—by the beauty of the place, by the beauty of the young man before him, by the power of the topic they have chosen to discuss. The dialogue also has a curious pace, stopping and starting and stopping again, its halting cadence a very apt imitation of the gentle-then-eruptive rhythms of love itself.

But Socrates' wide-wandering second speech and the discussion it elicits have two components that make it one of the most confusing presentations in the Platonic corpus. The speech begins in a manner that we have come to expect by now: with a discussion of the erotic. But its decisive moments come in two lovely mythic and metaphoric descriptions of the human soul (*Phaedrus* 245c–250b, 253d–254e). It is here that Socrates reminds us that *only* the gods can say what things are in themselves; human beings are especially good at saying what such things are *like* (*Phaedrus* 246a). There is no cartography of the human soul, but there are myths and metaphors. No sooner has he shared his own mythic vision with Phaedrus—the image of *erōs* giving the soul back its wings, as well as the more disturbing, and violent, metaphor of the human soul as a chariot—than he leads Phaedrus off into a curious tangential discussion that takes the form of still another set of myths: the curious and playful myth of the cicadas (*Phaedrus* 259a–d), and the vaguely Egyptian Myth of Theuth (*Phaedrus* 274d–275b), which is designed to explain the mystery of the invention of writing.

And it is here at last that our question comes into better focus. Is this one dialogue, or two, or three? What is the relation of the first speech to the second one, and what is their mutual relation to the third part of the dialogue? What, that is to say, can be the connection that Plato means to draw—between love, psychology, and writing?

PSYCHOLOGY

Briefly put, the question raised by this discussion of the human soul is a question that Plato himself posed already at the end of the Early Period, in several crucial discussions in the *Meno* and the *Gorgias*. It takes the form of a question we examined already in the introduction (*Meno* 70a): *didakton hē aretē;* "Can virtue be taught (or learned)?" It seems an innocuous enough question, yet it would haunt the next five hundred years of Greek moral enquiry. It is not a simple question at all, because what it really asks us to consider is whether we think moral *improvement* is a genuine human possibility or not.

Can virtue be taught, or learned, and if so, then how is this done? "Philosophy" is the Greek buzzword that provided one possible answer to that question, in much the same way that "ethics" does in our own day and age. The problem is that this answer doesn't tell us very much. In the *Meno*, Socrates suggests that "virtue is a kind of knowledge (*epistēmē*)" (*Meno* 87c). This proves to be a fascinating, and really rather radical claim, once it is unpacked.

If virtue is a kind of knowledge, then it would seem, at least in principle, that it can be learned. Moral philosophy has an important cognitive component, as I suggested in the introduction. If virtue is a kind of knowledge, then what is really being suggested by Socrates is the possibility that rationality may be a complete way of life. The point bears emphasizing: rationality may be a complete way of life.

If the moral agent knows—really knows, now—that doing X is wrong, then there is absolutely no rational explanation for doing so. The aspiration captured by that insight lies at the heart of most Socratic investigation. Either we will come to the realization that we do not know what we thought we knew, or else we will actually learn it. In one dialogue after another throughout the Early Period, we see self-styled experts claim a kind of knowledge—about courage, or piety, or even justice itself—and then we witness Socrates draw them elenchically to the painful realization that they do not know what they thought they knew. As Agathon discovered in the *Symposium* (201c), he did not even know what he was saying, although he said it very prettily.

The crucial point here—it was easy enough to miss even in antiquity, and I suspect that this is one of the reasons Socrates was killed—is that Socrates was not interested in the solely negative task of unmasking pretension and pretended knowledge. Socrates' moral agenda was ultimately a positive one. He wanted to force moral intuitions closer to the surface. He wanted superficially emotive appeals to become more disciplined, more intellectually rigorous, and thus more rational. Now, "rationality," on the Socratic model, seems to have something to do with being able to give an account (*logos*) of a conviction. He wanted moral convictions to be able to speak in their own defense, to be able to withstand close, and even hostile, scrutiny.

If we are able to get to the point where we can give an account of why we believe X to be wrong—to give an account of the wrongness of X—then we will, almost by definition, be rendered incapable of doing X again. If moral opinion is transformed into a kind of moral knowledge, then it would be, by definition, *irrational* to violate such knowledge through a failure of moral action. The astonishing claim that "virtue is knowledge"—at least until the later *Platonic* realization that "knowledge" itself is an idea that allows of no easy definition—implies a fairly rigorous kind of moral perfectionism. So, I suspect, did Socrates.

Plato's dilemma is somewhat different than Socrates' in the Erotic Period. His dilemma concerns how to explain the persistence of moral *failure*, not how to give an account of moral *knowledge*. Socrates seems to be suggesting that, if we come to realize the rational fact that any of these immoral practices is indeed wrong, then we will cease engaging in them. And up to a point, Plato agrees. Or rather, Plato wants to agree. But there is an essential problem with this account. It is the enduring problem of moral failure. Realizing this launched Plato on his own most creative period of reflection, the Erotic Period.

There is a problem with the rationalist account of moral behavior, and it is *the absence of desire*. It is true: the statement "I can't believe that I am about to . . ." *is* a profoundly irrational statement. Yet it is also all-too-recognizable. And no arena of human life is more fraught with the potential for such irrationality than the erotic. Plato's account of the human soul in the *Phaedrus* represents a powerful admission on his part of the sheer *power* of irrationality, symbolized here by a wild horse tethered to a well-trained one, forever dragging the entire assembly off the beaten track. The metaphor insists that *the soul is divided against itself*. This is a devastating admission, one that seriously qualifies, if it does not entirely subvert, Socrates' moral optimism. Plato seems to be confessing that the moral agent can indeed still do X, all the while admitting X to be wrong. He is concerned with finding an appropriately "moral science," one that can help to describe this experience, and perhaps to help explain it. He latches onto the rhetoric of *erōs* as an especially powerful way to get at the problems he has now identified. And the "science" he proposes is psychology: the giving of an account, not of morality, but of the human soul.

Perhaps now we begin to see what the *Phaedrus* is actually about. It is partly about Plato's coming to terms with the Socratic project, and of making it more fully his own. We see why the dialogue begins, as *all* the Erotic Dialogues begin, with *erōs*. For, of all human experiences, none is so rich as *erōs* with the potential for stepping outside of one's own mind, and in essence, for watching oneself fail. The power of desire—as the poets about whom Plato worried, and with whom Socrates was in love, all insist—is an almost overwhelming power.

A lot hinges on that qualification: *almost*. Plato raises the same issue in the *Republic* (607e–608b), where we see the same tripartite metaphor for the human soul. He does so in the selfsame dialogue in which he worries most explicitly about the power of poetry and its place in the ideal *polis*, not to mention in a proper moral pedagogy. He has seemed to many to want to be rid of poetry altogether. I hope that I have dispensed with that superficial view of the matter in this book. Socrates is erotically involved with poetry; he could not put poetry away if he tried. Even were he to break with it, he would not be able to get entirely away from it. And that meditation leads Plato now to still another question explicitly addressed in the *Phaedrus*: namely, the question of writing itself.

WRITING

The Myth of Theuth (*Phaedrus* 274c–275b) closes the circle of this curiously circular dialogue, bringing us back to the point at which we set off—that playful back and forth between Phaedrus and Socrates where, in effect, they compared the fidelity of oral and written forms of communication. The issue, we will recall, hinged on the question of memory. Would Phaedrus remember Lysias' speech exactly, or would it be preferable for him to read it? It appears to be better for Phaedrus to read the speech. Socrates, by contrast, never speaks from a script, least of all in this manic and inspired setting. The truth, for Socrates, "is either new or not at all."[5] He composes his speeches as he goes.

Now, anyone who has even a passing acquaintance with Platonic philosophy will sit up to take notice of such a claim, especially given this invocation of memory and remembering. For memory was explicitly related to this Platonic account of the human soul, as well as to the notion of knowledge that became prominent in the transitional dialogues which take us from the Early Period to the Erotic Period.

"Knowledge," Socrates also suggested in the *Meno* (81c, 85b–e), is not acquired out of thin air, nor is it planted in our otherwise empty heads by good and gifted teachers. Rather, Socrates prefers the metaphor which suggests that knowledge is a kind of recollection (*anamnēsis*)— recollection of things that the soul once knew but has now (temporally) forgotten. Education is thus an exercise in *retrieval*, in bringing back to consciousness moral truths the incarnate soul really does already know, somewhere. We are meeting the old Socratic challenge of bringing intuitions into the light, the light of *logos*.

The problem with which Plato has now elected to wrestle is the fact that writing, which was initially invented to aid the memory, actually hinders, where it does not destroy, the memory. As Theuth puts it, writing is a sort of drug (*pharmakon*) that is good at reminding (*hypomnēsis*), but not good at remembering (*mnēmēs*, *Phaedrus* 275a).

The archaeological evidence from the Bronze Age is instructive here.[6] Writing *is* a technology, a technology that *does* seem to have been invented to aid in remembering, in keeping track of supplies, supplies that were stored in the great palace complexes on Crete and on the mainland. Such writing is indeed a "reminder," in much the same way that our checkbooks are. For whatever reason, the human mind—with the notable exception of the *idiot savant*—is not well equipped to keep track of numbers and numerical accounts. Counting is best done in print.

After the collapse of the Bronze Age civilizations, there came a period of darkness in which we do not know a great deal about what was happening in the "Greek" world. There is little evidence of monumental architecture or of urban development, and thus there is little left for archaeologists to find. The technology of writing was also forgotten, so we do not know what these people were eating, or trading, and the like. Then, coming out of the so-called Greek Dark Ages, literacy was relearned, a new alphabet was created, and the technologies of writing were almost immediately put to dramatically new uses. The Homeric poems were written down. Sappho and others began recording their own highly personal and idiosyncratic erotic voices.[7] Hymns were written as they were sung; so, too, were various Olympic and Panhellenic victory songs. Tragedy and comedy came next in their train—written texts, all, designed for oral performance. "History" was born next, and Herodotus specifically tells us that he wrote his stories down so that they would not be lost in the bleached monochrome of time. Writing had become a big business in Plato's day.[8]

Still, there are arenas in human life where writing is not the aid to memory it wishes to be. The student who becomes so dependent on his or her notebook has been enslaved by the very technology that was supposed to liberate. If the notebook is lost or misplaced, then the student believes that he or she cannot possibly remember anything from the class at all. Ask a class full of bright-eyed students "where we left off last time," and they will all dutifully look it up—in their books. None will push away from the desk and, simply, reflect. And recollect.

That seems to be Plato's concern: If knowledge really is a kind of remembering—an active, as well as a passive, endeavor—then serious epistemic damage may be done by the technology of the written word. Writing, at the end of the day, may even stand in the way of knowing. This is a very sobering message, indeed, for a man such as Plato, who spent his life in literacy, and in the attempt to remember his mentor, Socrates, in print. Perhaps one message of the *Phaedrus* is that Plato knows well that he is not "remembering" Socrates this way at all—least of all when he is putting his own words into Socrates' mouth. What Plato aspires to do, in the Erotic Period certainly, is simply to *remind* us of Socrates, and of the way of life which he laid before us to consider.

TRAJECTORIES

These are a set of insights that emerged in what I am calling Plato's Erotic Period, and they emerge most clearly in his most deliberate attempts to think morally and philosophically about the erotic life. I have no final views about where Plato was headed intellectually in this period, but a constellation of four related ideas presents itself, here at the end of the *Phaedrus*, and thus at the end of this book. What is the connection that Plato so clearly means to underline here: between love, psychology, and writing?

First, you cannot have others write about love on your behalf. That is what is preeminently wrong with Lysias' speech. (To be sure, his fundamental assumptions are flawed as well. *Erōs* is a mania and that is a good thing, not a bad thing. There is no way to detach erotic pleasure from the possibility of pain. These insights have moral implications.) The larger idea lying behind the profession of rhetoric itself is what seems most misguided about the writerly enterprise. No one can seriously attempt to write an erotic speech on someone else's behalf, least of all when it is addressed to a third party whom the writer does not know. People who read erotic poetry too often, perhaps even addictively, may be in love with the idea of love, and thus may prove themselves incapable of loving—in full attention and in spiritual richness—another, indelibly separate human soul. Here again, it is not Socrates who is erotically problematic, as Martha Nussbaum suggests, so much as it is his great rival—Lysias here, and Alcibiades elsewhere.

Second, it is important to recall that rhetoricians did not normally write love speeches. They normally wrote forensic speeches, speeches for others to deliver on their own behalf in a court of law. If you think about it—and Plato thought about little else, it would seem—then the notion of the law virtually *requires* writing. If there is no written law, then there cannot really be a legal system in the way we normally conceive of one. Rabbinic Judaism and Sunni Islam are both religious traditions which are grounded in this insight. If there is not a written law—engraved on a marble stele and erected in the marketplace or some other central political location—then we have nothing in common to which to appeal. Writing regularizes, universalizes in its way, and that is an important quality to which the law may aspire.

But Plato is not ultimately interested in law; he is interested in justice. The distinction is crucial in Plato's mature work. Plato does not want to describe the legislator, so much as he wants to describe the statesman. The legislator, as he tells us in the *Cratylus*, is a mysterious figure lost in the mists of prehistory, pre-*literate* history, and there is little more to be said about him. Plato concludes the *Statesman* (and here the term is *politikos*, not *nomothetēs*) with much the same claim. He compares the statesman to a captain and the *polis* to a ship, arguing that both rely less on textbooks (*grammata*) than on technical experience and skill (*technēn*), and that such a skill—the craft of *politeia* itself—is "more powerful than whatever science might be derivable from the laws" (*Statesman* 297a).

Plato is thus involved in the vastly paradoxical enterprise of trying to describe, in writing, the *un*written wisdom of a Socrates—to describe it, and thus to pass it along to those of us who never had the chance to meet the man. Plato's writing, too, is best thought of as a reminder, not a rememberer. We who never knew Socrates cannot possibly "remember" him. We will have an entirely different, and entirely literary, relationship to the man. The same is true of their devotees' relationship to Abraham or Moses, Jesus or Muhammad. The three scriptural monotheisms have much to learn from Plato's attentive reflections on the power of writing and the power of the erotic in this, his Erotic Period.

Third, there is a crucial moral distinction to be made between law and education. If you take moral transgression—what I have been calling "moral failure"—as your starting point, then what the soul needs is law, a way to meet the problem that failure presents. But if you see moral failure as a more correctable problem, and if such correction is your starting point, then what the soul needs is education. Socrates seems to see the soul as potentially correctable, as "morable,"[9] if you will. Plato is less certain of this, less committed to that possibility across the board in the Erotic Period.

The *Laws*, for its part, is thus really a book about laws, not about education. Yet the *Laws* presents itself as a mere "prelude" (the word is *prooimion*, also used for the Homeric "hymns," *Laws* 722d–e), a prelude to the infinitely more complex *educational* project laid out in the *Republic*. To be sure, prisons and police are necessary constituents of the *polis*; there is a necessarily restrictive, even coercive, dimension to our social life. Such matters are a *prelude* to moral education, however, and the schools will be where philosophy does its important work, if it does it anywhere at all. Plato, even in a book as allegedly "conservative" and nomothetic as the *Laws*, allows a large place for the important institutions of civil society, from schools and gymnasia, to the companionship of wine (*tēs en oinōi sunousias*) and the essential social ritual of symposia (*Laws* 646d–650b, 652a–674c). It does not take a great deal of digging, in any case, to see a powerful argument for public education in Plato, especially given how concerned Socrates always was about money, and the access to moral education of various sorts that money provides.

Finally, what Plato realizes that he cannot describe in any simple way is knowledge itself. Explaining why this is the case is the explicit work of the post–Erotic Period in Plato's thought, especially in dialogues like *Theaetetus*, *Sophist*, and *Parmenides*. And ironically enough, this aporetic point returns me to the place from which I set out at the beginning of this book.

There is an intimate connection between loving and knowing in Platonic thought; that is the single greatest discovery, the charter metaphor of the Erotic Period. There is an intimate relation between the manner of our loving and the manner of our knowing as well. The topic of the *Phaedrus* is ultimately truth (*peri alētheias*, *Phaedrus* 247c), not *erōs* alone. The two are *intimately* related ideas.

For we do not exist in a perfect realm of certainty or presence to reality, such as the gods enjoy. We live *metaxu*—in between heaven and earth, in between the gods and the lives of animals, in between appearance and reality, partaking entirely of neither realm. We possess ideas, and aspirations to a kind of certainty and a kind of permanence that elude our grasp. We live with desires that are unfulfillable. We are restless, desiring, wanting souls, as well as finite, mortal bodies.

Yet we know what we know. That is the grandly human paradox which provides the pivot around which the thought of the Erotic Period endlessly revolves. The fact that you cannot "give an account" of why you love a singular other person who makes your head spin a little more swiftly, your heart beat a little more keenly, and your soul sing a little more poetically, does not make you seriously question the love. Love stands somewhere in between ignorance and pure knowledge (*Symposium* 202a). Much of Plato's life was devoted to an exploration of this complex territory, "in the middle." By examining that richly textured emotional territory—a kind of desire that we do not share with animals, but may share with the gods—Plato discovered that he could say some important things about the kinds of knowledge which are in fact accessible to us as finite and embodied souls. Love has the capacity to be elevating, ennobling, even apotheotic in its finest moments. And *erōs*, he suggests, throughout this period and in this manner, lends us the best metaphors with which to capture it.

Notes

1. An excellent review and substantiation of this large claim has recently appeared in an elegant collection of Platonic studies by Alexander Nehamas. He suggests that—since the late 1950s, and largely through the influential rehabilitation of these Platonic ideas by the late Gregory Vlastos (to whom the book is dedicated)—the theory of forms has been primarily understood to be a "theory of universals." Nehamas disagrees, suggesting instead—and properly using *Parmenides* and *Sophist* as charter texts for this interpretation—that the theory is rather designed to show how "predication" in language and thought is possible at all. That is to say, various things are grouped together under certain overarching umbrella concepts—ideas like "tallness" and "goodness" and "beauty," to be sure, but also concepts such as "religion" or "philosophy" as I will attempt to demonstrate in the Introduction—in a way that demands philosophical explanation. The mature theory of forms, Nehamas concludes, is Plato's attempt to deliver on such a philosophical demand.

See Alexander Nehamas, *Virtues of Authenticity: Essays on Plato and Socrates* (Princeton: Princeton University Press, 1999), xxvi–xxix, xxxiii–xxxiv, 142–44, 176–223. I regret that this wonderful book appeared too late for me to make better use of it.

INTRODUCTION: ON BEGINNING CAUTIOUSLY

1. See Barry A. Kosmin and Seymour P. Lachman, *One Nation under God: Religion in Contemporary American Society* (New York: Harmony Books, 1993), 1–17.

2. "Narrative" has, of course, become a sizeable topic in its own right in contemporary moral reflection. I do *not* mean to claim, as Alasdair MacIntyre does, that all moral arguments have a narrative character [see *After Virtue*, 2nd ed. (South Bend, Ind.: University of Notre Dame Press, 1984), 204–20, 265–72].

Maintaining some essential distinction between stories and critical moral arguments seems essential in an increasingly pluralistic world where "narrative traditions" are not held in common. See my "Of Coins and Carnage: Rhetorical Violence and the Macedonian Question," *Soundings* 77.3/4 (1994): 331–66.

3. For development of the idea, see Stanley Hauerwas, *The Peaceable Kingdom: A Primer in Christian Ethics* (South Bend, Ind.: University of Notre Dame Press, 1983), 2–6. For an intriguing discussion of its philosophical implications and applications, see Zygmunt Bauman, *Life in Fragments: Essays in Postmodern Morality* (Cambridge, Mass.: Blackwell Publishers, 1995).

4. MacIntyre, *After Virtue*, 1–5.

5. Jeffrey Stout, *Ethics After Babel: The Languages of Morals and Their Discontents* (Boston, Mass.: The Beacon Press, 1988).

In this citation and the following, I intend no criticism of the books and projects in question. I mean only to notice an interesting sense of "belatedness," and thus of implicit contemporary crisis. I have enormous respect especially for Stout's work on these matters, as it eschews the very posture of despair of which I have been so critical. I am honored to be considered a participant in his "vocation." See his "Commitments and Traditions in the Study of Religious Ethics," *Journal of Religious Ethics* 25.3 (1998), 23–56, esp. 35n7. Certainly our "correctives" do work simultaneously, and in tandem.

6. David J. Fasching, *Narrative Theology After Auschwitz: From Alienation to Ethics* (Minneapolis, Minn.: Augsburg Fortress Press, 1992).

7. David J. Fasching, *The Ethical Challenge of Auschwitz and Hiroshima: Apocalypse or Utopia?* (Albany: State University of New York Press, 1993).

8. I am thinking particularly of Alasdair MacIntyre's work: *After Virtue*, 1–35; and *Whose Justice? Which Rationality?* (South Bend, Ind.: University of Notre Dame Press, 1988), 326–48.

9. I refer to this as the age-old dilemma of living between the Akropolis and the Agora, the marketplace and the mountaintop, in *Afterwords: Hellenism, Modernism, and the Myth of Decadence* (Albany: State University of New York Press, 1996), 15 passim.

10. This point is well made by James Gustafson in *Can Ethics Be Christian?* (Chicago: University of Chicago Press, 1975), esp. 1–47.

11. Martha C. Nussbaum, "Reply," *Soundings* 72.4 (1989): 746.

12. For a stunning display of the new religious diversity in urban North America, see Gary Laderman, ed., *Religions of Atlanta: Religious Diversity in the Centennial Olympic City* (Atlanta, Ga.: Scholars Press, 1996).

13. For a closer critique of this scholarly apocalypticism, see my *Afterwords*, 127ff.

14. "In England muss man sich für jede kleine Emancipation von der Theologie in furchteinflossender Weise als Moral-Fanatiker wieder zu Ehren bringen. Das ist dort die *Busse*, die man zahlt" (Nietzsche, *Sämtliche Werke* 6:113).

15. "Wenn man den christlichen Glauben aufgibt, zieht man sich damit das Recht zur christlichen Moral unter den Füssen weg. Diese versteht sich schlechterdings nicht von selbst: . . . Das Christenthum ist ein System, eine zusammengedachte und *ganze* Ansicht der Dinge. Bricht man aus ihm einen Hauptbe-

griff, den Glauben an Gott, heraus, so zerbricht man damit auch das Ganze: man hat nichts Nothwendiges mehr zwischen den Fingern. Das Christenthum setzt voraus, dass der Mensch nicht wisse, nicht wissen *könne*, was für ihn gut, was böse ist: er glaubt an Gott, der allein es weiss. Die christliche Moral ist ein Befehl; ihr Ursprung ist transscendent; sie ist jenseits aller Kritik, alles Rechts auf Kritik; sie hat nur Wahrheit, falls Gott die Wahrheit ist, —sie steht und fällt mit dem Glauben an Gott" (Nietzsche, *Sämtliche Werke* 6:113–14).

16. Nietzsche concludes *Twilight of the Idols* with this same section ("The Hammer Speaks") from *Thus Spoke Zarathustra*, as it appears in *The Portable Nietzsche*, translated by Walter Kaufmann (New York: Penguin Books, 1954), 563.

17. MacIntyre, *After Virtue*, 113.

It is interesting to note that the passage I have been quoting continues with his withering criticisms of British appeals to intuition. "For the English," Nietzsche concludes with a sigh of exasperation, "morality is not even a problem yet."

18. For a fascinating sketch of this ethos in North America, see Michael Walzer, *Spheres of Justice: A Defense of Pluralism and Equality* (New York: Basic Books, 1983), 95–128.

19. I am indebted to Peter Murphy for this insight. See his "The Triadic Moment: The Anti-Genealogy of Hellenist Marxism," *Thesis Eleven* 53 (1998): 102–13.

20. Nietzsche, *Twilight of the Idols*, "Skirmishes," §23.

21. Nietzsche's classic statement of this kind of thinking is of course *Beyond Good and Evil: Prelude to a Philosophy of the Future*, translated by Walter Kaufmann (New York: Vintage Books, 1966).

22. "*Socrates*, um es nur zu bekennen, steht mir so nahe, dass ich fast immer einen Kampf mit ihm kämpfe" (*Sämtliche Werke* 8:97).

See also the fine analysis of "Nietzsche's Attitude Toward Socrates" in Walter Kaufmann, *Nietzsche: Philosopher, Psychologist, Antichrist* 4th ed. (Princeton: Princeton University Press, 1978), 391–411.

23. See my discussion of these developments in "Hellenism on Display," *Journal of Modern Greek Studies* 15 (1997): 247–60.

24. *Wir Philologen* 6[43]; *Sämtliche Werke* 8:114:

> Man bewundert jetzt das Evangelium der Schildkröte—ach, die griechen liefen zu rasch. Ich suche nicht nach glücklichen Zeiten in der Geschichte, aber nach solchen, welche einen gunstigen Boden für die *Erzeugung* des Genius bieten. Da finde ich die Zeiten vor den Perserkriegen. Man kann sie nicht genau genug kennen lernen.

For a discussion of the importance of this essay on subsequent Nietzschean developments, see my *Afterwords*, 23–63.

25. Says Alasdair MacIntyre: "the introduction of the word 'intuition' by a moral philosopher is always a signal that something has gone badly wrong with an argument" (*After Virtue*, 69).

26. Heidegger, *Plato's "Sophist*," translated by Richard Rojcewicz and André Schuwer (Indianapolis: Indiana University Press, 1997), 16–17.

27. Joseph Cropsey, *Plato's World: Man's Place in the Cosmos* (Chicago: University of Chicago Press, 1995), 149–52.

28. Romans 7:18–25.

29. John Boswell, *Christianity, Social Tolerance, and Homosexuality: Gay People in Western Europe from the Beginning of the Christian Era to the Fourteenth Century* (Chicago: University of Chicago Press, 1980), 116.

30. *Ecce Homo*, "Why I Am A Destiny," §6. In his calmer moments, Nietzsche is more specific, explaining that he is the first philosopher to undertake an honest investigation of the psychology of the moralist, and of the priest. See *On the Genealogy of Morals*, translated by Walter Kaufmann (New York: Vintage Books, 1967).

31. For a wonderful sketch of these philosophical developments, see Martha C. Nussbaum, *The Therapy of Desire: Theory and Practice in Hellenistic Ethics* (Princeton: Princeton University Press, 1994).

32. T. E. Lawrence, *Seven Pillars of Wisdom: A Triumph* (New York: Anchor Books/Doubleday, 1926, 1935), 41.

33. See my *Afterwords*, 201–31.

I. SYMPOSIUM, THE FIRST: PLATO

1. See, for instance, the telling comments made at *Republic* 392d and 394b–c, and again at *Symposium* 205c–d.

2. This tradition is preserved in the *Palatine Anthology* (IX.506):

Nine are the Muses, as the many say.
But this is careless.
For here is Sappho, the Lesbian.
She is the tenth.

See D. A. Campbell, *Greek Lyric I: Sappho and Alcaeus* (Loeb Classical Library of Harvard University Press, 1982), 48–49.

3. For an extraordinary and exhaustive examination of these traditions, see Alice Swift Riginos, *Platonica: The Anecdotes Concerning the Life and Writings of Plato* (Leiden: E.J. Brill, 1976), 43–51.

4. Riginos, *Platonica*, 43.

5. These same categories, of *epistēmē* and *orthē doxa*, appear centrally in the *Symposium*, as I will demonstrate in the next chapter.

6. Proclus' comments are printed in Riginos, *Platonica*, 45. The translation is my own.

7. Perhaps no translator has captured the dramatic quality of one such Platonic dialogue better than my good friend, Avi Sharon, whose *Symposium* appeared earlier this year (Newburyport, Mass.: Focus Philosophical Library, 1998), 13ff.

8. For a concise summary of this point, see Frances M. Cornford, *Before and After Socrates* (Cambridge: Cambridge University Press, 1966), ix, 32.

9. Carl Sagan, *Cosmos* (New York: Ballantine Books, 1980).

10. Ibid., 139–60.

11. Ibid., 140–41, emphasis mine.

12. Ibid., 149.

13. Ibid., 156.

14. For a more favorable and balanced view than the one I am offering, albeit briefly here, see John Boslough, *Masters of Time: Cosmology at the End of the Age of Innocence* (New York: Addison-Wesley, 1992).

15. See my review of Sagan's last book, *Pale Blue Dot: A Vision of the Human Future in Space* (Reading, Mass.: Random House, 1994) in the *Journal of the American Academy of Religion* 64.2 (1996): 459–63.

16. Stephen Hawking, *A Brief History of Time: From the Big Bang to Black Holes* (New York: Bantam Books, 1988), 94.

I do not know which is finally the more morally troubling aspect of this statement, the cavalier manner in which commitments to theories are made, then remade, or the deeper moral deformation in the use of such a magazine as the "stake." But it is admittedly far too early for me to be moralizing the "erotic" life in this book.

17. The image is a remarkable one, grounded in the Old Attic saying, "If the wind won't move the boat, then use the oars." See Liddell and Scott, *A Greek-English Lexicon, Abridged Edition* (Oxford at the Clarendon Press, 1980), 566. That is to say, a second-sailing is also a *second-best* manner of locomotion. That Socrates should say this of his own method is a remarkably chastened account of the philosophical enterprise as Socrates conceives it.

See also R. Hackforth's commentary in *Plato's Phaedo* (The Cambridge University Press, 1972), 127, note 5, as well as Seth Bernadete's *Socrates' Second Sailing: On Plato's "Republic"* (Chicago: University of Chicago Press, 1989), 1–5.

18. The example used is, interestingly enough, homosexual activity. By defining this as "against nature," Plato is essentially undercutting the lion's share of the discussion in the *Symposium*, where same-sex male love is the predominant model. This passage from the *Laws* thus clearly bears far greater attention than it normally receives.

Ironically enough, the passage received a virtual explosion of recent attention at the Colorado State Supreme Court, where the matter of gay sexuality recently became an issue again. In the 1995 case, *Romer v. Evans* (which was later argued at the Supreme Court in 1996: 116 S. Ct. 1620) the question before the court concerned the constitutionality of a Colorado state referendum that denied gays the right to appeal for relief from discrimination on the basis of their sexual orientation. In three full days of testimony, classicists and philosophers such as John Finnis and Martha Nussbaum quarreled over this precise passage from the *Laws*, among other things.

See John Finnis, "'Shameless Acts' in Colorado: Abuse of Scholarship in Constitutional Cases," *Academic Questions* (Fall 1994): 10–41; John Finnis, "Law, Morality, and 'Sexual Orientation,'" *Notre Dame Law Review* 69.5 (1994): 1049–76; and Martha Nussbaum, "Platonic Love and Colorado Law: The Relevance of Ancient Greek Norms to Modern Sexual Controversies," *Virginia Law Review* 80 (1994): 1515–1651, reprinted and abridged with a response by Richard Posner in Robert B. Louden and Paul Schollmeier, eds., *The Greeks and Us: Essays in Honor of Arthur W. H. Adkins* (Chicago: University of Chicago Press, 1996), 168–223.

19. *Mēdeis ageōmētrētos eisitō*, it read over the door of the Academy: "Let no one who is unmathematical enter here."

20. A fresh approach was recently suggested by Joseph Cropsey in his *Plato's World: Man's Place in the Cosmos* (Chicago: University of Chicago Press, 1995). Cropsey suggests that we attend to the *internal* chronology Plato himself clearly enunciates, an extended story running from *Theatetus*, to *Euthyphro*, *Cratylus*, *Sophist*, *Statesman*, *Apology*, *Crito*, and *Phaedo*. Cropsey's is a fascinating and elegant thesis, I think, strange in places, but not wholly incompatable with what I am offering here.

21. This position is neatly summarized by A. E. Taylor in his now-classic *The Mind of Plato* (Ann Arbor, Mich.: Ann Arbor Paperbacks, 1922, 1960), 26–29. Even more pertinent is Gregory Vlastos' *Socratic Studies*, edited by Myles Burnyeat (Cambridge: Cambridge University Press, 1994), 135. For an interesting, slightly different and more nuanced chronology, see Alexander Nehamas, *The Art of Living: Socratic Reflections from Plato to Foucault* (Berkeley: University of California Press, 1998), 196n33.

22. I have not dated the extremely difficult *Menexenus*, nor the two *Hippias'*. And I do not include the probably spurious (however interesting) pseudo-Platonic dialogues *Epinomis*, *Lovers*, *Theages*, and the two *Alcibiades'*. I will however speak briefly of these dialogues in the third chapter, and then again about the longer *Alcibiades* in the conclusion.

23. See the remarkable text, *"An Apology for Actors" (1612) by Thomas Heywood and "A Refutation of the Apology for Actors" (1615) by I.G.*, edited by Richard H. Perkinson (New York: Scholars' Facsimiles & Reprints, 1941) for a wonderful illustration of the contours of this fascinating religious debate.

24. Julius A. Elias presents an interesting thesis about that in *Plato's Defense of Poetry* (Albany: State University of New York Press, 1984). He notices that Socrates suggests that poetry *might* need to be excised from the ideal

republic, *unless* someone can offer a compelling defense of it. Elias argues, and I agree, that dialogues like the *Phaedrus* constitute that defense.

25. This same word, "republic" (*politeia*), of course, gives us the title to Plato's other great utopian tract.

26. This word has a negative connotation in the *Republic* whose metaphysical hierarchy places imitation at three removes from the truth [601d–602c]. The word is rehabilitated by Aristotle, who makes it the cornerstone of his definition of "tragedy," at *Poetics* 1447a.

See also S.H. Butcher's essay "'Imitation' As an Aesthetic Term," in *Aristotle's Theory of Poetry and Fine Art* (New York: Dover, 1951), 121–62.

27. I will develop this point at some length in the next chapter.

28. *Iliad* VI.484.

29. There is, Socrates and Plato are quick to add, a "craft" (*technē*) of justice, rather than a "form" (*eidos*) of it. This trope has been nicely developed by Richard D. Parry in *Plato's Craft of Justice* (State University of New York Press, 1996). In that analysis, Parry makes much more of the doctrine of the forms than I do, and he argues for the centrality of the soul-body distinction in Plato's Middle Period in much the way that I am trying to think against. This leads him to read Diotima's speech in the *Symposium* as far more consistent within the larger context of the dialogue than I do. Even with these differences—and they *are* significant—Parry's book helps me to make the point I am trying to make here: that there is no form of *erōs*. Rather, loving well, on the Platonic model, is better thought of as a craft, as perhaps *the* crucial instantiation of one's apprenticeship to virtue.

30. See Cephalus' telling remarks about *erōs* and old age, at *Republic* 329a–c.

31. Hans-Georg Gadamer, *Dialogue and Dialectic: Eight Hermeneutical Studies On Plato*, translated by P. Christopher Smith (New Haven, Conn.: Yale University Press, 1980), 118.

32. This is one of the *Athenaum Fragments* (no. 84) translated by Peter Firchow and available in *Friedrich Schlegel: Philosophical Fragments* (Minneapolis: University of Minnesota Press, 1991), 28.

For more on the implications of the idea of "beginning in the middle," see Andrew Bowie, *From Romanticism to Critical Theory: The Philosophy of German Literary Theory* (New York: Routledge, 1996), esp. 104–6, as well as my review of the book, "So You Do Theory, Do You?," *Philosophy Today* 42.4 (1998): 440–48.

2. SYMPOSIUM, THE SECOND: THE EROTIC

1. Recent work on this important social institution in the archaic and classical periods suggests some necessary qualification of this statement. In particular, it serves to qualify the impact of that word 'just'. These dinner—or rather,

drinking—parties served an important social function, creating a setting in which certain aristocratic values could be celebrated, even as they were being challenged in the face of profound democratic reforms in *poleis* like Athens.

See Oswyn Murray, *Early Greece*, 2d Ed. (Cambridge, Mass.: Harvard University Press, 1993), 207–19, as well as his indispensible edited volume, *Sympotica: A Symposium on the "Symposion"* (Oxford: The Clarendon Press, 1990), 3–13, 135–45, 238–60. For an interesting attempt to sketch out some of the parallels to these social affairs in aristocratic *women's* lives, see Margaret Williamson, *Sappho's Immortal Daughters* (Cambridge, Mass.: Harvard University Press, 1995), esp. 69–72.

2. By the time the war is over, Agathon had gone into exile in Macedonia, Euripides had died there, and Sophocles had died at home, in Athens, some months later. Alcibiades was exiled as well, though not voluntarily, then still later, he was killed in Asia Minor. Finally, several years after the final defeat of Athens in the war, Socrates himself was executed there.

3. John Boswell made this point one of the mainstays of his historical method, with varying degrees of success. Each of his massive medieval studies begins with a long discussion of certain essential words, and the difficulty of translating them into a modern idiom. See *Christianity, Social Tolerance, and Homosexuality: Gay People in Western Europe from the Beginning of the Christian Era to the Fourteenth Century* (Chicago: University of Chicago Press, 1981), 41–59; *The Kindness of Strangers: The Abandonment of Children in Western Europe from Late Antiquity to the Renaissance* (New York: Pantheon Books, 1988), 22–39; and *Same-Sex Unions in Premodern Europe* (New York: Vintage Books, 1994), 3–27.

4. This is much clearer in Greek than it can be made in translation. Not only does the whole dialogue take place in quotation marks, as it were ("then he said," "then she added," etc.), but Greek grammar insists upon the difference when phrases appear in dependent clauses ("he said *that* . . ."). Thus the verb-forms throughout this entire dialogue—its heavy reliance upon the optative, the infinitive, and the passive voice—all serve as constant reminders to the reader that this story is being told at a considerable emotional and temporal distance.

For more on this point, see Martha Nussbaum's *The Fragility of Goodness: Luck and Ethics in Greek Tragedy and Philosophy* (Cambridge: Cambridge University Press, 1986), 167–68.

For my Greek text of the *Symposium*, I am using the critical edition by Sir Kenneth J. Dover (Cambridge: Cambridge University Press, 1980).

5. Actually Glaukon has heard the story already from an anonymous third party who heard it in *his* turn from a man named Phoinix (the same man, so it seems, who was told the story by Aristodemus), but Glaukon insists that he didn't tell the story very well, and it was all mixed up.

6. Martha Nussbaum hotly contests this reading, at *Soundings* 72.4 (1989): 760, claiming that Socrates cannot have had an erotic relationship with Diotima: "he doesn't pursue, or really love, anyone." The Greek at *Symposium*

201d seems to tell a different story: *ē dē kai eme* ta erōtika *edidaxen*, "she taught me *erōtika*."

See also Dover's editorial comments on this passage in his critical edition of the *Symposium*, 137.

7. Two excellent resources in this attempted reconstruction are Margaret Williamson, *Sappho's Immortal Daughters* (Cambridge, Mass.: Harvard University Press, 1995), and Ellen Greene, ed., *Reading Sappho: Contemporary Approaches* (Berkeley: University of California Press, 1996). I am currently engaged in a book-length study of Sappho, tentatively entitled *In Sappho's Name*, which examines the broader, and so-to-speak "archaic," feminine sexuality we see embodied in her poetry.

8. Actually, the scholarly consensus has been, rather uncritically and simplistically, that Plato has created this character, and given her a hometown that sounds roughly like *mantis*, or "prophetess." The fact that we can say no more than this is an appalling statement about our own listless lack of creativity as readers and listeners to this story. There is *much* more than this to be said, I think. See *Phaedrus* 244b–c.

9. This last point is slightly overstated. We *are* told, parenthetically, that Aristodemus is from Kydathenaium (*Symposium* 173b) and that Phaedrus is from Myrrhinous (*Symposium* 176d), but nothing is made of these facts and they are not amplified. The strangeness, and foreignness of Diotima, however, is emphasized and her home city is mentioned three times in the dialogue (*Symposium* 201d, e; 209d; 211d). It seems to me that Mantineia *is* made an issue, in a way that these other places are not.

10. I will be making heavy use of Pausanias' second-century record of the antiquities in mainland Greece in answering this question, just as I will be making extensive use of Plutarch's biographies in asking the same questions of Alcibiades. In both cases I am less interested in these authors' "scientific" or historical objectivity than in how they tell stories and what stories they repeatedly tell.

That is to say, this essay is meant to be an exploration of what a fourth-century Greek would have thought when he or she heard the names 'Mantineia' and 'Alcibiades', 'Socrates', and 'Diotima'. For *that* kind of question—what we will be calling "love's knowledge"—Plutarch's and Pausanias' folksy stories are really perfect.

11. There is also a second Pausanias at our dinner party, who delivers one of the speeches on Love. I will try, therefore, to be clear in my essay about which Pausanias I have in mind. In most cases, it will be clear enough.

12. Pausanias, *Guide to Greece*, 2 volumes, translated by Peter Levi (New York: Penguin Books, 1971).

For the Greek text of Pausanias, I am using *Pausaniae: Graciae Descriptio*, edited by Frederico Spiro in three volumes (Stuttgart: B. G. Teubner Verlagsgesellschaft, 1959).

13. Pausanias, *Guide to Greece* VIII.2.4–5 and Spiro, *Pausanias: Graeciae Descriptio*, 2:260. See also the fascinating, if extreme, discussion by Paul Veyne,

Did the Greeks Believe Their Myths? An Essay on the Constitutive Imagination, translated by Paula Wissig (Chicago: University of Chicago Press, 1988), 72–74 and 95–102 on "the Pausanias question." For a marvelous contemporary reconstruction of this picture of the heroic age, see Roberto Calasso, *The Marriage of Cadmus and Harmony,* translated by Tim Parks (New York: Vintage Books, 1993).

14. For a marvelous nineteenth-century travelogue, with an engaging description of the topography and the ruins in this area, see William Martin Leake, *Travels in the Morea* [1830, 3 Volumes] (Amsterdam: Adolf M. Hakkert, 1968), I:101–15.

15. Pausanias, *Guide to Greece* VIII.6.1–3; cf. *Iliad* II.603–11.

16. Pausanias, *Guide to Greece* X.20.2; cf. Herodotus, *Histories* VII.202.

17. See Robert A. Bauslaugh, *The Concept of Neutrality in Classical Greece* (Berkeley: University of California Press, 1991), 3–165.

18. Pausanias, *Guide to Greece* V.4.7, VIII.8.6.

19. The conditions of this alliance, a sort of mutual nonaggression pact with further guarantees of military aid, may be found in Thucydides, *The Peloponnesian War* V.47.

The conditions of the alliance were carved into a *stēlē* that was then erected in the central marketplace of Mantineia.

20. See Thucydides, *The Peloponnesian War* V.43; and Plutarch, *Life of Alcibiades* §15.

For the Greek text of Plutarch's biographies, I am using the edition by Konrad Ziegler, *Plutarchi: Vitae Parallelae* (Leipzig: B.G. Teubner, 1959), 226–79.

21. Thucydides, *The Peloponnesian War* V.63–80; and Leake, *Travels in the Morea,* 3:44–77.

22. Pausanias, *Guide to Greece* VIII.8.6; cf. Thucydides, *The Peloponnesian War* VI.29.

23. Pausanias, *Guide to Greece* VIII.8.6–10; cf. Xenophon, *Hellenika* I.5.2–I.6.5. In a remarkable feat of military engineering, the Spartans caused the river that ran through the city to flood; the waters essentially ate away the mud-brick fortifications surrounding the city.

24. Using this rhetorical aside as a marker, we know that Plato must have penned the *Symposium* sometime *after* 385 BCE.

25. Pausanias sketches out very quickly the subsequent history of the place. After the Theban defeat of Sparta at Leuktra, the Mantineians were caught trying to negotiate a private peace with Sparta—the temptation to neutrality, again—but then war sucked them back in on the Spartan side. As soon as possible, they broke the alliance, and became the most steadfast member of the anti-Spartan Achaean League. Given the Mantineians' remarkable gift for backing the wrong side, Pausanias concludes in astonishment that they fought *for* Augustus and *against* Antony at Actium in 31 BCE. The Roman period thus proved to be among the happiest and most stable in Mantineian memory.

26. Pausanias, *Guide to Greece* VIII.5.2.

27. Granted, there *are* male deities present here, but they are all less interesting, somehow. There are the predictable temples to Zeus the Saviour, to Poseidon (who seems to have been the patron god of Mantineia [VIII.5.5]), to Helios the Sun, shrines to several local heroes, and one very unusual temple to "the generous god." My point is simply that this is all pretty standard stuff, as the *female* cults at Mantineia seem not to have been.

Hence I am wondering, when we hear that Diotima is from *Mantineia*, are we perhaps meant to think of femininity, of love, and of the feminine *difference*?

28. Pausanias, *Guide to Greece* VIII.5.11, whose priestess is always a young virgin girl.

29. Already in the *Iliad* (IV.50–52), Hera mentions Argos, Sparta, and Mycenae as her three favorite cities in the Greek world. This greatest of goddesses, the consort of Zeus himself, has had a very long and very special affinity for this part of the Greek world, which we might loosely call "Arkadia."

30. Pausanias, *Guide to Greece* VIII.6.5.

31. Pausanias, *Guide to Greece* VIII.8.1, VIII.9.6.

32. Which is precisely how Sappho invokes her, as *symmachos*, in the one complete Sapphic hymn (dedicated to Aphrodite) that we still possess.

33. Pausanias, *Guide to Greece* VIII.6.5; VIII.9.6 and Spiro, *Pausanias: Graeciae Descriptio*, 2:271, 278. The allusion to Aphrodite in her "heavenly" (*Ouranian*) and her "common" (*Pandēmon*) aspects, which lies at the heart of Eryximachus's speech (*Symposium* 180D) is made later at IX.16.2 and Spiro, *Pausanias: Graeciae Descriptio*, 3:35.

34. Pausanias, *Guide to Greece* VIII.9.1 and Spiro, *Pausanias: Graeciae Descriptio*, 2:277.

35. This semidivine hero also makes an appearance in the *Symposium* at 186e.

36. Martha Nussbaum, *The Fragility of Goodness*, 165–99.

37. "Narrative Emotions: Beckett's Genealogy of Love" as reprinted in Nussbaum, *Love's Knowledge: Essays on Philosophy and Literature* (New York: Oxford University Press, 1990), 287. This essay appeared originally in *Ethics* 98:2 (1988): 225–54.

38. See the remarkable discussion in Kenneth J. Dover, *Greek Homosexuality* (Cambridge, Mass.: Harvard University Press, 1977, 1989), 68–73.

39. Aristotle, *Metaphysics* 997b–998a, 1011b–1012a, 1023a, 1055a–b, 1056a, 1058a–b.

40. I am indebted to Christine Downing's very fine essay, "Diotima and Alcibiades: An Alternative Reading of the *Symposium*" in *Soundings* 72.4 (1989): 631–55, especially 637, 645–46, 654.

41. This is the essential point that, behind the at times overdrawn polemics, has animated Camille Paglia's passionately argued views of the matter. It also

accounts for her astonishing rise to short-lived kind of media prominence. See her provocative suggestions in "No Law in the Arena: A Pagan Theory of Sexuality" in *Vamps and Tramps* (New York: Vintage Books, 1994), xxiii, 67–92.

Better and more balanced is Richard Carp's "Perception and Material Culture: Historical and Cross-Cultural Perspectives," *Historical Reflections* 23.3 (1997): 269–300, esp. 283.

42. The apparent paradox—that these erotic relationships are designed to be short-lived, given the apparent importance of the age differential and the assumed youth of the *erōmenos*—is addressed explicitly in Pausanias's speech at our party (*Symposium* 181e and 183d–e).

43. For these and subsequent comments, I am indebted to Kenneth J. Dover's extraordinary and pioneering study, *Greek Homosexuality*, esp. 183–84. It is the real, and almost single-handed contribution of this volume to get classicists to talk about this dimension of "the Greek experience." It is astonishing only after one has read the book that it had not all been discussed before.

44. Kenneth J. Dover, *Greek Homosexuality*, 6.

45. Plutarch, *Life of Alcibiades* 1.5 and Konrad Ziegler, *Plutarchi: Vitae Parallelae* I.2:227.

46. One of the nicest cases in point is Ismene's comment in the opening argument of the *Antigone*, where she tells her sister: *all' amēchanon erāis*, "you want the impossible."

In the course of the argument, she means to be saying that Antigone, as a woman, ought not take it upon herself to fight with men. But there is a deeper, darker meaning. Not clear at the outset of the drama, it is nevertheless well befitting a child of Oedipus: Antigone wants, lusts after, the one thing that is not permitted to her, *the body* of her dead brother.

See Nussbaum's rather dismissive remarks on this point in *Soundings* 72.4 (1989): 743. Still, she makes some fascinating, if unconscious, remarks on this same idea in *The Fragility of Goodness*, 175–76.

47. This term is Michel Foucault's, used suggestively in his monumental *History of Sexuality*, vol. 2, translated by Robert Hurley (New York: Random House, 1985), 10.

48. Nussbaum, *The Fragility of Goodness*, 188. See also Dover, *Greek Homosexuality*, 15–17.

49. "Those who are pregnant," she observes, "in a bodily sense, turn in preference to women, and in this way they are lovers" (*Symposium* 208e).

50. Dover, *Greek Homosexuality*, 81–109. See also Jeffrey Henderson, *The Maculate Muse: Obscene Language in Attic Comedy* (New Haven, Conn.: Yale University Press, 1975), 204–22.

51. David Konstan suggests that the artistic picture of *erōs* changed in the Hellenistic and Roman periods, when the ancient novel (of which five significant examples survive) presented an ideal of heterosexual love as importantly mutual, and as a love between equals. See his *Sexual Symmetry: Love in the Ancient*

Novel and Related Genres (Princeton: Princeton University Press, 1994), esp. 26–30 on "the pederastic paradigm."

52. With the interesting exception of Aristophanes. His comic imagery clearly exhibits a sensitivity to the mutuality of any genuine love-commitment. I cannot explore this dimension of the dialogue, except peripherally, because of the complexity of Aristophanes' dramatic position in the whole drama. Suffice it to say here that his vision is closest to Socrates' *and* to Diotima's: "he started to say something about how Socrates in his speech had made reference to his own" (*Symposium* 212c).

Aristophanes, that is to say, takes the bittersweet erotic vision of Diotima and makes it comical. See also Nussbaum, *The Fragility of Goodness*, 171–76.

53. It is interesting that the terms for "correct opinions" are *ta ortha doxazein* and *orthē doxa*, the very "orthodoxy" to which I alluded above, with one key difference. This one is *true*. Such, it seems, is *love's* knowledge.

54. Martha Nussbaum, *Love's Knowledge: Essays on Philosophy and Literature* (Oxford: The Clarendon Press, 1990).

55. My own comments, "Martha Nussbaum on Tragedy and the Modern Ethos," appeared in *Soundings* 72:4 (1989): 589–605. Nussbaum's brief response was printed in the same volume, at pages 741–47.

56. *Soundings* 72:4 (1989) 743–44. See also remarks that anticipate this in *The Fragility of Goodness*, 197. That long-awaited volume on Hellenistic philosophy is *The Therapy of Desire: Theory and Practice in Hellenistic Ethics* (Princeton: Princeton University Press, 1994), 359–483.

57. Nussbaum, *The Fragility of Goodness*, 166, 180–81, 184–87.

58. Ibid., 184.

59. Ibid., 240–45.

60. Ibid., 185.

61. I am indebted to my good friend and colleague, James J. Winchester, now director of the honors program at Spelman College, who has lectured on this point, and who first alerted me to this dimension of both Plato's and Nussbaum's arguments.

62. Nussbaum, *The Fragility of Goodness*, 195; see also 183–84, 199.

63. This idea, with all of its destructive potential, is brilliantly explored by Sam Shephard in his one-act play, *Fool for Love* (Boston: Faber and Faber, 1983, 1984).

64. There is a curious remark from Aristoxenos (fragment 55) that attributes an uncharacteristically strong heterosexual appetite to Socrates which he whetted, but "without injustice" of any kind.

See Dover, *Greek Homosexuality*, 153ff.

65. Plutarch, *Life of Alcibiades* 19–22.

66. Plutarch's anecdote, in his *Life of Alcibiades* 9 and Konrad Ziegler *Plutarchi: Vitae Parallelae* I.2, 235, is instructive:

"Alcibiades owned an exceptionally large and handsome dog, which he had bought for seventy minae, and it possessed an extremely fine tail, which he had cut off. His friends scolded him and told him that everyone was angry for the dog's sake. Alcibiades, laughing, retorted, 'That has happened exactly as I wanted. I want the whole of Athens to chatter about this—in order that they not say anything worse about me.'"

67. See Plutarch, *Life of Alcibiades* 19–20 and Walter M. Ellis, *Alcibiades* (New York: Routledge, 1989), 58–62.

68. Plutarch, *Life of Alcibiades* 4–6.

69. The oddly mingled eroticism, objectification, and sadism are marked so as not to be missed.

70. Plutarch, *Life of Alcibiades* 8 and Ellis, *Alcibiades*, 32–33.

This extraordinary and strong-willed woman was already the divorced wife of Perikles. It is less clear whether she was successful in her divorce suit against Alcibiades.

71. Plutarch, *Life of Alcibiades* 23.

72. Nussbaum, *The Fragility of Goodness*, 199.

73. Ibid.

74. For the sexual implications of this term, see Dover, *Greek Homosexuality*, 34–39.

75. Plutarch, *Life of Alcibiades* 39.

76. Plutarch, *Life of Alcibiades* 2.1 and Konrad Ziegler, *Plutarchi: Vitae Parallelae*, 227–28. It is fascinating that Plutarch uses the term *tois paidikois*, which is an idiomatic equivalent for the *erōmenos*. Plutarch seems to be suggesting that this aspect of Alcibiades' character derived from his need to be loved, to be "the pursued" in every relationship of substance.

For more on the term *paidika*, see Dover, *Greek Homosexuality*, 17, 85.

77. Plutarch, *Life of Alcibiades* 16. See also Nussbaum, *The Fragility of Goodness*, 192–93.

78. *Soundings* 72.4 (1989): 756, 758. It is interesting that Downing's paper was titled "Diotima and Alcibiades: An Alternative Reading of the *Symposium*." She, too, it seems, thinks that we need to attend to what we are expected to know and learn about Diotima, at least as much as about Alcibiades.

79. Nussbaum, *The Fragility of Goodness*, 228–33.

80. Sheldon M. Cohen, "Luck and Happiness in the *Nicomachean Ethics*" *Soundings* 73.1 (1990): 218.

81. Nussbaum, *The Fragility of Goodness*, 15 note.

82. Louis A. Ruprecht Jr., "Martha Nussbaum on Tragedy and the Modern Ethos," *Soundings* 72.4 (1989): 601.

83. Friedrich Nietzsche, *Ecce Homo*, "Why I Am a Destiny," §9.

84. As Nietzsche does. I have been extremely critical of this dimension to

Nietzsche's thought in my first book, *Tragic Posture and Tragic Vision: Against the Modern Failure of Nerve* (New York: Continuum Press, 1994), 128–80.

I then go on to perform a reading of Mark's gospel which draws out its tragic dimensions, reading it *within* this continuous tradition of human inquiry, not *against* it.

85. Nussbaum's harshest words on this point appear in "Narrative Emotions: Beckett's Genealogy of Love," but the seeds of it are already sown in her reply to Stanley Hauerwas' criticisms in *Soundings* 72.4 (1989): 769–70.

86. See Michel Foucault, *The History of Sexuality*, 2:14–15, 245–50.

87. See *The New York Times Book Review*, 10 November 1985, pages 13–14. It is worth noting that Christine Downing, with her greater appreciation of the positive eroticism of the *Symposium*, appreciates the very qualities about Foucault's book to which Nussbaum objects.

88. See Hilary Putnam, *Reason, Truth and History* (Cambridge: Cambridge University Press, 1981), 161–62.

89. Michel Foucault, *The History of Sexuality*, vol. 1, translated by Robert Hurley (New York: Random House, 1978), 8, 17–35.

90. Nussbaum, *The Fragility of Goodness*, 420.

91. D. A. Campbell, *Greek Lyric I: Sappho and Alcaeus* (Cambridge, Mass.: Loeb Classical Library of Harvard University Press, 1982), 146–47.

92. See Nussbaum's important admission at *Soundings* 72.4 (1989): 736–38.

93. For Alcibiades—the man who will later cut off these same *phalloi*—as the embodiment of such erotic laughter, see *Symposium*, 213a, 222c.

94. See Kenneth J. Dover's *Aristophanic Comedy* (Berkeley: University of California Press, 1972), 218–20; and *Greek Homosexuality*, 124–53.

95. It is interesting to reflect on this matter of gender, although I puzzle over it and do not know exactly what it means. Male characters who are also erotic characters in tragedy—and here I am thinking chiefly of Oedipus and Hippolytos—seem to speak with voices of sexuality repressed, almost as though there were common agreement that the *women* understand, for better and for worse, what *erōs* really means. If that is the case, then it becomes all the more important that Diotima, she who "teaches" the teacher, is a woman.

I am, as I have indicated, currently attempting to discern more about femininity, *erotic* femininity, in antiquity, through a book-length study of Sappho's poetry.

3. SYMPOSIUM, THE THIRD: MORAL VALUE

1. Zygmunt Bauman, *Life in Fragments: Essays in Postmodern Morality* (Cambridge, Mass.: Blackwell Publishers, 1995), 269.

2. I am indebted to Catherine H. Zuckert's marvelous *Postmodern Platos: Nietzsche, Heidegger, Gadamer, Strauss, Derrida* (Chicago: University of

Chicago Press, 1996) for making this point so elegantly. I had the rare privelege of hearing Professor Zuckert lecture on this vast topic at the NEH Institute to which I alluded in my acknowledgments; I recall her gracious accessibility at that time with great appreciation.

3. An excellent demonstration of this caricaturing of "Greek" thought appears in Vassilis Lambropoulos, *The Rise of Eurocentrism: Anatomy of Interpretation* (Princeton: Princeton University Press, 1994). For his specific discussion of Levinas, as often as not juxtaposed with the views of Derrida, see pages 215–20, 261–67, 320–26.

4. Emmanuel Levinas and Richard Kearney, "Dialogue," in *Face to Face with Levinas*, edited by Richard A. Cohen (Albany: State University of New York Press, 1986), 22.

See related comments in "Time and the Other," translated by Richard A. Cohen, in Seán Hand, ed., *The Levinas Reader* (Cambridge, Mass.: Blackwell Publishers, 1989), esp. 48–54, where Levinas again addresses himself to what he calls "eros and freedom," but, for all of his insights, insists on making his larger point by condemning a pure caricature of Platonic thought, what he calls "the Platonic law of participation where every term contains a sameness and through this sameness contains the Other" (48). Finally, see the more systematic remarks in *Totality and Infinity*, translated by Alphonso Lingis (Pittsburgh: Duquesne University Press, 1969), 254–85.

5. For several accounts of the medieval version of this claim (*amor ipse notitia est*, "love is itself a knowledge"), see Louis Dupré, *Passage to Modernity: An Essay in the Hermeneutics of Nature and Culture* (New Haven, Conn.: Yale University Press, 1993), 35–37; and Lee Yearley, *Mencius and Aquinas: Theories of Virtue and Conceptions of Courage* (Albany: State University of New York Press, 1990), 142, 230n35.

6. Martha Nussbaum, *Love's Knowledge: Essays on Philosophy and Literature* (New York: Oxford University Press, 1990), 329. Articulating this connection, between love and knowledge, has been the single most unifying factor in Martha Nussbaum's recent work. It goes without saying, I trust, that I would never have begun to work on these topics myself had she not made these texts and these questions come alive so eloquently.

7. "The more solitary and isolated I am," he said in a letter, "the more I come to love myths."

See Werner Jaeger's *Aristotle: Fundamentals of the History of His Development* (New York: Oxford University Press, 1934, 1967), 321, as well as *Metaphysics* 982b: "Even the lover of myths is in a way a lover of wisdom, since a myth is made up of wonders."

8. I am certainly well aware of the fact that positive accounts of Socrates and his philosophical positions exist. Gregory Vlastos was an especially eloquent defender of the Socratic model, and his edited collection, *The Philosophy of Socrates: A Collection of Critical Essays* (Notre Dame, Ind.: University of Notre

Dame Press, 1971, 1980) as well as *Socrates: Ironist and Moral Philosopher* (Cambridge: Cambridge University Press, 1991) are among the finest in their genre. But such studies do not take away from my larger point, which is that Socrates, these days, is a man who badly *needs* defending.

For a directly opposing thesis—namely, that the nineteenth century was suspicious of Socrates in a way that *we* have overcome—see Martha Nussbaum, "Aristophanes and Socrates on Learning Practical Wisdom," *Yale Classical Studies* 26 (1976): 44–50.

9. This is already the implicit argument of *The Birth of Tragedy* (1872), where Socrates is viewed as representative of Greek thought in decline. For Nietzsche's latest (1888) articulation of "the problem," see *Twilight of the Idols*, "The Problem of Socrates," §§1–9, where he insists that the cultural image of "the sage" is, itself, inescapably decadent.

10. See, for example, Seneca, *De Ira* III.12–13 and *De Vitae* 1–5; and Martha Nussbaum, *The Therapy of Desire: Theory and Practice in Hellenistic Ethics* (Princeton: Princeton University Press, 1994), 91–93.

11. A comparison, say, of Seneca's Medea with Euripides' is quite telling on this point. While clearly not defending infanticide, Euripides does feel that Medea has a right to her outrage, and he puts some of the best lines of the play in her mouth. Seneca goes out of his way to undercut Medea's position, and to underscore the horror of "unnaturalness" in what she does and who she is. On this view, he is insensitive to precisely the kinds of erotic complexities and commitments that Socrates explicates so well.

12. John D. Barrow, *Pi in the Sky: Counting, Thinking and Being* (New York: Oxford University Press, 1992), 102.

13. As I noted in the first chapter, Joseph Cropsey suggests that the trilogy is actually part of a massive seven-dialogue series in *Plato's World: Man's Place in the Comsos* (Chicago: University of Chicago Press, 1995).

14. Seth Bernadete, *The Rhetoric of Morality and Philosophy: Plato's Gorgias and Phaedrus* (Chicago: University of Chicago Press, 1991), 2. "It is characteristic of the *Phaedrus*," Bernadete concludes, "that it treats the members of the triplet two at a time" (152).

15. For a fascinating discussion of these and other mathematical matters, see Barrow, *Pi in the Sky*, 6–8, 26–105, 249–97.

See also Peter Murphy, "Architectonics," from a work-in-progress tentatively entitled *Xenopoiesis*.

> The great insight of ancient Greek mathematics (an insight forged in response to the ancients' horror at incommensurable numbers) was the conclusion that even if two quantities (a and c) were not equatable directly, they could still be equated via their relation to a third quantity (b). Indeed the whole of Greek thought was attuned to such tripartite schemas.

16. Barrow, *Pi in the Sky*, 81–101.

17. Jean-Pierre Vernant, "One . . . Two . . . Three: Eros," translated by Deborah Lyons, in Winkler and Zeitlin, eds., *Before Sexuality: The Construction of Erotic Experience in the Ancient Greek World* (Princeton: Princeton University Press, 1990), 472ff.

18. Which seems also to be the Augustinian view, one that had such an impact on subsequent Christian attitudes toward marriage and erotic relations. See *De bono coniugali* XVIII.21.388.

19. This is the whole point of the Myth of Theuth (*Phaedrus*, 274c–276a), as well as the passionate conclusion of the *Seventh Letter* (341c–345d).

20. I think it significant that the second of Socrates' loves, *philosophia*, and this alone among the four, is feminine. The power of this feminine force will eventually cause Socrates to *forget* Alcibiades altogether, as we saw already at *Protagoras* 309b.

It is interesting that this entire discussion takes place in the *dual voice*. See Bernadete, *The Rhetoric of Morality and Philosophy*, 64.

21. Eva Cantarella's *Bisexuality in the Ancient World*, translated by Cormac O. Cuilleanáin (New Haven, Conn.: Yale University Press, 1992) is an intriguing analysis that covers an impressive range of material, but her reading of the Socratic and Platonic tradition (54–63) is odd, to say the least. It is profoundly at odds with my own attempt here, to *rehabilitate* the Platonic philosophy of the Erotic Period.

22. For more on this, see Anne Carson, *Eros the Bittersweet* (Princeton: Princeton University Press, 1986), 70–77, 168–73.

23. I acknowledge the powerful poetry and prose of Anne Carson as that which has instructed me most helpfully, and even inspirationally, about this essential Platonic insight. In "The Glass Essay," Carson reveals herself within the grips of this age-old dilemma:

> Everything I know about love and its necessities
> I learned in that one moment
> when I found myself
> thrusting my little burning red backside like a baboon
> at a man who no longer cherished me.
> There was no area of my mind
> not appalled by this action, no part of my body
> that could have done otherwise.
> But to talk of mind and body begs the question.
> Soul is the place,
> stretched like a surface of millstone grit between body and mind,
> where such necessity grinds itself out.
> Soul is what I kept watch on all that night.
>
> —Anne Carson, *Glass, Irony, and God*
> (New York: New Directions, 1995), 11–12

24. Dame Rebecca West, *Black Lamb and Grey Falcon: A Journey Through Yugoslavia* (New York: Penguin Books, 1940, 1968), 665.

25. See the notable discussion in Caroline Walker Bynum, *Holy Feast and Holy Fast: The Religious Significance of Food to Medieval Women* (Berkeley: University of California Press, 1987), 254.

26. Nussbaum, *The Fragility of Goodness*, 195.

27. Ibid.

28. Especially those detractors who live in late modern societies, with their own rather bizarre reinvention of the human body. For a rich discussion of some of the latest technologies of the body, see Bauman, *Life in Fragments*, 163–79.

29. "If someone is going to think these things through in a correct manner, he must necessarily examine the nature of friendship, of desire, and of what are called 'the erotic desires.' For there are two entities here, and from their combination comes yet a third . . . but because they are all given just one name, total confusion and obscurity is created" (*Laws* 837a).

30. Charles Reynolds, of the University of Tennessee at Knoxville, has asked if I am not really interested in defending the traditional language of Trinitarian thought. I am embarrassed to say that I do not know. I have not been dealing primarily with Christian language or thought, in part, because no cognate of *erōs* found its way into the Greek of the New Testament.

But I can say that I have always found the Christological dimension of this debate, despite its deep confusions and occasional hyperlexicality, a fascinating contribution to the philosophical debate over the relationship between the soul and the body, a relationship in which *neither* term can be reduced.

31. See Frances M. Cornford, *Before and After Socrates* (Cambridge: Cambridge University Press, 1966).

See also Suzanne K. Langer, *Philosophy in a New Key* (Cambridge, Mass.: Harvard University Press, 1942), 7–10.

32. See Jean-Paul Sartre, *Being and Nothingness*, translated by Hazel E. Barnes (New York: Modern Library, 1956), 209–28.

33. Ibid., 206.

34. Ibid., 389–406.

35. Simone Weil, "The *Iliad*, or, The Poem of Force," translated by Mary McCarthy (Wallingford, Pa.: Pendle Hill Pamphlet No. 91, 1943, 1993), 7.

36. Zygmunt Bauman, *Postmodern Ethics* (Cambridge, Mass.: Blackwell Publishers, 1993), 110–45.

37. For a fascinating discussion of Dyadic and Triadic metaphors for human being, I am deeply indebted to Walker Percy's *The Message in the Bottle* (New York: Farrar, Straus & Giroux, 1975), 159–88; and also *Signposts in a Strange Land*, edited by Patrick Samway (New York: Farrar, Straus & Giroux, 1991), 111–29, 271–91.

38. Thomas C. MacCary, *Childlike Achilles: Ontogeny and Phylogeny in*

the Iliad (New York: Columbia University Press, 1982), 127–36. See also Carson, *Eros the Bittersweet*, 12–17, 26–31.

39. For the full implications of this idea, I am indebted to Thomas R. Flynn's *Sartre and Marxist Existentialism: The Test Case of Collective Responsibility* (Chicago: University of Chicago Press, 1984), 51–93.

40. See, for example, Stanley Hauerwas, *After Christendom? How the Church is to Behave if Freedom, Justice and a Christian Nation Are Bad Ideas* (Nashville, Tenn.: Abingdon Press, 1991), 113–31.

41. See John Boswell, *Christianity, Social Tolerance, and Homosexuality: Gay People in Western Europe from the Beginning of the Christian Era to the Fourteenth Century* (Chicago: University of Chicago Press, 1980), 22, 51–52, 70.

42. This could be taken, and I suspect that it *was* taken, as an argument for monotheism in the Hellenistic era. One's relationship to the divine, according to everything I have been suggesting, would be profoundly altered if it involves us in relation to one other being or else to more than one. Monotheism, when it was transplanted to the Greek-speaking world from Judea, thus became a matter of mathematical and numerical, as well as moral, reflection.

43. It is worth reflecting, I think, upon this image of what Socrates calls "orthodoxy" and its position "in between" (*metaxu*) knowledge and ignorance.

44. This observation is made by way of objecting to Alasdair MacIntyre's almost outrageously anti-intuitive comment in *After Virtue*, 2nd ed. (Notre Dame, Ind.: University of Notre Dame Press, 1984), 69: "One of the things that we ought to have learned from the history of moral philosophy is that the introduction of the word 'intuition' by a moral philosopher is always a signal that something has gone badly wrong with an argument."

MacIntyre equates the commitment to the metaphor of "human rights" with a belief in witches and unicorns on this same page.

45. For this and other insights, I am indebted to Christine Downing's fine essay, "Diotima and Alcibiades: An Alternative Reading of the *Symposium*," *Soundings* 72.4 (1989): 631–55.

For other resources, see Xenophon, *Memorabilia* II.6.28; and *Symposium* VIII.2; Aiskhines, *Socratikos*, fragment 11; Kenneth J. Dover, *Greek Homosexuality* (London: Oxford University Press, 1979), 153–60; and Gregory Vlastos, "Socratic Irony," *Classical Quarterly* 37 (1987): 88–93.

46. Nietzsche, *Sämtliche Werke*, 6:71.

47. See Werner J. Dannhauser, *Nietzsche's View of Socrates* (Ithaca, N.Y.: Cornell University Press, 1974), 192–232.

48. An interesting, if rather unexpected, parallel insight appears in Augustine: "Certainly I am not deceived in this knowledge that I am. And, consequently, neither am I deceived in knowing that I know. For, as I know that I am, so I know this also, that I know. And when I love these two things, I add to them a certain thing, namely, my love, which is of equal moment. For neither am I deceived in this, that I love" (*The City of God* XI.26).

49. Anne Carson, *Eros the Bittersweet* (Princeton: Princeton University Press, 1986), 152–53.

50. Like Aristotle, he is trying to speak of things for which there are, finally, no words, things that Aristotle calls *anōnymos* (*Nicomachean Ethics* 1107b2, 1115b25, 1125b17, 1127a12–14).

Erōs itself is, it seems to me, the ultimate example of such a thing. One would never think to look to the lexicon for assistance in "thinking love through," nor of "defining" it.

51. How many Platonic dialogues, after all, end with a whimper rather than the bang we might otherwise expect?

Hegel went so far as to call the *Parmenides* "the greatest literary product of ancient dialectic," precisely because it has this open-ended character (*The Phenomenology of Mind*, Preface, §71).

52. I have been much impressed by Jürgen Habermas' *A Theory of Communicative Action*, 2 volumes, translated by Thomas McCarthy (Boston: Beacon Press, 1984, 1988) for a defense of this notion of "consensual truth" and "communicative rationality." It is, among other things, a defense of the Socratic way of proceeding over against its genealogical detractors, from Nietzsche to Foucault. Communication—on this one point Habermas, like Socrates, is adamant—is ideally about truth, not power.

53. Naturally enough, we *do* see Socrates passionately inspired by others, especially by Phaedrus in the dialogue that bears his name. See Nussbaum, *The Fragility of Goodness*, 200–33.

54. Ibid., 195.

55. Ibid., 184, 198–99.

56. Martin Heidegger, "The Thinker as Poet," in *Poetry, Language, Thought*, translated by Albert Hofstadter (New York: Harper & Row, 1971), 6.

57. As does Martha Nussbaum on his behalf. See *Love's Knowledge*, 325.

58. Nussbaum, *Love's Knowledge*, 220–29. See also Mark William Roche, *Tragedy and Comedy: A Systematic Study and Critique of Hegel* (Albany: State University of New York Press, 1998), 21–47.

59. See Allan Bloom's posthumously published essay, "The Death of Eros: Did Romeo and Juliet Have a *Relationship*?" *New York Times Magazine* (23 May 1993): 27, 83–84.

60. I recognize the historical problem of attempting to use a Shakespearean play to illuminate a Platonic dialogue. All I mean to point out is that in both places we meet the assumption of the existence of an experience that we might call "true love," as well as a profound sensitivity to the agony and the ecstasy that are *necessarily* combined in this experience. While I recognize the farcical dimension of the play—my reading in fact hinges upon it—things turn deadly serious in the end. Loving and dying are as connected in Shakespeare's sonnets and plays as they are in Sappho, another erotic poet who laughs at herself in the midst of her most intense erotic longing.

There are, in any case, Classicists who adhere to the commitment to making precisely such connections. The editorial mission of the journal *Arion* reads as follows: "We value most the contributor who speaks across disciplines: the author who can write on Sophocles, say, in a way that engages the student of Shakespeare." And vice versa, I assume.

61. For this, and much of what follows, I am indebted to René Girard's masterful reading of the play in a lecture delivered at Emory University in the spring of 1991, as well as to his discussion of "Rhetorical Figures in the Sonnets" in *A Theater of Envy* (New York: Oxford University Press, 1991), 297–307.

62. Shakespeare, *Romeo and Juliet* I.i.178–85.

63. Ibid., I.i.186.

64. Ibid., I.ii.61.

65. Ibid., I.iv.160–69.

66. Ibid., I.iv.227.

67. Ibid., V.iii.91–115.

68. Nussbaum, *The Therapy of Desire*, 359–401.

69. Ibid., 140–91.

70. For a fascinating survey of Southern culture in the United States as a curious amalgam of "Judeo-Christian" and "Stoic" sensibilities, see Walker Percy, *Signposts in a Strange Land*, 83–88, 90.

71. See the moral letter "On Suicide" in Moses Hadas' reader, *The Stoic Philosophy of Seneca* (New York: Doubleday & Company, Inc., 1968), 202–7.

72. This is a particular emphasis of the later Roman, rather than the Hellenistic, Stoic philosophers.

See Seneca's "On the Shortness of Life" in Hadas, *The Stoic Philosophy of Seneca*, 47–73; Epictetus, *Conversations* I.29, III.4; and Marcus Aurelius, *The Meditations* XII.36.

73. The term is Alasdair MacIntyre's, coined in his popular diagnosis of modern society, *After Virtue*, 2nd ed. (Notre Dame, Ind.: University of Notre Dame Press, 1984), 6–22. For several ambivalent, and probing, analyses of what this cultural image has meant in our "permissive society," see Philip Rieff, *Freud: The Mind of a Moralist* (Garden City, N.Y.: Doubleday, 1961) and *The Triumph of the Therapeutic: Uses of Faith After Freud* (San Francisco: Harper & Row, 1966).

For some damning indictments of the North American bourgeois character-type of "the therapist," see MacIntyre, *After Virtue*, 29–31, and Robert M. Bellah et al., *Habits of the Heart: Individualism and Commitment in American Life* (Berkeley: University of California Press, 1985), x–xi, 119–22, 138–41.

Finally, for some stunning and creative juxtapositions of Freudian and Greco-erotic imagery, see Norman O. Brown, *Life Against Death: The Psychoanalytical Meaning of History* (Middletown, Conn.: Wesleyan University Press, 1959), 23–73, 307–22, and *Love's Body* (New York: Random House, 1966).

74. Nussbaum, *The Therapy of Desire*, 13–47.

75. To put it another way, while we clearly do have certain *ethical* responsibilities of self-respect, and even of self-love, I am talking about *erotics*, not ethics. And the erotic is the more primordial entity.

76. For this discussion, I am deeply indebted to the uncanny conclusion of Caroline Walker Bynum's *Holy Feast and Holy Fast*, 299–301.

77. See Sharon D. Welch, *A Feminist Ethic of Risk* (Minneapolis, Minn.: Fortress Press, 1990), 23–47, 83–99.

78. Curiously, Carl Sagan, in an entire book devoted to the future of space exploration, had hardly a word to say about it. In a book that is over four hundred pages long, he mentions the *Challenger* only once, in a single short paragraph (*Pale Blue Dot: A Vision of the Human Future in Space* [New York: Random House, 1994], 319).

79. I have been much instructed by my friend and former colleague, Gary Laderman, on this point. See his *The Sacred Remains: American Attitudes Toward Death, 1799–1883* (New Haven, Conn.: Yale University Press, 1996) for an analysis of the creation of a North American "death industry" in and around the period of the Civil War. Laderman's point is that the material fact of the dead body presented a practical problem of transportation and preservation that was largely resolved through the emergence of the embalmer's art. He is now involved in research for a second volume which will trace out the interesting contours of that story into the twentieth century.

80. This phrase embodies the essential thesis of Caroline Walker Bynum in *Holy Feast and Holy Fast*, 5, 30. She later devotes an entire book to the idea, *The Resurrection of the Body in Western Christianity, 200–1336* (New York: Columbia University Press, 1995).

81. Marguerite Yourcenar puts this point beautifully, time and again, in *Fires*, translated by Dori Katz (New York: Farrar, Straus & Giroux, 1981):

Loneliness . . .

I don't believe as they do, I don't live as they do, I don't love as
they do . . .

I will die as they die. (4)

82. Perhaps the best way to put the matter is to say that we can possibly, just possibly, love our neighbor as our*selves*, but we certainly can *not* love our neighbor as we love a lover.

83. G. W. F. Hegel, *The Phenomenology of Mind*, Preface, §5, where, as he puts it, philosophy must "lay aside the name of *love* of knowledge and be actual *knowledge*."

CONCLUSION: ON ENDING GRACIOUSLY

1. Anne Carson, *Eros the Bittersweet* (Princeton: Princeton University Press, 1986), 34–38.

2. See bell hooks, *Teaching to Transgress: Education as a Practice of Freedom* (New York: Routledge, 1994), 191–207.

3. It would seem that *erōs*, as a kind of passionate attachment, cannot really have had a place in Paul's world. Stoic that he is in such matters, Paul's theological revolution was in part a linguistic one—replacing *erōs* by a different word for love, a distinctive sort of love he called *agapē*.

> You were called to freedom, my brothers. Not freedom of opportunity for the flesh, but rather a freedom which commands you to be servants of one another, in love [*agapē*]. For the whole law is fulfilled in this one word: Love. "Love [*agapēseis*] your neighbor as yourself." But if you bite and devour one another, then see that you are not consumed by one another in the process. (*Galatians* 5:13–15)

This seems a pretty clear reference to the kinds of behavior the lyric poets wrote about. The story told in Kleist's disturbing play, *Penthesileia*, raises it explicitly. Contrastingly, Jesus himself seems far more aware, however tantalizingly so, of the fact that such erotic realities exist, and that they will not go away quite so simply.

4. John D. Barrow, *Pi in the Sky: Counting, Thinking, and Being* (New York: Oxford University Press, 1992), 249–97.

5. Carl Sagan, *Pale Blue Dot: A Vision of the Human Future in Space* (New York: Random House, 1994), 25–39. For my highly critical review of the book, see *Journal of the American Academy of Religion* 64.1 (1997): 459–63.

6. Louis Dupré, *Passage to Modernity: An Essay in the Hermeneutics of Nature and Culture* (New Haven, Conn.: Yale University Press, 1993), 252.

7. G. W. F. Hegel, *The Phenomenology of Spirit* §§178–81.

8. See Louis A. Ruprecht Jr., *Tragic Posture and Tragic Vision: Against the Modern Failure of Nerve* (New York: Continuum Press, 1994), 71–127.

9. For more on this, see my "The Ethos of Olympism: On the Religious Meaning of the Modern Olympic Movement," *Soundings* 80.4 (1997): 1000–36.

10. See H. A. Harris, *Greek Athletics and the Jews* (University of Wales Press, 1976).

11. See, for instance, Edward Stein's *Forms of Desire: Sexual Orientation and the Social Constructionist Controversy* (New York: Garland Publications, 1990), especially John Boswell's "Categories, Experience, and Sexuality," 133–73.

12. Anne Carson, *Eros the Bittersweet*, 35ff.

Actually, it would be fairer to say that *written* words have boundaries and clear edges. Spoken words do not. Their edges are always expanding and contracting; they are softer, more malleable. Spoken words are *metaxu*. And who can measure the sweet murmurings of the lover in love, the words which one never thinks to write down until it is too late?

13. Aristotle, *Politics* 1295a–97a.

14. For an appreciative review of this critical Marxian legacy, see Beverly Wildung Harrison, *Making the Connections: A Preliminary Feminist Social Ethic* (Boston: Beacon Press, 1985), 51–55.

15. For an interesting exploration of the sorts of things money means in our own North American context, and the sorts of reforms that would be commensurate with some of these beliefs, see Michael Walzer's *Spheres of Justice: A Defense of Pluralism and Equality* (New York: Basic Books, 1983), 95–128.

16. Toni Morrison's *Playing in the Dark: Whiteness and the Literary Imagination* (New York: Vintage Books, 1992) presents a stunning analysis of this important cultural fact.

17. I am delighted to acknowledge my indebtedness to Dr. Arturo Lindsay, who was responsible for my original invitation to Panama City, where I delivered a lecture in conjunction with the opening of his new show in the Museum of Contemporary Art. Arturo took all of us on a month-long whirlwind tour of his country thereafter, during which I learned a tremendous amount—about myself and the country I call home.

I currently have a semiserious short monograph, entitled *Panamanian Peregrinations*, submitted to several presses for review.

18. For more on this, see my "Classics at the Millennium: An Outsider's View of a Discipline," forthcoming in *Soundings* (Summer 1999).

19. Derek Walcott, *The Antilles: Fragments of Epic Memory* (New York: Farrar, Straus & Giroux, 1992), 12, 19.

20. John Boswell, *Christianity, Homosexuality, and Social Tolerance: Gay People in Western Europe from the Beginning of the Christian Era to the Fourteenth Century* (Chicago: University of Chicago Press, 1980), 41–46.

21. Nietzsche, *Wir Philologen* 5[64]; *Sämtliche Werke* 8:58–59, my emphasis.

> Erziehung ist erst Lehre vom *Nothwendigen*, dann vom *Wechselnden und Veränderlichen*. Man führt den Jüngling in die Natur, zeigt ihm überall das Walten von Gesetzen; dann die Gesetze der bürgerlichen Gesellschaft: hier wird schon die Frage rege: *musste* dies so sein? Allmählich braucht er Geschichte, um zu hören, wie das so geworden ist. Aber damit lernt er, dass es auch anders werden kann. Wie viel Macht über die Dinge hat der Mensch? dies ist die Frage bei aller Erziehung. Um nun zu zeigen, wie ganz anders es sein kann, zeige man z.B. die Griechen. Die Römer braucht man, um zu zeigen wie es so *wurde*.

22. Frank M. Snowden, Jr., *Before Color Prejudice: The Ancient View of Blacks* (Cambridge, Mass.: Harvard University Press, 1983).

23. *Oxford English Dictionary* (New York: Oxford University Press, 1989), 15: 665–67.

24. Even putting the matter this way is problematic in two distinct ways. First and foremost, I am applying contemporary categories—homosexuality, heterosexuality, and bisexuality—in what may appear to be an uncritical manner, categories, all, that may or may not have made much sense to the Greeks. The difficulty here is a *translational* one. We must use our own terms and categories in the never-ending attempt to make sense of, and thus to reconstruct, the past. There is an inescapability about proceeding in this way, it seems to me.

The second dilemma is more acute. The matter of Greek sexual identity simply seems to be too *under*determined by the textual evidence before us. It is not even clear what would count as evidence for one or another of the various reconstructions of Greek sexual attitudes. In general, six arenas have been identified as sources of significant evidence of sexual attitudes in antiquity: Visual Art, primarily vase-paintings; Forensic Speeches; Comic Drama; Lyric Poetry; the Greek philosophical tradition; and finally some intriguing Roman imperial dream analyses, primarily those of Artemidorus. Each of these arenas, excepting the last, was mined first by Sir Kenneth Dover in 1979, in his groundbreaking study, *Greek Homosexuality* (Cambridge, Mass.: Harvard University Press, 1979), 1–17; each would be further worked by nearly everyone who labored subsequently in this area. The problem presented here is *interpretive*, and it is a far more complex problem. How, after all, ought one to interpret deliberately comic sexual pronouncements? Or forensic speeches in which the character of one's opponent is expected to be defamed? Or pictorial renderings? Fantastically orgiastic scenes involving satyrs and women and men are hardly to be taken as literal representations of acceptable Athenian behavior. And even the philosophical record—especially the Platonic record, as I have tried to demonstrate repeatedly in this book—is far from clear, and never speaks in a single voice. That is the whole point of the dialogical method, after all.

A fascinating, if overly polemical, recent attempt to move beyond the limited evidence mustered by Dover, one in which better attention is paid to matters of *class structure* in Classical Athenian society, is T. K. Hubbard's "Popular Perceptions of Elite Homosexuality in Classical Athens," *Arion, Third Series* 6.1 (1998): 48–78.

25. John Boswell, *Christianity, Homosexuality, and Social Tolerance*, 61–87, 169–206.

Some of Boswell's work, which attended only to the world of men in antiquity, has been amplified and thoroughly enriched by Bernadete J. Brooten, whose *Love Between Women: Early Christian Responses to Female Homoeroticism* (Chicago: University of Chicago Press, 1996) is a paradigmatic example of how refreshingly candid and reasoned discussion of difficult topics can be.

26. It was attention to the evidence of such painting that best characterized the intellectual strategy of Sir Kenneth Dover in his groundbreaking *Greek Homosexuality*.

27. Camille Paglia, *Sexual Personae: Art and Decadence from Nefertiti to Emily Dickinson* (New Haven, Conn.: Yale University Press, 1990), 1; *Sex, Art*

and American Culture: Essays (New York: Vintage Press, 1992), 101–24, 182; and especially *Vamps and Tramps: New Essays* (New York: Vintage Press, 1994), 19–94.

28. I hesitate to say 'irrational' if for no other reason than because I am convinced by Plato's claim that *erōs* is, almost by definition, a sort of *mania*. Mania is *not* the same thing as *alogia* or *amathia* in Plato's Erotic Period.

29. I particularly appreciate the wonderful sketch of Romantic philosophy in Andrew Bowie, *From Romanticism to Critical Theory: The Philosophy of German Literary Theory* (New York: Routledge, 1997).

See my review essay of the book, "So You Do Theory, Do You?," *Philosophy Today* 42.4 (1998): 440–48.

30. George Steiner, *Antigones: How the Antigone Legend Has Endured in Western Literature, Art, and Thought* (New York: Oxford University Press, 1984), 129–30.

31. Byron, *Don Juan* I.lxiv. He continues in the next stanza:

Alfonso was the name of Julia's lord,
A man well looking for his years, and who
Was neither much beloved nor yet abhorred:
They lived together as most people do,
Suffering each other's foibles by accord,
And not exactly either *one* or *two*;
Yet he was jealous, though he did not show it,
For Jealousy dislikes the world to know it.

32. The publication of Richard Herrnstein and Charles Murray's *The Bell Curve: Intelligence and Class Struggle in American Life* (New York: The Free Press, 1994) generated a veritable firestorm of controversy on the nation's campuses. My own concern about the book is less that it endeavors to speak of "biology," or of "race"—I am more than willing to do that—than with its crude *scientism*. The book begins (1–24) with an interesting historical genealogy, and a defense, of the science of "psychometrics," the comparative measurement of intelligence, or what they call "cognitive ability." It is a chilling feature of such testing, unaddressed by the authors, that these tests were consistently created and promoted by advanced industrial military bureaucracies in England and the United States. IQ tests, that is to say, are always already implicated in the military-industrial complex.

Having defended the continued utility of such tests, the authors then use statistical analysis (an even "softer" science than psychometrics itself) to deal with the comparative cognitive abilities of Hispanics, blacks, whites, and Asians (their terms, and their taxonomies, instructively enough). They conclude with some astonishing connections—between crime rates, illegitimate birth rates, poverty rates, and the alleged distribution of native intelligence. Surely the authors cannot have been surprised by the vociferous reaction to the book, although they claim to have been shocked.

Now, the authors are not racists—except in the technical sense of the term, that they use pretty crude racial categories as fundamental to their analysis. But they *are* crude scientists—who seem not to see, or at least not to say with sufficient clarity, that biology is impossible to "measure" in a neutral environment where it has been fully detached from other cultural forces. One simply cannot test "race" in a vacuum; human beings are not those kinds of creatures. Particularly in North America, race is profoundly overlaid with economic inequities, inequities *The Bell Curve* assigns more to natural variation in intelligence than to these distortive social and cultural forces.

For a critique, especially of the crude scientism of the book, see Russell Jacoby and Naomi Glaubermann, eds., *The Bell Curve Debate: History, Documents, Opinions* (New York: Random House, 1995), esp. 3–13, and Charles Murray's 1995 "Afterword" (553–75).

33. For some representative texts, see Philip Rieff, ed., *The Sexual Enlightenment of Children* (New York: Collier Books, 1963) and *Sexuality and the Psychology of Love* (New York: Collier Books, 1963), as well as *Three Contributions to the Theory of Sex* in A. A. Brill, ed., *The Basic Writings of Sigmund Freud* (New York: Modern Library, 1938), 553–629, esp. 580–93.

34. For more on these debates, see my "Hellenism on Display," in *Journal of Modern Greek Studies* 15 (1997): 247–60.

35. This connection has been made, passionately and with a decidedly public edge, by Martha Nussbaum in *Cultivating Humanity: A Classical Defense of Reform in Liberal Education* (Cambridge, Mass.: Harvard University Press, 1997). Some important reservations have been voiced about this project—again, sketched on too broad a canvas and with some unfortunate polemics and oversimplification—by Bruce S. Thornton in "Cultivating Sophistry," *Arion, Third Series* 6.2 (1998): 180–204. The main issue dividing these thinkers, at least as it seems to me, is the relative affinity they posit between the cosmopolitan ethos of the Hellenistic Stoic tradition and the identity-pluralism of more contemporary curricular reform.

My own political sympathies lie with Nussbaum here, and I resonate especially with her pleas for a better reasoned educational ethos, one more attentive to the twin notions of globalism and civility. But I am dismayed by the almost shocking ratio of assertion to argument in the book. Clearly, hers is intended as a manifesto rather than a reasoned defense of what she lauds as "interculturalism." Whether a reasoned defense of "reform in liberal education" is in fact possible is the disturbing question I can no longer avoid, and am trying to confront here, with Plato's dubious assistance. For more on this see David A. Hollinger, *Postethnic America* (New York: Basic Books, 1995), esp. 79–104.

36. An excellent explication and analysis of these difficult Levitical passages may be found in Saul M. Olyan, "'And With a Male You Shall Not Lie the Lying Down of a Woman': On the Meaning and Significance of Leviticus 18:22 and 20:13," *Journal of the History of Sexuality* 5.2 (1994): 179–206.

37. I am thinking in particular of the diagnosis made by Alasdair MacIntyre

in *After Virtue*, 2nd ed. (South Bend, Ind.: University of Notre Dame Press, 1984), which then becomes the springboard for the thesis I summarize here and for which I argue at some length in *Afterwords: Hellenism, Modernism and the Myth of Decadence* (Albany: State University of New York Press, 1996).

38. It has been both helpful and instructive to see MacIntyre address this issue more substantively in his later work. The question of how what he calls "rival traditions" may in fact converse with, rather than against, one another is the problem to which he turns in his next book, *Whose Justice? Which Rationality?* (South Bend, Ind.: University of Notre Dame Press, 1988). His third book in this vein, *Three Rival Versions of Moral Enquiry: Encyclopedia, Genealogy and Tradition* (South Bend, Ind.: University of Notre Dame Press, 1990) represents an attempt to display what such intertraditional discussion might begin to look like, and enjoys some limited success, although the anti-modern, anti-encyclopedic polemics still hamper the project.

I am especially indebted to Jeffrey Stout for his rigorous exposition of the intriguing new trajectories in MacIntyre's later work. For the second book, see his "Homeward Bound: MacIntyre on Liberal Society and the History of Ethics," *Journal of Religion* 69.2 (1989): 220–32. For a broader and more textured overview of the issues I am also tracking, see "Commitments and Traditions in the Study of Religious Ethics," *Journal of Religious Ethics* 25.3 (1998): 23–56, esp. 38–48. It is a delight for me to be able to express this debt.

39. That is the essential insight of Boswell's *Christianity, Homosexuality, and Social Tolerance*, 303–34. His larger theory, right or wrong, is that appeals to "nature" became the means to ground normative moral judgments only in the High Middle Ages. The weaker argument is its corollary—namely, that "nature" has been invoked historically to defend a really astonishing, and astonishingly contradictory, array of moral perspectives.

40. Nietzsche, *Twilight of the Idols*, "Skirmishes," §7; *Sämtliche Werke*, 6:115:

> Die Natur, künstlerisch abgeschätzt, ist kein Modell. Sie übertreibt, sie verzerrt, sie lässt Lücken. Die Natur ist der *Zufall*. Das Studium "nach der Natur" scheint mir ein schlechtes Zeichen: es verräth Unterwerfung, Schwäche, Fatalismus, — dies Im-Staube-Liegen vor *petit faits* ist eines *ganzen* Künstlers unwürdig.

41. Nietzsche, *Twilight of the Idols*, "Skirmishes," §48; *Sämtliche Werke*, 6:150:

> Auch ich rede von "Rückkehr zur Natur," obwohl es eigentlich nicht ein Zurückgehn, sondern ein *Hinaufkommen* ist—hinauf in die hohe, freie, selbst furchtbare Natur und Natürlichkeit, eine solche, die mit grossen Aufgaben spielt, spielen *darf*. . . . Um es im *Gleichniss* zu sagen: Napolean war ein Stück "Rückkehr zur Natur," so wie ich sie verstehe. . . . Aber Rousseau—wohin wollte der eigentlich zurück?

42. It is also a crucial revision to which I have devoted a book, *Afterwords*, 23–63.

43. Nietzsche, *Wir Philologen* 5[167]; *Sämtliche Werke*, 8:88–89:

> Das Griechenthum durch die That zu *überwinden* wäre die Aufgabe. Aber dazu müsste man es erst kennen!—es giebt eine Grundlichkeit, welche nur der Vorwand der Thatenlosigkeit ist. Man denke, was Goethe vom Alterthum verstand; gewiss nicht soviel als ein Philologe und doch genug, um fruchtbar mit ihm zu ringen. Man *sollte* sogar nicht mehr von einer Sache wissen, als man auch schaffen könnte. Überdies ist es selbst das einzige Mittel, etwas wahrhaft zu *erkennen*, wenn man versucht es zu *machen*. Man versuche alterthümlich zu leben—man kommt sofort hundert Meilen den Alten näher als mit alle Gelehrsamkeit.—Unsre Philologen zeigen nicht, dass sie irgend worin dem Alterthum *nacheifern*—deshalb ist ihr Alterthum ohne Wirkung auf die Schüler.

44. This kind of moral cobbling has been ably defended by Jeffrey Stout in *Ethics After Babel: The Language of Morals and its Discontents* (Boston: Beacon Press, 1988).

45. Nietzsche, *Twilight of the Idols*, "'Reason' in Philosophy," §5; *Sämtliche Werke*, 6:78:

> Die "Vernunft" in der Sprache: oh was für eine alte betrügerische Weibsperson! Ich fürchte, wir werden Gott nicht los, weil wir noch an die Grammatik glauben.

46. For an analysis of the way in which this was particularly true for women in the European Middle Ages, see Caroline Walker Bynum, *Holy Feast and Holy Fast: The Religious Significance of Food to Medieval Women* (Berkeley: University of California Press, 1987), 22–23, 196–97, 262, 273.

47. See George Bernard Shaw's telling comments in his preface to the play *Saint Joan* (New York: Penguin Books, 1951):

> Joan of Arc, a village girl from the Vosges, was born about 1412; burnt for heresy, witchcraft, and sorcery in 1431; rehabilitated after a fashion in 1456; designated Venerable in 1904; declared Blessed in 1908; and finally canonized in 1920. She is the most notable Warrior Saint in the Christian calendar, and the queerest fish among the eccentric worthies of the Middle Ages. (7)

48. Marguerite Yourcenar has sketched a wonderful portrait of nineteenth-century northern Europe for us with careful attention to just this feature of the society, in *Dear Departed: A Memoir*, translated by Maria Louise Ascher (New York: Farrar, Straus & Giroux, 1991).

For more on Yourcenar's exceptional *ouevre*, see my "Clio and Melpomene:

In Defense of the Historical Novel," *Historical Reflections* 23.3 (1997): 389–418.

For examples of these same ideas in Hellenistic literature, see David Konstan, *Sexual Symmetry: Love in the Ancient Novel and Related Genres* (Princeton: Princeton University Press, 1994).

49. See the wonderful discussion of these matters in Margaret Williamson, *Sappho's Immortal Daughters* (Cambridge, Mass.: Harvard University Press, 1995), 72–75, 90–132.

50. Federico Garcia Lorca, *Three Tragedies*, translated by James Graham-Lujan (New York: Scribners, 1941, 1955), 34–99. This play, composed in 1933, is an enormously and enduringly popular play in modern Greece.

51. Walter Hinderer, ed., *Heinrich von Kleist: Plays* (New York: Continuum Press, 1982), 165–268. Intriguingly, Leni Riefenstahl long planned a film version of the play, although the war aborted this project permanently. See *Leni Riefenstahl: A Memoir* (New York: St. Martin's Press, 1992), 66, 142, 152–53, 168.

APPENDIX: ON LANGUAGE AND LITERACY

1. Jean-Jacques Rousseau, *Essay on the Origin of Languages*, in Victor Gourevitch, trans. and ed., *The First and Second Discourses Together with the Replies to Critics, and Essay on the Origin of Languages* (New York: Harper & Row, 1986), 239–95.

Much of my thinking about Rousseau has been influenced by Clifford Irwin and Nathan Tarcov, eds., *The Legacy of Rousseau* (Chicago: University of Chicago Press, 1997), an altogether remarkable collection of critical essays.

2. Rousseau, *Essay on the Origin of Languages*, 246–47.

Still more intriguing for my purposes is the insight with which Rousseau begins: "Love, it is said, was the inventor of drawing. Love might also have motivated speech, though less happily" (240–41).

3. A classic text in this area is still Walter J. Ong, *Orality and Literacy: The Technologizing of the Word* (New York: Methuen & Co., 1982), although Ong is building on Milman Parry's definitive work on "oral epic composition" and the revolution in Homeric studies that work subsequently inspired.

For more on Parry's work, see Albert B. Lord, *The Singer of Tales* (Cambridge, Mass.: Harvard University Press, 1960) and Adam Parry, ed., *The Making of Homeric Verse: The Collected Papers of Milman Parry* (Oxford: Oxford University Press, 1987). For Rousseau's reflections on Homeric illiteracy, see *Essay on the Origin of Languages*, 254–55.

4. Jacques Derrida, *Of Grammatology*, translated by Gayatri Chakravorty Spivak (Baltimore: Johns Hopkins University Press, 1974, 1976). Especially notable in this volume are Derrida's treatment of Rousseau's *Essay on the Origin of Languages* (165–268), and a rather idiosyncratic section, also on Rousseau, entitled ". . . That Dangerous Supplement . . ." (141–64).

Derrida's definitive essay on the Platonic matters before us is "Plato's Pharmacy," in *Dissemination*, translated by Barbara Johnson (Chicago: University of Chicago Press, 1981), 63–171. See also Catherine Zuckert, *Postmodern Platos: Nietzsche, Heidegger, Gadamer, Strauss, Derrida* (Chicago: University of Chicago Press, 1996), 201–53.

5. Norman O. Brown, *Love's Body* (New York: Random House, 1966), 234.

6. See John Chadwick, *Linear B and Related Scripts* (London: Trustees of the British Museum, 1987).

7. Peter Green, *The Shadow of the Parthenon: Studies in Ancient History and Literature* (London: Maurice Temple Smith Limited, 1972), 152–92.

8. Eric A. Havelock, in *Preface to Plato* (Cambridge, Mass.: Harvard University Press, 1963), goes so far as to suggest that Plato's quarrel with the poets, and thus with the traditional performative role of the Homeric *rhētōr*, was in actuality a response to the dawning literacy of the late classical age.

9. I am indebted to my former colleague at Emory University, Andre J. Nahmias, Department of Pediatrics, for this wonderful term.

Select Bibliography

No attempt has been made to be inclusive here. I simply wished to provide some indication of some of the books that have had the greatest impact on me as I have reflected on the vastness of the Platonic project in the Erotic Period, as well as some of the English translations of the relevant dialogues that seem to me to have something important to offer to every student of Platonic thought.

PHAEDO

Gallop, David. *Plato: Phaedo*. New York: Oxford University Press, 1975.

Grube, G.M.A. *Plato's Phaedo*. Indianapolis, Ind.: Hackett Publishing Company, 1977.

Hackforth, R. *Plato's Phaedo: Translated with an Introduction and Commentary*. Cambridge: Cambridge University Press, 1955, 1992.

SYMPOSIUM

Griffith, Tom. *Symposium of Plato*. Berkeley: University of California Press, 1990.

Groden, Suzy Q. *The Symposium of Plato*. Amherst: University of Massachusetts Press, 1970.

Nehamas, Alexander and Paul Woodruff. *Plato: Symposium*. Indianapolis, Ind.: Hackett Publishing Company, 1989.

Sharon, Avi. *Plato's Symposium*. Newburyport, Mass.: Focus Philosophical Library, 1998.

REPUBLIC

Bloom, Allan. *The Republic of Plato*. 2nd Ed. New York: Basic Books, 1968, 1991.

Jowett, Benjamin. *The Republic and Other Works*. Garden City, N.Y.: Anchor Press/Doubleday, 1973.

Sterling, Richard and William Scott. *Plato: The Republic*. New York: W.W. Norton, 1985.

PHAEDRUS

Nehamas, Alexander and Paul Woodruff. *Plato: Phaedrus*. Indianapolis, Ind.: Hackett Publishing Company, 1995.

SECONDARY LITERATURE

Benardete, Seth. *On Plato's "Symposium": Über Platons "Symposion."* Carl Friedrich von Siemens Stiftung, 1993.

———. *The Rhetoric and Morality of Philosophy: Plato's "Gorgias" and "Phaedrus."* Chicago: University of Chicago Press, 1991.

———. *Socrates' Second Sailing: On Plato's "Republic."* Chicago: University of Chicago Press, 1989.

Boswell, John. *Christianity, Social Tolerance and Homosexuality: Gay People in Western Europe From the Beginning of the Christian Era to the Fourteenth Century*. Chicago: University of Chicago Press, 1981.

Brooten, Bernadette J. *Love Between Women: Early Christian Responses to Female Homoeroticism*. Chicago: University of Chicago Press, 1996.

Bury, R. G. *The Symposium of Plato*. Cambridge: Cambridge University Press, 1973.

Bynum, Caroline Walker. *Holy Feast and Holy Fast: The Religious Significance of Food to Medieval Women*. Berkeley: University of California Press, 1987.

———. *The Resurrection of the Body in Western Christianity, 200–1336*. New York: Columbia University Press, 1995.

Calasso, Roberto. *The Marriage of Cadmus and Harmony*, trans. by Tim Parks. New York: Vintage Books, 1993.

Carson, Anne. *Eros the Bittersweet: An Essay*. Princeton: Princeton University Press, 1986.

———. *Glass, Irony, and God*. New York: New Directions Books, 1995.

Cornford, Frances M. *Before and After Socrates*. Cambridge: Cambridge University Press, 1932.

Derrida, Jacques. "Plato's Pharmacy." In *Dissemination*, translated by Barbara Johnson, 63–171. Chicago: University of Chicago Press, 1981.

Dover, Sir Kenneth J. *Greek Homosexuality*. Cambridge, Mass.: Harvard University Press, 1979.

————, ed. *Plato: Symposium*. Cambridge: Cambridge University Press, 1980.

Halperin, David, John J. Winkler, and Froma I. Zeitlin, eds. *Before Sexuality: The Construction of Erotic Experience in the Ancient Greek World*. Princeton: Princeton University Press, 1990.

Konstan, David. *Sexual Symmetry: Love in the Ancient Novel and Related Genres*. Princeton: Princeton University Press, 1994.

————. *Friendship in the Classical World*. Cambridge: Cambridge University Press, 1997.

Murray, Oswyn, ed. *Sympotica: A Symposium on the "Symposion."* Oxford: Clarendon Press of Oxford University, 1990.

Nehamas, Alexander. *The Art of Living: Socratic Reflections from Plato to Foucault*. Berkeley: University of California, 1998.

————. *Virtues of Authenticity: Essays on Plato and Socrates*. Princeton: Princeton University Press, 1999.

Nussbaum, Martha C. *The Fragility of Goodness: Luck and Ethics in Greek Tragedy and Philosophy*. Cambridge: Cambridge University Press, 1986.

————. *Love's Knowledge: Essays on Philosophy and Literature*. New York: Oxford University Press, 1990.

————. *The Therapy of Desire: Theory and Practice in Hellenistic Ethics*. Princeton: Princeton University Press, 1994.

Nussbaum, Martha C. and Saul M. Olyan, eds. *Sexual Orientation and Human Rights in American Religious Discourse*. New York: Oxford University Press, 1998.

Paglia, Camille. *Sexual Personae: Art and Decadence from Nefertiti to Emily Dickinson*. New York: Vintage Books, 1990.

Price, A. W. *Love and Friendship in Plato and Aristotle*. New York: Oxford University Press, 1989.

Riginos, Alice S. *Platonica: The Anecdotes Concerning the Life and Writings of Plato*. Leiden: E. J. Brill, 1976.

Taylor, Alfred E. *The Mind of Plato*. Ann Arbor: University of Michigan Press, 1920, 1960.

————. *Socrates: The Man and His Thought*. Garden City, N.Y.: Doubleday Anchor Books, 1954.

Vlastos, Gregory, ed. *The Philosophy of Socrates: A Collection of Critical Essays*. Notre Dame, Ind.: University of Notre Dame Press, 1971.

————. *Plato: A Collection of Critical Essays*. 2 Volumes. Notre Dame, Ind.: University of Notre Dame Press, 1971, 1978.

————. *Platonic Studies*. 2nd ed. Princeton: Princeton University Press, 1973, 1981.

————. *Socratic Studies*. Myles Burnyeat, ed. Cambridge: Cambridge University Press, 1994.

Williamson, Margaret. *Sappho's Immortal Daughters*. Cambridge: Harvard University Press, 1995.

Winkler, John J. *The Constraints of Desire: The Anthropology of Sex and Gender in Ancient Greece*. New York: Routledge Press, 1990.

Yourcenar, Marguerite. *Fires*, trans. by Dori Katz. New York: Farrar, Straus & Giroux, 1957, 1981.

———. *Memoirs of Hadrian*, trans. by Grace Frick with the author. New York: Farrar, Straus & Giroux, 1954, 1957.

Zuckert, Catherine. *Postmodern Platos: Nietzsche, Heidegger, Gadamer, Strauss, Derrida*. Chicago: University of Chicago Press, 1996.

Index